C000072038

Rabbinic Authority
and
Personal Autonomy

Rabbinic Authority
and
Personal Autonomy

edited by Moshe Sokol

The Orthodox Forum Series
A Project of the Rabbi Isaac Elchanan Theological Seminary
An Affiliate of Yeshiva University

JASON ARONSON INC.
Northvale, New Jersey
London

This book was set in 11 point Goudy by Lind Graphics of Upper Saddle River, New Jersey, and printed by Haddon Craftsmen of Scranton, Pennsylvania.

Library of Congress Cataloging-in-Publication Data

Rabbinic authority and personal autonomy / edited by Moshe Sokol.
    p. cm.
  Includes bibliographical references and index.
  ISBN 0-87668-581-5
  1. Jewish law—Decision making—Congresses. 2. Tradition
(Judaism)—Congresses. 3. Judaism—20th century—Congresses.
4. Orthodox Judaism—Congresses. 5. Autonomy (Psychology)-
-Religious aspects—Judaism—Congresses. I. Sokol, Moshe.
BM521.R23 1992
293.3'1—dc20   91-25301

Manufactured in the United States of America. Jason Aronson Inc. offers books and cassettes. For information and catalog write to Jason Aronson Inc., 230 Livingston Street, Northvale, New Jersey 07647.

THE ORTHODOX FORUM

The Orthodox Forum, convened by Dr. Norman Lamm, President of Yeshiva University, meets each year to consider major issues of concern to the Jewish community. Forum participants from throughout the world, including academicians in both Jewish and secular fields, rabbis, *rashei yeshivah*, Jewish educators, and Jewish communal professionals, gather in conference as a think tank to discuss and critique each other's original papers, examining different aspects of a central theme. The purpose of the Forum is to create and disseminate a new and vibrant Torah literature addressing the critical issues facing Jewry today.

THE ORTHODOX FORUM
First Conference

September 10–11, 1989, 10–11 *Elul* 5749
The Jewish Center, New York City

PARTICIPANTS

Dr. Norman Lamm, Yeshiva University
Rabbi Marc Angel, Spanish-Portuguese Synagogue, New York
Dr. David Berger, Brooklyn College and Yeshiva University
Rabbi Louis Bernstein, Yeshiva University
Dr. Moshe Bernstein, Yeshiva University
Rabbi Yosef Blau, RIETS/Yeshiva University
Dr. Judith Bleich, Touro College
Dr. Jay Braverman, Yeshivah of Flatbush
Rabbi Shalom Carmy, Yeshiva University
Rabbi Zevulun Charlop, RIETS/Yeshiva University
Rabbi Emmanuel Feldman, Congregation Beth Jacob, Atlanta,
  GA
Dr. Marvin Fox, Brandeis University
Rabbi Robert S. Hirt, RIETS/Yeshiva University
Dr. Jerry Hochbaum, Memorial Foundation for Jewish Culture
Dr. Ephraim Kanarfogel, Yeshiva University
Dr. Lawrence Kaplan, McGill University
Dr. Aaron Kirschenbaum, Tel Aviv University
Dr. Sid Leiman, Brooklyn College and Yeshiva University
Dr. Israel Miller, Yeshiva University
Rabbi Yaakov Neuburger, REITS/Yeshiva University

Rabbi Michael Rosensweig, REITS/Yeshiva University
Rabbi Sol Roth, Yeshiva University and Fifth Avenue Synagogue,
  New York
Dr. Jonathan Sacks, Jews College, London, England
Rabbi Yonason Sacks, Yeshiva University High Schools
Dr. Jacob J. Schacter, The Jewish Center, New York
Rabbi Mayer Schiller, Yeshiva University High Schools
Dr. David Shatz, Yeshiva University
Dr. Moshe Sokol, Touro College
Rabbi Shubert Spero, Bar Ilan University
Dr. Moshe Tendler, RIETS/Yeshiva University
Dr. Chaim Waxman, Rutgers University and Yeshiva University
Rabbi Mordechai Willig, RIETS/Yeshiva University
Dr. Joel Wolowelsky, Yeshivah of Flatbush High School
Rabbi Walter Wurzberger, Yeshiva University and Congregation
  Shaarey Tefilah, Long Island

Contents

Preface

Moshe Sokol

According to Peter Berger, the sociologist of religion, "the theme of individual autonomy is perhaps the most important theme in the worldview of modernity."[1] A product of Enlightenment thinking, the impact of individual autonomy can be felt in every sphere of contemporary life, from the political to the personal. Such ideas as individual rights, responsibility and freedom, and the importance of making one's own decisions and finding things out on one's own are all associated with the concept of autonomy.

Yet, religion in general naturally places great stress upon religious authority. Indeed, the deterioration of religious life and institutions following the Enlightenment, a process whose effects we still feel, is intimately connected with the rise of personal

---

[1] P. Berger, B. Berger, and H. Kellner, *The Homeless Mind* (New York: Vintage Books, 1974), 196.

autonomy and the concomitant breakdown in the authority of religious leaders and institutions.

If this tension between religious authority and personal autonomy is a central problem for Western religions generally, it can be a particularly sharp problem for Jews who maintain a commitment to the observance of *halakhah*. The *halakhah*, after all, stresses minute details of observance relating to even the most personal of matters, and it often entails the need to consult rabbinic authorities for halakhic decisions. Thus, for modern halakhic Jews the question of autonomy is a particularly troubling one.

This generalization does need some qualification, however. There are in fact large numbers of Jews, notably many traditionalist Orthodox, who deny that personal autonomy has any value at all. They believe that little good, and perhaps much harm, can come from working things out on one's own; that subservience to a religious authority, like subservience to God, is an important religious value. Such persons are quick to seek expert guidance from their rabbinical leaders on halakhic, and often nonhalakhic matters, from public policy issues even to personal decisions. These Jews will take such guidance to be binding, and will behave accordingly. Since they typically do not see any value in autonomous decision-making, and do see great practical and religious value in seeking binding religious guidance, such Jews feel quite comfortable and secure with their approach.

On the other hand, many sincere Jews committed to the *halakhah* believe that there is significant value in working things out on one's own, as do most modern Westerners. They also believe that by virtue of their exposure to Western culture and ideas, they have a distinct and positive contribution to make to Jewish life and decision-making. Yet, they recognize their own limitations as well. Like many traditionalist Orthodox, the great majority are not sufficiently expert in *halakhah* to make their own informed decisions about difficult Jewish legal matters, and therefore they often require halakhic guidance. Moreover, they respect and admire the spiritual and intellectual achievements of great religious authorities, and therefore are inclined to respect the positions taken by such authorities. Thus, the tension between personal autonomy and rabbinic authority.

Belief in the value of religious authority naturally leads to an inquiry into the nature and scope of its counterweight, personal autonomy. What exactly is personal autonomy, and to what extent is it consistent with any approaches to mainstream normative Judaism? Similarly, belief in the value of personal autonomy naturally leads to an inquiry into the exact nature and scope of *its* counterweight, rabbinic authority. Does rabbinic authority extend to nonhalakhic areas, as it does to halakhic areas? To what extent is halakhic decision-making influenced by subjective factors? Do sociological considerations play a role in halakhic queries, halakhic decision-making, and in the popular choice of halakhic authorities? Are there grounds for halakhic pluralism within the halakhic system itself? How is halakhic innovation possible, given the weight of the past and of traditional authority?

The answers to these questions are certainly of great practical significance in delineating the scope of rabbinic authority. They are also central to the very self-definition of modern Jews committed to the *halakhah*.

The chapters in this volume are intended to respond to these questions directly. Their authors are distinguished experts in the fields of Jewish law, rabbinics, sociology, and philosophy, and the methodology they employ is objective and scholarly rather than apologetic. The chapters were originally commissioned by Yeshiva University and presented at the first conference of the Orthodox Forum, September 10–11, 1989, under this author's chairmanship. The Forum, a think tank for Orthodoxy organized by the Rabbi Isaac Elchanan Theological Seminary, an affiliate of Yeshiva University, meets once or twice annually and takes up issues of significance to Orthodoxy, and to Judaism and Jewish life generally.

Gratitude for the appearance of this volume is due to numerous persons. First, to Yeshiva University and its president, Dr. Norman Lamm, for spearheading this project and for making available the resources to see it to fruition. The cochairmen of the conference, Professor Aaron Kirschenbaum and Rabbi Michael Rosensweig, contributed to the formulation of the questions posed to the authors and provided much help and sound advice, as did the members of the Orthodox Forum Steering Committee as a whole. The participants of the Orthodox Forum, and the commentators on the papers, raised numerous valuable points, many of which had an impact on the final versions of the essays as they appear in this volume. Finally, special thanks are due to Rabbi Robert Hirt, vice president of Rabbi Isaac Elchanan Theological Seminary, for overseeing the work of the Orthodox Forum with devotion and skill, and to Mr. Daniel Ehrlich, assistant director of the Max Stern Division of Communal Service, for providing competent and genial staff support.

1

Daas Torah: A Modern Conception of Rabbinic Authority

Lawrence Kaplan

The concept of *Daas Torah* is, at one and the same time, both precise and delimited, and broad and elusive. It is precise and delimited for, as historians have argued, *Daas Torah* appears to be a specific modern concept of rabbinic authority that has arisen and developed in a clear and definite historical context. It is broad and elusive, first of all, because of the wide range of varying meanings that—incorrectly, I believe—have been attributed to it, but also because of certain inherent ambiguities in the concept. Most important, the proponents of *Daas Torah* have argued that in fact it is

I benefited greatly from the comments and criticisms of all the participants in the Orthodox Forum. In particular, I would like to thank the following for calling my attention to important source materials: Rabbis Yosef Blau, Norman Lamm, Yonasan Saks, and J. J. Schacter, and Professors David Berger and Moshe Sokol. I would also like to thank Rabbi Joshua Shmidman of Congregation Tifereth Beth David Jerusalem of Montreal for his help.

not a new concept at all, but that it is identical with the fundamental notion of rabbinic authority as that notion is to be found in
the classical sources of rabbinic Judaism. One proponent has gone
so far as to argue that if the concept of *Daas Torah* is not "mentioned
per se in the Talmud," it is because it forms the entire basis of the
Talmud's authority, because it is "implicit in every line of every
piece of every *masechta* of the Talmud."[1] One might think that this

---

[1]See Avi Shafran, "The Enigma of Moses Mendelssohn," *The Jewish
Observer* 19:9 (December 1986): 17. Ironically, Shafran's own article,
despite its valiant advocacy of the concept of *Daas Torah*, was itself sharply
criticized in the issue immediately following of *The Jewish Observer* 19:10
(January 1987): 13, in a statement by Rabbi Yaakov Perlow, the Novominsker Rebbe, written "in response to an invitation by members of the
Moetzes Gedolei ha-Torah," for treating Mendelssohn "too kindly" and for
not condemning him from "a perspective that rests on the truths of Torah
[as] keenly sensed by the sages of his [Mendelssohn's] and later days." Thus
Rabbi Shafran, the advocate of *Daas Torah*, is weighed in the balance and
found wanting by the Novominsker Rebbe speaking in the name of the
Moetzes Gedolei ha-Torah, by, in other words, an authoritative expression
of *Daas Torah* itself! In this connection, it might also be worth noting that
Rabbi Perlow's assumption that the negative attitude toward Mendelssohn taken by the Hatam Sofer is representative of the general view of
Gedolei Yisrael toward Mendelssohn is, in truth, despite the air of authority with which it is set forth, completely lacking in any foundation
and a distortion of undeniable historical facts. See Steven Lowenstein,
"The Readership of Mendelssohn's Bible Translation," *HUCA* 53 (1982):
179–213; Meir Hildesheimer, "Moses Mendelssohn in Nineteenth-
Century Rabbinic Literature," *PAAJR* 55 (1988): 79–133; and the ap-
pendix to the responsum of the Maharam Schick in *Likkutei Teshuvot:
Hatam Sofer*, ed. E. Stern (London: G. J. George and Co. Ltd., 1965), no.
82, 75, trans. Shnayer Z. Leiman in "R. Moses Schick: The Hatam Sofer's
Attitude Toward Mendelssohn's *Biur*," *Tradition* 24:3 (Spring 1989):
83–86. I should add that there is a reliable oral tradition to the effect that
the "well-known" anonymous gaon who according to the Maharam
Schick studied the *Bi'ur*, in particular the *Bi'ur* to Leviticus, and who was
strongly criticized by the Hatam Sofer for so doing, was none other than

is a classic example of converting a weakness into a strength,[2] but it serves to show the strong nature of the claim being made.

In this chapter, I have set myself three interrelated tasks. First, I will seek to determine the exact nature of the view of rabbinic authority being propounded in the concept of *Daas Torah* and examine the historical context or contexts in which this concept developed, as well as the functions it has served in those contexts. Second, I will try to locate the roots of this concept in traditional notions of rabbinic authority and see to what extent the concept of *Daas Torah* resembles these traditional notions and to what extent it differs from them. Finally, I will look at the fortunes of *Daas Torah* on the contemporary scene and engage in a few, necessarily tentative, speculations as to its prospects for the future. An epilogue consisting of a troubling but, I trust, instructive historical narrative will serve as a conclusion.

THE IDEOLOGY OF *DAAS TORAH*: A HISTORICAL OVERVIEW

Several years ago I wrote an article in which I made a few brief critical remarks about the concept of *Daas Torah*.[3] As might have

---

that halakhic giant, pillar of rabbinic Judaism, and the Hatam Sofer's own father-in-law, R. Akiva Eger! (On R. Akiva Eger's attitude toward the *Bi'ur*, see Lowenstein, 188–89; and Hildesheimer, 97.) Or, perhaps R. Akiva Eger, R. Moses Schick, R. Samson Raphael Hirsch, R. Azriel Hildesheimer, R. Mordecai Baneth, R. Yosef Zechariah Stern, and the rest, all of whom, although at times sharply critical of Mendelssohn, saw some value—indeed, at times, much value—in the person and his writings, also ought to stand condemned by the authoritative pronouncement of *Daas Torah* for the "sin" of treating Mendelssohn "too kindly"?!

[2]Certainly the doctrines of God's existence, the election of Israel and the revelation of the Torah are "implicit in every line of every piece of every *masechta* of the Talmud," and yet, if memory has not failed me, they are, every now and then, "mentioned *per se* in the Talmud."

[3]"Rabbi Isaac Hutner's 'Daat Torah Perspective' on the Holocaust: A Critical Analysis," *Tradition* 18:3 (Fall 1980): 235–48.

been expected, a number of people, three to be exact, wrote to take issue with me.[4] As, however, might not have been expected, these three correspondents, interestingly enough, defined the concept of *Daas Torah* in three different ways. One correspondent identified *Daas Torah* with halakhic *pesak*, another with the *talmid*-rebbe relationship, while the third—coming closest to the mark—identified it with the voluntary acceptance by the heterogeneous traditional community of the consensus of the *Moetzes Gedolei ha-Torah*, the Council of Torah Sages of Agudas Yisrael, on questions that involve the Jewish community as a whole.[5] These widely varying definitions may point to certain ambiguities that are inherent in the concept of *Daas Torah*. Without denying these ambiguities, I would argue that the concept of *Daas Torah* should not be identified with any of the three suggested definitions—especially not with either of the first two; on the other hand, it does bear certain resemblances to all of them, especially with the third.

While the term *Daas Torah* does appear in earlier rabbinic literature, it only begins to be used as a designation for a specific notion of rabbinic authority sometime in the late nineteenth or early twentieth century.[6] Gershon Bacon, who has devoted several

---

[4]See "Letters to the Editors," *Tradition* 21:2 (Summer 1983): 180–87, for two critical responses to my article by Rabbi Leonard Isbee (180) and Rabbi Aaron Reichel (181–82) and my reply (183–87). A third critical response by Rabbi Meir Belsky was sent to *Tradition* as a private communication.

[5]The views of Rabbis Isbee, Belsky, and Reichel, respectively.

[6]See my article cited above in n. 3, 248 n. 5. Rabbi Hillel Goldberg has recently argued that Rav Yisrael Salanter in a letter written in 1883 (R. Yisrael Salanter, *Iggerot u-Mikhtavim*, ed. S. Wilman [Brooklyn, 1970], 70) already used the term *Daas Torah* in its modern sense. See Hillel Goldberg, "Israel Salanter and *Orhot Zaddikim*: Restructuring Musar Literature," *Tradition* 23:4 (Summer 1988): 38 n. 18. However, a careful examination of the relevant passage in the letter referred to by Goldberg indicates that there is much *less* to the use of the term there than meets the eye. In the

letter, Rav Salanter, in the course of discussing his position on a particular communal matter, writes:

> My son-in-law wrote me . . . that his view inclines [in a direction different from mine] because it is a matter of necessity [*daato notah mipnei ha-hekhre'ah*], but that he will nullify his view because of my view which is *Daas Torah*. This [formulation of his] suggests that, in truth, he is not nullifying his view, and he is a person of judgement. Perhaps, then, his honor will be so kind as to travel to Vilna to meet with Rabbi . . . and discuss the matter calmly with my son-in-law; and the counsel of the Lord will be established.

What emerges from a close reading of this passage is the following. (1) It was not Rav Salanter who used the phrase *Daas Torah* here. Rav Salanter was just quoting his son-in-law's formulation; (2) Rav Salanter's son-in-law used the phrase in order to play upon the talmudic antithesis between *daat notah* and *daat torah* (*Hullin* 90b); (3) in stating that he was nullifying his view in favor of his father-in-law's *Daas Torah* view, Rav Salanter's son-in-law was simply engaging in an act of personal deference to the stature and authority of his father-in-law and was not really abandoning his own view; (4) Rav Salanter was very well aware of the fact that his son-in-law's statement was just an act of personal deference and that his son-in-law was still maintaining his own view; (5) precisely because of the above, Rav Salanter felt that his son-in-law's contrary view should not be simply dismissed or ignored, and for that reason he suggested that the matter be discussed further with him.

In light of our analysis, it is difficult to agree with Goldberg's contention that *Daas Torah* in its modern sense is being invoked in this letter. The *disciples* of Rav Salanter did develop a notion of *Daas Torah* in its modern sense, but that is another story. See n. 81, below.

Even more recently, Mendel Piekarz, in his exceptionally important and thorough work, *Hasidut Polin: Megamot Raayoniyot bein Shetei ha-Milhamot u-bi-Gezerot 1940–1945* (Jerusalem: Mossad Bialik, 1990), 81–96, has found extensive evidence for the use of the term *Daas Torah* in its modern sense in the writings of hasidic rebbes beginning in the late nineteenth century. On the other hand, we cannot agree with Piekarz's

studies to this subject,[7] has argued that we must view the emergence and formation of the concept of *Daas Torah* within the context of the rise of Agudas Yisrael as a political party devoted to defending and espousing the interests of Orthodox Jewry in the challenging and often hostile modern environment in which traditional Jewry found itself, both the modern environment in general and, more specifically, the modern Jewish environment.

The process whereby the traditional Jewish community, in response to the challenges of modernization, became a self-consciously Orthodox community has been the subject of much recent study.[8] One facet of this process was the Orthodox community's adoption of certain modern techniques, strategies, and modes of operation and organization, the better to combat modernity and defend traditional Judaism. One of these modern methods of organization was the political party.

The beginning of the twentieth century saw the rise of a secular Jewish leadership and secular ideological Jewish movements—most prominent among them the Bund and Zionism—that organized themselves as political parties and fought for their interests and for positions of communal power under party banners. This political challenge posed by secular Jewry to traditional Jewry gave rise to the need for traditional Jewry to respond in like fashion. It was in this

---

claim (389 n. 23) that the term in its modern sense is already to be found in the writings of the Maharal of Prague. For the significance of Piekarz's work for this discussion, see below, n. 84.

[7]See Gershon Bacon, *Agudath Israel in Poland, 1916–1939: An Orthodox Jewish Response to the Challenge of Modernity* (Ph.D. dissertation, Columbia University, 1979), in particular chap. 2 (48–76); and his essay "Daat Torah ve-Hevlei Mashiah," *Tarbiz* 53:3 (1983): 497–508. A revised version of Bacon's thesis, *Agudat Yisrael in Poland, 1916–1939: The Politics of Tradition*, has been announced for publication.

[8]See the many works of Jacob Katz, Eli Schweid, Moshe Samet, Michael Silber, Emmanuel Etkes, Robert Liberles, David Ellenson, and Mordecai Breuer, for more on this subject.

context that Agudas Yisrael grew and developed and, particularly in Poland during the interwar years, took on the form of a political party. Yet, this mode of political organization did not come easily to traditional Jewry. Obviously it was (and remains?) paradoxical and disturbing for traditional Jewry to adopt modern political guises, even if such guises are necessary in order to defend traditional interests. And can traditional Jewry simply see itself as a party like all parties?! It was in response to this politicization of traditional Jewry and the dilemmas it posed—so Bacon claims[9]—that the concept of *Daas Torah* arose.

The Agudah, in its own self-perception, was not one party among many parties; indeed, it was not really a political party, in the normal sense, at all. For at its head stood the great rabbis of the era, as embodied in the institution of *Moetzes Gedolei ha-Torah*, The Council of Torah Sages. The views of these Torah giants on all issues, whether on more "narrowly" conceived religious and halakhic issues or on "broader" communal and political issues, were authoritative and binding for the Agudah and its followers. Their views were binding precisely because these giants, as a result of their immersion in Torah, were, in all their pronouncements, the authentic spokesmen for, the quintessential embodiment of, the Jewish tradition. Their views, in a word, were *Daas Torah*, the authentic and authoritative Torah viewpoint on the issues in question. Thus, the Agudah itself, under the leadership of these *Gedolim*, was not just another political party, but *the* authoritative spokesman for and representative of traditional Judaism and the traditional Jewish community. Moreover, the Agudah could counterpose its authentic rabbinic leadership to what it saw as the inauthentic, indeed subversive, secular leadership of the other Jewish parties.

Perhaps the clearest and most forceful presentation of the ideology of *Daas Torah* is to be found in the following statement, attributed to the Hafetz Hayyim.

---

[9]But see below, n. 84.

The person whose view [*daato*] is the view of Torah [*Daas Torah*] can solve all worldly problems, both specific and general. However, there is one condition attached. The *Daas Torah* must be pure, without any interest or bias. However, if there is a person who possesses *Daas Torah* but it is intermingled even slightly with other views from the marketplace or from the newspapers, then this *Daas Torah* is turbid, intermingled with dregs. Such a person cannot penetrate into the heart of the matter.[10]

Thus, paradoxically, or maybe not so paradoxically, it is the rabbis who are completely immersed in the world of Torah and seemingly removed from the outside world who, in truth, possess a unique penetrating insight into the challenges and needs of the situation; and it is only they who, consequently, can draw upon "the spirit of tradition" in order to formulate the policies needed to meet these challenges and needs.

Another very forceful expression of this ideology, deriving from the interwar period, is to be found in an address—not cited by Bacon—of Rav Joseph B. Soloveitchik, in a eulogy delivered in 1940 upon the passing of Rav Hayyim Ozer Grodzinski.[11] In his eulogy, Rav Soloveitchik—although he does not use the term *Daas Torah*—speaks of the need to unite in one person, as in the high priest of old, the *tzitz*, the symbol of halakhic scholarship and *pesak*, and the *hoshen*, the symbol of policy decisions on critical communal issues. In one striking passage Rav Soloveitchik states:

The very same priest, whose mind was suffused with the holiness of the Torah of R. Akiva and R. Eliezer, of Abbaye and

---

[10]*Hafetz Hayyim al ha-Torah*, ed. Rabbi S. Greineman (Bnei Brak, n.d.), 30.

[11]"A Eulogy for R. Hayyim Ozer Grodzinski," *Ha-Pardes* 14:7 (September 1940): 5–9; reprinted in *Divrei Hagut ve-Haarakhah* (Jerusalem: World Zionist Organization: Dept. of Torah Education and Culture in the Diaspora, 1981), 187–94.

Raba, of the Rambam and Rabad, of the Beth Yosef and the Rema, could also discern with the holy spirit [roeh be-ruah ha-kodesh] the solution to all current political questions, to all worldly matters, to all ongoing current demands.[12]

It is no coincidence that this eulogy was delivered at the second annual conference of the Agudas Yisrael of the United States, at a time, moreover, when Rav Soloveitchik was a vice president of the Agudah. Nor is it a coincidence that in the eulogy, Rav Soloveitchik contrasted this type of all-embracing leadership, as embodied, for example, by Rav Hayyim Ozer, with the secular leadership of nontraditional movements wishing to reserve communal leadership for themselves and reduce the rabbis to religious functionaries who rule only on purely ritual or technical, halakhic matters.[13] We have here, then, an elegant expression of the Agudah ideology of Daas Torah.

Bacon's analysis, which we have largely followed up to this point,[14] is correct as far as it goes, but it does not go far enough. Indeed, Bacon perhaps places too much emphasis on the rise of Agudas Yisrael as a political party, finding in this the primary context for understanding the development of Daas Torah and slighting other factors that nurtured this development.

It needs to be noted that Daas Torah came into its own—at least in nonhasidic circles—only after the Second World War, and not during the interwar period. As evidence for this contention, we may cite the following two observations. First, there are not really many clearly articulated and publicly presented expressions of the ideology of Daas Torah, again in nonhasidic circles, from the

---

[12]Divrei Hagut ve-Haarakhah, 192.

[13]Ibid., 193–94. For the possible historical background to this eulogy, see Aharon Rakeffet-Rothkoff, "Hanhagat Am Yisrael be-Mishnato shel ha-Rav Yosef Soloveitchik," in Itturim, ed. Moshe Ishon (Jerusalem: World Zionist Organization: Dept. of Torah Education and Culture in the Diaspora, 1986), 298–313.

[14]But see below, n. 84.

interwar period. The statement of the Hafetz Hayyim, cited earlier, which is the clearest and most forceful of all such statements, is not to be found in any of his published works. Rather, it was an oral comment noted by his disciple Rav Shmuel Greineman (the brother-in-law of the Hazon Ish) and incorporated in the latter's book *The Hafetz Hayyim on the Torah*, published in 1943, after the Hafetz Hayyim's death. As for the statement of Rav Soloveitchik cited earlier, it cannot be considered a full-blown expression of the ideology of *Daas Torah*. For Rav Soloveitchik was referring specifically to the communal authority of someone like Rav Hayyim Ozer, who derived much of that authority from his position as communal Rav of Vilna and not simply from his personal charisma and learning, as great as they might have been. Or, to put it another way, it was Rav Hayyim Ozer's personal charisma and learning, *filtered through and mediated by* his position of communal Rav, that was the source of his authority.[15] Second, as Bacon himself shows,

---

[15] A more muted conception of *Daas Torah* may be found in Rav Aaron Lewin, *Ha-Derash ve-ha-Iyyun*, vol. 2, *Parshat Yitro* (Bilgoray, 1931), 198, cited in Piekarz, *Hasidut Polin*, 80 n. 22. (Piekarz mistakenly refers to *Parshat Bo*.) A clear and succinct expression of the doctrine, if lacking the force of the statement of the *Hafetz Hayyim*, is set forth in an essay by Alexander Zusya Friedman, perhaps the leading ideologist of Agudas Yisrael in Poland. See "Agudat Yisrael," in *Darkenu*, Jubilee Volume (*Tishrei* 1935), 57; cited in Piekarz, *Hasidut Polin*, 88 n. 21. A particularly critical reference to and use of the notion of *Daas Torah*, unaccompanied, however, by a definition or exposition of the concept, can be found in the famous letter Rav Hayyim Ozer Grodzinski wrote to R. Meir Hildesheimer in 1934 opposing the latter's attempt to transplant the Hildesheimer Rabbinical Seminary from Berlin to the land of Israel. See *Ahiezer: Collected Letters*, vol. 2 (Bnei Brak, 1970), 443–44 [= *Kovetz Iggerot Hazon Ish* 2:171–73]. (For further discussion of this letter, see n. 33, below.) It is worth noting that all the statements we have cited come from the 1930s when the storm clouds were gathering.

One figure from the interwar period who is often cited in connection with the concept of *Daas Torah* is Rav Elhanan Wasserman. It is true that

the *Moetzes Gedolei ha-Torah*, the quintessential embodiment of the ideology of *Daas Torah*, was never really an active and functioning organization during the interwar period, but rather was "a largely theoretical institution."[16] This second observation may be further corroborated by the recently published autobiography of Dr. Isaac Breuer, *Darki (Mein Weg)*, in which Breuer describes the *Moetzes*

Rav Elhanan, in his more publicizing and popular writings, was perhaps the most articulate spokesman of the Agudah ideology of that period. He presents time and again with force and clarity the basic positions of the Agudah: for example, its critique of both secular Jewish nationalism as well as the religious nationalism of Mizrahi, and its perception of the manifold defections from traditional Judaism and of the growing persecutions of the Jewish people as evidence of the "birth pangs of the Messiah." It is also true that he refers to these views as being "*Daas Torah* gathered from *Sofrim* and *Sefarim*," "as ideas . . . taken from the Torah" (*Kovetz Maamarim*, 153) and uses the term *Daas Torah* rather freely in his essays (*Kovetz Maamarim*, 98, 104, 128, 140, 155). It is all the more striking, then, that there is no ideology of *Daas Torah* to be found in any of Rav Elhanan's essays. Particularly noteworthy is the absence in any of the essays of a role accorded to the *gedolim* in formulating *Daas Torah*. It is also of interest that Rav Elhanan uses the terms *Daas Torah*, *Daas ha-Torah*, *Atzas ha-Torah*, and *Daatah shel ha-Torah* interchangeably.

The term *Daas Torah* was also used freely in many of the placards of the *haredi* community of Jerusalem in the 1920s and 1930s condemning Zionism and all "deviations" from the tradition (e.g., speaking Hebrew). See *Torat Rebbe Amram*, vol. 1 (Jerusalem, 1977), pt. 2, docs. 3, 4, 24, 48, and 60. Note that in doc. 60, the Agudas Yisrael itself is accused of acting in violation of *Daas Torah*. Cf., as well, doc. 52 for the conception of *Daas Torah*—though the term itself is not used—set forth by *Hevrat ha-Hayyim* (named after Rav Yosef Hayyim Sonnenfeld), the society which was the forerunner of the *Neturei Karta*. Indeed, even the more "moderate" elements of the Jerusalem Orthodox community would also, at times, brandish the term *Daas Torah* in their placards. See Menahem Friedman, *Hevrah ve-Dat* (Jerusalem: Yad Yitzhak Ben-Zvi, 1978), 329.

[16]Bacon, *Agudath Israel in Poland*, 106–15, 462.

Gedolei ha-Torah as a council "which never enjoyed any real existence."[17]

It was only after the Second World War that there emerged, even in nonhasidic circles, a much more explicit, developed, and ongoing presentation of the ideology of *Daas Torah*, as set forth in statements by Rav Eliyahu Dessler, the *Hazon Ish* and his disciples, Rav Yaakov Kanevsky, and, may he be distinguished for a long life, Rav Eliezer Schach, and many others. Moreover, it was only after the war that the *Moetzes Gedolei ha-Torah* became a functioning, active, and influential organization. Finally, and perhaps most important, it was only after the war that rabbinic leaders, speaking in the name of and invoking the authority of *Daas Torah*, took the initiative on such crucial communal issues as *sherut leumi*, membership in "mixed" synagogue organizations, for example, the Synagogue Council of America, and, more recently, the return of the *shetahim*. This leads one to believe that a key factor, if not the key factor, in the rise of the ideology of *Daas Torah* was, as Rabbi Shubert Spero has suggested,[18] the breakdown of traditional Jewish communal structures, the concomitant weakening of the power of communal rabbis and lay religious leaders, and the emergence of

---

[17]Isaac Breuer, *Darki*, trans. from the German manuscript by M. Schwartz (Jerusalem: Mossad Yitzhak Breuer, 1988), 170. The continuation of this passage is particularly striking for its exceptionally biting tone. It is impossible to imagine any Agudah ideologist today writing about the *Moetzes Gedolei ha-Torah* in a manner even remotely approaching the sharpness of Breuer's critical remarks.

It is worth noting that the recent Agudah "house" history, *The Struggle and the Splendor: A Pictorial Overview of Agudath Israel of America* (New York: Agudath Israel of America, 1982), 21–25, not surprisingly, portrays the *Moetzes Gedolei ha-Torah* as the vital and active nerve center of the Agudah from the very beginning of the movement. How wonderful to be able to bask in the glow of current pieties, unconstrained by such a mundane consideration as concern for historical truth!

[18]Shubert Spero, "Daas Torah" in *Divrei Ha-Rav* (Cleveland, OH: Young Israel of Cleveland, 1976), 18–19.

the *rashei yeshivah*, with their Torah scholarship and personal charisma, to center stage. This process has, of course, been going on since the nineteenth century,[19] but it reached its climax only with the Second World War and the destruction of the great traditional Jewish communities of Eastern Europe. Thus, the climax of this process, of this change of leadership, coincides with and would seem to be partially, if not largely, responsible for the emergence of a full-blown concept of *Daas Torah*.

A striking symbol of this change of leadership, particularly relevant to the issue of *Daas Torah*, is the passing of the mantle of leadership of the traditional Orthodox Jewish community from Rav Hayyim Ozer before the war to the *Hazon Ish* after the war. As we have already noted, Rav Hayyim Ozer was, of course, a great talmudic scholar, but first and foremost he was the communal rav of the great city of Vilna. His standing thus reflected the traditional role of communal rav as leader of the Jewish community. The *Hazon Ish*, who was Rav Hayyim Ozer's confidante in Vilna, left Vilna and, by implication, the Jewish world of Eastern Europe in the mid 1930s for the land of Israel. Upon his arrival there, the *Hazon Ish* did not settle in Jerusalem but in the new community of Bnei Brak. Thus, the *Hazon Ish* functioned as a halakhic authority outside of already established traditional Jewish communal structures. Moreover, the *Hazon Ish* never (with the exception of a very brief stint as a communal rav during the First World War necessitated by the emergency situation) held an official position, either as rav or even as *rosh yeshivah*. His halakhic authority and his *Daas Torah* derived purely from his greatness as a Torah scholar and his personal charisma.

---

[19]See, for example, Emmanuel Etkes, "Bein Lamdanut le-Rabbanut be-Yahadut Lita shel ha-Me'ah ha-Yod-Tet," *Tziyyon* 53 (1988): 385–403; Mordecai Breuer, "Tradition and Change in European Yeshivot: Seventeenth to Nineteenth Centuries," paper delivered at a conference on "Tradition and Crisis Revisited: Jewish Society and Thought on the Threshold of Modernity," Center for Jewish Studies of Harvard University, October 1988; and Piekarz, *Hasidut Polin*, 17–23.

We are suggesting, then, that the ideology of *Daas Torah*, in large part, is intended to provide a basis for a new type of rabbinic authority, a type of authority that can serve as a substitute for the traditional mechanisms whereby both the lay and rabbinic leadership of functioning Jewish communities dealt with new challenges, whether through *takkanot* (be they *takkanot ha-kahal* or rabbinically instituted *takkanot*), *gezerot*, the ban, and the like.

In this respect, it is again instructive to focus on the *Hazon Ish*, this time contrasting him not with his predecessor, Rav Hayyim Ozer, but with a great luminary of an earlier generation to whom he has often been compared, and with much justice, the Gaon of Vilna. Both the *Hazon Ish* and the Gaon of Vilna were private individuals. Neither served as rav or rosh yeshivah. Each derived his immense authority from his unparalleled Torah learning and unique charisma. But in the time of the Gaon of Vilna, the traditional communal structures were still in place. Therefore, when the challenge of Hasidism arose, the Gaon, working in tandem with the lay leaders, lent his immense prestige to the communal ban issued against the *hasidim* by those lay leaders representing the community of Vilna.[20] By contrast, when the *Hazon Ish* spoke out on the issue of *sherut leumi*, he expressed his opposition purely on his own authority, presenting his view as *Daas Torah*.[21] He was the community.

This reliance on the ideology of *Daas Torah* as a basis for promulgating an *issur*, an *issur* that in previous generations would

---

[20]See S. Dubnow, *Toldot ha-Hasidut* (Tel Aviv: Dvir, 1967), 114–17. One ban was signed by the Gaon himself, by the Rav of Vilna, Rav Samuel, and by the *dayyanim*; another ban was signed by Rav Samuel, the *dayyanim*, and the *parnassim*. An examination of the various bans and proclamations against the hasidim will easily reveal the preeminent role played in the entire episode by the lay leaders of the various communities.

[21]*Hazon Ish*, *Kovetz Iggerot*, vol. 1, letters 111–113 (122–26); cf. the public announcement of the *Daas Torah* of the *Hazon Ish* on *sherut leumi* in Shimon Finkelman, *The Chazon Ish* (New York: Mesorah Publications Ltd., 1989), 252.

have been set forth as a communal ban, may be seen in the famous *issur* against Orthodox participation in the Synagogue Council of America. Once again it is not coincidental that the *issur* was issued by eleven *rashei yeshivah*, nary a communal rav among them.[22] The one communal rav who was asked to sign the *issur*, R. Eliezer Silver, refused. While agreeing in principle with the *issur*, he felt that issuing the *issur* at that time and in that form was partially motivated by anti-Yeshiva University considerations and would only exacerbate a difficult situation.[23] The difference in sensibilities here is quite telling.[24]

Three statements from the postwar era should give us a good picture of the contemporary ideology of *Daas Torah*.

The first statement comes from the pen of the *Hazon Ish*. In a famous letter to a leader of Po'alei Agudat Yisrael on the issue of *sherut leumi*, the *Hazon Ish* sets forth the ideology of *Daas Torah* in a passage reminiscent of Rav Soloveitchik's eulogy for Rav Hayyim Ozer, but phrased in much sharper terms.

The viewpoint that divides the Torah in two: questions of *issur ve-heter* on the one hand and guidance in everyday life on

---

[22]Rav Aharon Kotler, perhaps the major signatory of the *issur*, referred to it in a private letter as an "issur of the Ramim." See *Mishnat Rav Aharon*, vol. 2 (Jerusalem: Makhon Yerushalayim, 1985), 165.

[23]See Aharon Rakeffet-Rothkoff, *The Silver Era* (New York: Yeshiva University, 1981), 292. In a recent interview, Rabbi Emanuel Rackman recalls Rav Silver telling him to pay no attention to the *issur*. See *Jewish Review* (September–October 1990), 12.

[24]In this connection, a reliable informant related to me that he was present at a meeting of the *Agudas ha-Rabbanim* where Rav Silver publicly rebuked Rav Aharon Kotler for what he considered unwarranted interference in an internal communal matter. It should be mentioned parenthetically that the change in the character of the *Agudas ha-Rabbanim* in the 1950s from an organization dominated by communal rabbis to one dominated by *rashei yeshivah* is both a part and a symbol of the entire story being told here.

the other; and that holds that for *issur ve-heter* one should subjugate oneself to the sages of one's time, while leaving other matters to one's own free choice—this is the viewpoint held by the heretics of old in Germany who drove their brethren to assimilate with the other nations. . . . For one to distinguish between instruction regarding *issur ve-heter* and matters of legislation constitutes denigration of *talmidei hakhamim* and places one in the category of those who have no portion in the world to come.[25]

The second statement may be found in Rav Eliyahu Dessler's famous and oft-cited response to a correspondent who raised the argument that many Jews might have been spared the ravages of the Holocaust had the rabbinic authorities in Eastern Europe encouraged the masses of the Jews to emigrate to the land of Israel. Rav Dessler writes:

Whoever was present at their meetings [the Hafetz Hayyim, Rav Hayyim Brisker, and Rav Hayyim Ozer] . . . could have no doubt that he could see the *Shekhinah* resting on the work of their hands and that the holy spirit was present in their assemblies. . . . Our rabbis have told us to listen to the words of the Sages, even if they tell us that right is left, and not to say, heaven forbid, that they certainly erred because little I can see their error with my own eyes. Rather, my seeing is null and void compared with the clarity of intellect and the divine aid they receive. . . . This is the Torah view [*Daas Torah*] concerning faith in the Sages [*Emunat Hakhamim*]. The ab-

---

[25]*Hazon Ish, Hitorrerut* (Bnei Brak, 1988), 41–42. An English translation can be found in Finkelman, *Chazon Ish*, 249. It is worth noting that the *Hazon Ish* does not use the phrase *Daas Torah* in this letter. The only place in his writings, to my knowledge, where he does use the phrase is *Kovetz Iggerot*, vol. 1, letter 108 (121). Rabbi Shalom Carmy informs me that his search for the phrase *Daas Torah* in the writings of the *Hazon Ish* has been similarly unsuccessful, seeming to confirm my impression.

sence of self-negation toward our rabbis is the root of all sin and the beginning of all destruction, while all merits are as naught compared with the root of all—faith in the Sages.[26]

The third statement—perhaps the clearest exposition of *Daas Torah*—comes from the pen of one of the most articulate spokesmen for traditional Orthodoxy in the United States, Rabbi Bernard Weinberger. Rabbi Weinberger sets down the premise that

> *Gedolei Yisrael* possess a special endowment or capacity to penetrate objective reality, recognize the facts as they really are and apply the pertinent halakhic principles. This endowment is a form of *ruah ha-kodesh*, as it were, bordering, if only remotely, on the periphery of prophecy.

From this premise Rabbi Weinberger draws the following conclusion:

> *Gedolei Yisrael* inherently ought to be the final and sole arbiters of all aspects of Jewish communal policy and questions of *hashkafah* and . . . even knowledgeable rabbis who may differ with the *gedolim* on a particular issue must submit to the superior wisdom of the *gedolim* and demonstrate *Emunat Hakhamim.*[27]

These statements appear clear enough.[28] Yet, there is still an ambiguity in the concept of *Daas Torah*; and resolving this ambi-

---

[26]Eliyahu Dessler, *Mikhtav Me-Eliyahu* 1:75–77; cf., as well, his discussion on p. 59.

[27]Bernard Weinberger, "The Role of the Gedolim," *Jewish Observer* 1:2 (October 1963): 11.

[28]Many other statements on *Daas Torah* can be found in the writings of Rav Kanevsky, Rav Shach, and the various English, Hebrew, and Yiddish journals of Agudas Yisrael. In this connection, see the lucid and thoughtful, if somewhat journalistic, exposition and defense of *Daas Torah* by the exceptionally able and articulate leader of the Agudah, Rabbi Moshe

guity, or at least bringing it to light, may help to clarify the notion of *Daas Torah* as well as to suggest other functions it serves.

One may ask to what extent *Daas Torah* is analogous to, or is, a special type of halakhic *pesak*. Rav Soloveitchik's presentation and that of others suggest that while *Daas Torah* is dependent on great halakhic expertise, an actual decision involving *Daas Torah* on a communal question is more of an intuitive matter, nurtured to be sure by the halakhic intellect, but differing fundamentally from halakhic *pesak*. This is corroborated by a statement of the Hazon Ish who, when challenged to cite the paragraph in the *Shulhan Arukh* that prohibits *sherut leumi*, replied: "It is to be found in the fifth section of the *Shulhan Arukh*, the one which is not written and is the province of only true *talmidei hakhamim*."[29]

On the other hand, the *Hazon Ish*, on another occasion, in setting forth how he arrived at a *Daas Torah* decision, stated: "When I am asked for a decision about such matters I do not simply shake them from my sleeve. Rather, I study all the relevant sources: *Gemara*, Rashi, Tosafos, *Rishonim* and *Aharonim*, and clarify the matter. Only after studying the entire *sugya*, when the matter is

---

Sherer, "Gedolei Yisrael ve-Politikah," in *Bi-Shtei Einayim* (Brooklyn: Mesorah, 1988), 244–49. (This article originally appeared in Yiddish in the Agudah journal, *Dos Yiddishe Vort*.) A very striking collection of statements by leading American *rashei yeshivah* espousing the ideology of *Daas Torah* in a rather extreme form may be found in the *Jewish Observer* (February 1987), 43–45. See, in particular, Rabbi Elya Svei's article in that issue "Torah: A Source for Guidance in Every Phase of Jewish Activity," 7–9. It is especially worth noting how many of these statements blur *Daas Torah* with *kavod ha-Torah* and *kevod hakhamim*. Thus, refusing to accept the *Daas Torah* pronouncement of a particular *gadol* is equated with *bizzayon ha-Torah* and *bizzayon talmidei hakhamim!* An even more recent collection of essays where the term *Daas Torah* is used very freely is *Ve-Zarah ha-Shemesh: Yisudah ve-Mishnatah shel Degel ha-Torah* (Bnei Brak, 1990). Of course, *Degel ha-Torah* claims to be the "true" inheritor of the "original" Agudah, of the Agudah, that is, before it became "corrupted."

[29]Finkleman, *The Chazon Ish*, 254.

clear, do I give an answer."[30] This description clearly identifies the decision-making process for arriving at a *Daas Torah* decision with that of halakhic *pesak*.

A similar ambiguity is found in the famous *issur* forbidding Orthodox participation in the Synagogue Council of America. On the one hand, participation in the Synagogue Council was declared to be forbidden according to *Din Torah*, suggesting that the *issur* should be viewed as a classic halakhic *pesak*, based on halakhic sources. On the other hand, no formal responsum was ever issued and the *issur* has often been described and defended as an expression of *Daas Torah*.[31]

---

[30]See E. Shulsinger, *Al Mishkenot Ha-Ro'im* (Bnei Brak, 1988), 69–70. A somewhat garbled version of this account can be found in Finkelman, *The Chazon Ish*, 199–200.

[31]Rabbi Moshe Tendler, who is both the son-in-law of Rav Moshe Feinstein and a noted rabbinic scholar in his own right, insists that Rav Moshe always saw the ban on Orthodox participation in the Synagogue Council of America as being a matter of strict *pesak halakhah*. On the other hand, as I have argued in this chapter, the whole way the ban was issued, the fact that no formal responsum was ever forthcoming, and the manner in which the ban has generally been presented by its defenders all point to a different conclusion. In this connection, I should also mention that Rabbi Tendler has stated that Rav Moshe in private would allow himself to make critical remarks about the concept of *Daas Torah*. "Why are people talking about *Daas Torah*—Rav Moshe was wont to exclaim—when they don't even know a Shakh or a Taz!" See, however, Rav Moshe's forceful exposition and defense of the notion of *Daas Torah* in "Following the Guidance of the Torah Personality," *Jewish Observer* 12:9 (December 1977): 20–23, a transcription of an oral address of Rav Moshe at a convention of the Agudas Yisrael. Assuming the transcription of the *Jewish Observer* to be accurate, we are confronted with an apparent discrepancy. Perhaps—and I venture this suggestion with great diffidence and hesitation—we have here an example of the inconsistencies we sometimes encounter between the public affirmations of a public figure and his more private doubts and reservations.

For Rav Aharon Kotler's view of the *issur* regarding the Synagogue

In truth, the issues in connection with which *Daas Torah* has most often been invoked—participation in the Synagogue Council of America; relations with the non-Orthodox; *sherut leumi*; attitudes to the State of Israel and Zionism; the *shetahim* and *meridah be-umot*, and so on—are all of a mixed nature. Technical halakhic considerations merge with broad considerations of *hashkafah* and policy analysis. Moreover, to a large extent, although not entirely, the considerations of *hashkafah* and policy analysis determine which halakhic considerations are invoked and how they are analyzed and applied. Finally, these questions of *hashkafah* and policy analysis are highly charged insofar as they center around the cluster of challenges that the modern world has presented to traditional Judaism, and particularly insofar as the traditional world is sharply divided on how best to meet these challenges and thereby to secure the future of traditional Judaism.

The above leads me to suggest two further functions for the ideology of *Daas Torah*. In a very rich and stimulating paper,[32] Rabbi Jonathan Sacks writes:

> The transformations of Jewish modernity—emancipation and its social and intellectual implications—have been . . . profound. But there were deep disagreements as to what would constitute continuing the covenant in such a way as to maintain a *strict identity with the Jewish past*. . . . Was the emancipation a lessening, continuation, or deepening of *galut*? Was Jewish segregation from general culture in the Middle Ages an aberration or an ideal? What was the role of secular action in bringing about the independent sovereignty of

---

Council, see the letter referred to in n. 22. Rav Aharon's language in this letter seems more ideological than strictly halakhic, although one perhaps shouldn't make too much of this, given the personal and somewhat informal context of his statement.

[32]See Rabbi Jonathan Sacks's essay, "Creativity and Innovation in *Halakhah*," in this volume.

Israel? To what extent is Israel still *galut?* In an age where Jews
identify as Jews but not through *halakhah,* should such Jews
be, as far as possible, included or excluded by the halakhic
system? Approaches to these and similar questions, more than
any other factor, have been decisive in the halakhic process
for the past two centuries.

Let us develop Rabbi Sacks's line of thought further. It is
certainly no coincidence that it is precisely "approaches to these
and similar questions" that have been decisive in *all* issues where
Daas Torah has been invoked.[33] For, as Rabbi Sacks correctly states

---

[33]See, for example, the range of issues covered in the anthology, *Yalkut
Daas Torah me-Et Gedolei ha-Dor ha-Aharon,* printed as the second part of
the "Nezah" edition of Rav Elhanan Wasserman's *Ikveta de-Meshiha* (Bnei
Brak, 1989). In this connection, it is particularly worth noting R. Hayyim
Ozer's invoking of the notion of *Daas Torah* in his famous letter to R. Meir
Hildesheimer opposing the latter's attempt to relocate the Hildesheimer
Rabbinical Seminary. See n. 15, above. R. Hayyim Ozer and R. Hil-
desheimer in their clash concerning the propriety of this relocation were,
of course, disagreeing about an issue in which questions of *hashkafah* and
policy played the critical role, the key question being how traditional
Judaism in the area of higher Jewish education could best respond to the
challenges posed to it by the modern world. In light of our analysis, it
comes as no surprise, then, that R. Hayyim Ozer invoked the notion of
Daas Torah in his letter to lend weight to his strongly held view as to what
that response should be, a view that, of course, reflected his generally
rejectionist approach to modernity, and to squelch R. Hildesheimer's
attempt at implementing a very different response, a response that, of
course, reflected R. Hildesheimer's more positive and accommodationist
approach to the modern world. Since the issue in this letter involved the
relocation of the Hildesheimer Seminary from *Berlin* to the *land of Israel,*
and these two areas were not in R. Hayyim Ozer's Eastern European
rabbinic bailiwick, R. Hayyim Ozer could not, in espousing his view, rely
upon his position as communal rav of Vilna or as the head of various
Eastern European rabbinical organizations, but only upon his own personal authority as one whose opinion constituted *Daas Torah.* For a

and as we have similarly noted, the traditional Jewish community has become deeply divided on these issues. While large segments of the Orthodox community have adopted various rejectionist approaches to modernity, viewing modernity in most or all of its manifestations as empty at best, and, at worst, corrupt and dangerous and a threat to traditional religious values, other segments of the Orthodox community, while not unaware of the dangers the modern world poses to tradition, have adopted, again with variations, a more positive and affirmative attitude to the modern world and its values. And it is precisely on this point that one critical difference between the concept of *Daas Torah* and that of halakhic *pesak* enables the notion of *Daas Torah* to serve as an important weapon in the hands of the antimodern rejectionist Orthodox camp in their ongoing struggle with the more modern affirmative camp.

The methodology of halakhic *pesak*—even halakhic *pesak* involving questions of *hashkafah*—with its citation and analysis of sources, use of argumentation, and all the rest, acknowledges the possibility and, more important, the legitimacy of different viewpoints, based upon differing modes of argumentation, analysis, and interpretation. Halakhic *pesak* allows for, nay, encourages, halakhic debate and halakhic pluralism. An expression of *Daas Torah*, however, presents itself, sans argumentation and analysis, as the authentic Torah viewpoint on the issue in question, thus implicitly—and, at times, explicitly—branding all other positions as inauthentic and illegitimate. Thus, the rejectionist camp invokes *Daas Torah* with respect to its approach to the wide range of issues and challenges posed by the modern world and the breakdown of

---

thorough account of the abortive attempt to relocate the Hildesheimer Seminary, see Christhard Hoffman and Daniel Schwartz, "Early but Opposed—Supported but Late: Two Berlin Seminaries Which Attempted to Move Abroad," *Leo Baeck Institute Yearbook* 36 (1991): 267–304. (The section on the Hildesheimer Seminary was written by Daniel Schwartz and is to be found on 267–83, 296–300.)

tradition, issues over which it and the modern camp sharply disagree, precisely in order to present *its* approach, both to itself and others, as the sole legitimate *Torah* approach and to *delegitimate* thereby the more accepting approach of the modern Orthodox camp.[34]

But more. *Daas Torah* does not only serve the function of underwriting the sole and exclusive legitimacy of the rejectionist approach to modernity; it is an essential constitutive element of that approach. And at this point we come to another, perhaps even deeper, difference between *Daas Torah* and halakhic *pesak*. For the difference between the two is not just a matter of halakhic—and particularly hashkafic!—pluralism versus halakhic—and hashkafic—uniformity. The difference also touches upon profound epistemological and axiological matters. For whereas halakhic *pesak* allows for, indeed encourages, reasoned debate and disagreement—within, of course, the framework of the halakhic system—*Daas Torah*, as indicated by the comments of Rav Dessler and Rabbi Weinberger, requires the suppression of one's own critical faculties and submission to the superior, if at times incomprehensible, wisdom of the *gadol*. And one must submit to the views of the *gadol* not simply because the halakhic system, in terms of its complex rules for resolving disputes, ascribes greater authority to his decisions. Rather, the views of the *gadol* are true and authentic, while my differing views are false and inauthentic. What is required of me, then, is, again, intellectual submission and faith in the *gadol* and his superior wisdom.

This being the case, it follows that the ideology of *Daas Torah* is a central, perhaps the central, element in the ethic of submission that characterizes the rejectionist approach. For at the heart of the rejectionist approach is the view that unquestioning submission to authority, the authority of *halakhah*, of the *gadol*, of God, is the

---

[34]For a similar explanation, see M. Herbert Danzger, *Returning to Tradition: The Contemporary Revival of Orthodox Judaism* (New Haven: Yale University Press, 1989), 167.

highest religious value and one that is absolutely opposed to the
modern values of intellectual autonomy and self-expression. It is,
therefore, only to be expected that two of the greatest representatives and thinkers of the rejectionist community, the *Hazon Ish* and
Rav Dessler, who were, as we have seen, forceful proponents of the
ideology of *Daas Torah*, were also profound exponents of the ethic
of submission. It would take us beyond the confines of this discussion to examine this ethic of submission in any depth and how it
finds expression in—indeed, is the cornerstone of—the writings of
Rav Dessler and the *Hazon Ish*.[35] Here two statements made by the
Hazon Ish must suffice.

First, in a letter replying to a correspondent who was apparently critical of certain aggadic statements of the Sages, the *Hazon
Ish* begins by arguing that it is "our obligation to keep far from
speculation [*mehkar*]," goes on to say that he just wishes to be a
"simple Jew" who is concerned with the "what," not the "why" of
Judaism, and climaxes his letter with the remarkable statement:
"We recoil upon hearing the casting of doubt on any statement of
Hazal, whether *halakhah* or *aggadah*, and view [such critical re-
marks] as constituting blasphemy, heaven forbid."[36]

---

[35]In a paper, "The Hazon Ish: Haredi Critic of Traditional Orthodoxy,"
to be published in a volume of essays, *The Uses of Tradition: Jewish
Continuity Since The Emancipation*, ed. Jack Wertheimer, I discuss at some
length the issue of the ethic of submission as found in the writings of the
Hazon Ish.

[36]*Kovetz Iggerot*, vol. 1, letter 15 (43). Cf. *Kovetz Iggerot*, vol. 3 (Bnei
Brak, 1990), letter 14 (43), where the *Hazon Ish's* insistence that all *aggadot*
in the Talmud are authoritative results in a rather forced interpretation on
his part of a statement of the Rashba. Contrast this view of the Hazon Ish
with the views on *aggadah* of Rav David Tzevi Hoffman in his Introduction to his commentary on *Va-Yikra* and Rav Samson Raphael Hirsch in
his two Hebrew letters to Rav Hile Wechsler, published by Mordecai
Breuer in *Ha-Maayan* (*Tevet* 5736) and trans. into English by Joseph Munk
in *L'Eylah* 27 (Pesah 5749): 30–35. The attempt on the part of Rav Yosef
Avraham Wolf, the well-known head of the Beth Jacob movement in *Eretz*

Second, at the beginning of Chapter 4 of *Emunah U-Bitahon*, the *Hazon Ish* states that "at the root [of man's manifold evil traits] there is only . . . one evil trait. This evil trait is allowing one's natural life to flow along its natural course."[37] The *Hazon Ish* goes on to argue, in that chapter, that the only way to rectify this evil trait is through absolute submission to the precise, extensive, and exceptionally difficult requirements of *halakhah (dikduk ha-din).*[38]

Of course, I hasten to add, any Orthodox approach, be it traditionalist or modern, must make room for authority and sub-mission within its worldview. However, the modern Orthodox approach, precisely because it is both modern and Orthodox, also seeks — within, of course, the authoritative framework of *halakhah* — to make room for such modern values as intellectual autonomy, creativity, critical independence, and self-expression. The writings of Rav Soloveitchik, in particular his classic essay "U-Bikashtem Mi-Sham," constitute, in my view, the most extensive and pro-foundest attempt in our age to establish a delicate and exquisite balance between these two poles.[39] Here, in an attempt to draw as

---

Yisrael and confidante of the *Hazon Ish*, to reconcile the view of the *Hazon Ish* with that of Rav Hoffman — Rav Wolf was unaware of the two at that time as yet unpublished letters of Rav Hirsch — in his essay, "Shiluv Emunat Torah she-be-al Peh be-Horaah," in *Ha-Tekufah u-Baayotehah* (Bnei Brak, 1981), 125–26, is exceptionally strained and singularly uncon-vincing, as indeed is Rav Wolf's entire valiant but quixotic and ultimately misguided attempt to reconcile the *haredi* ideology of the *Hazon Ish* with the *Torah im Derekh Eretz* ideology of Rav Hirsch, Rav Hoffman, and Rav Yehiel Yaakov Weinberg. There really are limits as to how far one can go in attempting to square the circle!

[37]*Hazon Ish, Emunah U-Bitahon*, 44.

[38]I discuss this matter in full in my forthcoming article, "The Hazon Ish."

[39]See Aviezer Ravitsky, "Kinyan ha-Daat be-Haguto: Bein ha-Rambam le-NeoKantianism," in *Sefer ha-Yovel li-Kebod ha-Rav Yosef Soloveitchik Shlit'a*, ed. R. Shaul Yisraeli et al. (Jerusalem: Mossad ha-Rav Kook, 1984),

sharp a contrast as possible, I would merely like to set down beside the statement of the *Hazon Ish* in Chapter 4 of *Emunah U-Bitahon* cited above, a statement of a contemporary modern Orthodox thinker.

> [My approach] . . . is a kind of theistic humanism . . . grounded in the doctrine of *Imagio Dei*, . . . [Since] human beings were created in the image of God . . . it follows that since God is all good, all human characteristics must be essentially good as well.[40]

The difference between the "theistic humanism" represented in this statement and the "theistic antihumanism," if we may term it such, of the *Hazon Ish* could not be clearer!

It is precisely because the modern Orthodox reject the ethic of submission that they are highly suspicious of the entire ideology of *Daas Torah*. Indeed, one astute observer has gone so far as to argue that it is precisely their opposing views on the issue of *Daas Torah* that serve as the key difference between the rejectionist camp and the modernist camp.

> We suggest . . . that the critical feature distinguishing the modernist [orthodox] from the traditionalist orthodox is *the nature and scope of the authority to which each is committed.* Traditionalists allow their leaders authority in political and

---

125–51 [= "Rabbi Joseph B. Soloveitchik on Human Knowledge: Between Maimonides and NeoKantianism," *Modern Judaism* 6:2 (May 1986): 157–88]; Lawrence Kaplan, "Rabbi Joseph B. Soloveitchik's Philosophy of Halakhah," *The Jewish Law Annual* 7 (1987): 139–97. I will discuss this issue as well in two forthcoming articles on Rabbi Soloveitchik: "From Freedom to Necessity and Back Again: Man's Religious Odyssey in the Thought of Rabbi Joseph Soloveitchik," and "Rabbi Joseph Soloveitchik as a Modern Halakhic Thinker."

[40]Moshe Sokol, "Personal Autonomy and Religious Authority," in this volume, p. 204.

personal matters, and the leadership attempts to exercise authority beyond the specifics of halakhah. . . . Modernists, in contrast, seek maximum scope for personal decision making and their leadership limits its authority only to halakhah.[41]

We would state matters somewhat differently. While the disagreement over *Daas Torah* between the modern Orthodox and the traditionalist Orthodox is certainly important, it is, as we have sought to show, symptomatic of a deeper division between them, namely, the different relative weights they assign to submission, authority, and self-overcoming, on the one hand, and autonomy, independence, and self-expression on the other. In a word, the debate over *Daas Torah* is ultimately a debate over the ethic of submission, over what is the proper posture of the halakhic Jew standing in the presence of God.[42]

In sum, this analysis of the differences between halakhic *pesak* and *Daas Torah* and between the rejectionist traditionalist Orthodox and the affirmative modern Orthodox has, I believe, brought to light two additional functions of the ideology of *Daas Torah*. First, the ideology of *Daas Torah* enables the traditionalist Orthodox to present their rejectionist approach to modernity as being the sole legitimate approach, thereby delegitimating the more affirmative approach of the modern Orthodox. Second, and even more important, the ideology of *Daas Torah* is a key element of that

---

[41]Danzger, *Returning to Tradition*, 164.

[42]After I had completed this essay, I came across Aryeh Fishman's important monograph, *Bein Dat le-Ideologiyah: Yahadut ve-Modernizatziah be-Kibbutz ha-Dati* (Jerusalem: Yad Yitzhak Ben-Zvi, 1990). In chap. 8 of his book, "Between Autonomous Religious Authority and Heteronomous Religious Authority" (164–88), Fishman discusses the issue of *Daas Torah* in the context of the manifold tensions that have arisen between the religious kibbutz movement and the established rabbinate and, as the chapter title indicates, approaches this issue from a perspective similar to my own.

rejectionist approach, being perhaps the quintessential expression of the traditionalist ethic of submission.[43]

DAAS TORAH AND CLASSICAL CONCEPTIONS OF RABBINIC AUTHORITY

A proponent of the ideology of *Daas Torah* might offer the following reply to the preceding analysis. "Even were your analysis correct—which, of course, I deny—it would still be irrelevant and, worse, misleading. For *Daas Torah* is not really a new concept of rabbinic authority at all, but just a reformulation, in modern terms, of a classical type of rabbinic authority. And if certain modern needs and challenges have led us to stress this concept, this does not mean that the concept itself is a modern one. And if *Daas Torah* is, as you say, the quintessential expression of the ethic of submission, perhaps this simply demonstrates that this ethic itself is well grounded in the classical sources of Judaism."

What, then, are the roots in the classical sources of the concept of *Daas Torah?*

The two key classical concepts in which *Daas Torah* is supposedly grounded are provided by Rav Dessler in his already cited letter. Rav Dessler stated:

> Our rabbis have told us to listen to the words of the Sages even if they tell us that right is left, and not to say, heaven forbid, that they certainly erred because little I can see their error with my own eyes. . . . This is the Torah view [*Daas Torah*] concerning faith in the Sages [*Emunat Hakhamim*].

Rav Dessler refers to two concepts as forming the basis for the ideology of *Daas Torah:* (1) *lo tasur,* according to the interpretation of the *Sifre* as cited by Rashi in his commentary on Deuteronomy 17:11, and (2) *Emunat Hakhamim.* Let us look at each in turn.

---

[43]See below, nn. 70 and 84.

The Torah in Deuteronomy in speaking of the authority of the Great Court *(Bet Din ha-Gadol)* states: "You shall not deviate [*lo tasur*] from the verdict that they announce to you either to the left or to the right" (Deuteronomy 17:11).

The meaning and implication of the phrase "to the left or to the right" *(yamin u-semol)* are the subject of two differing and perhaps conflicting explanations dealing with the question as to whether one is obliged or forbidden to submit to a ruling of the Great Court if one believes or is convinced they erred.

The *Sifre* in commenting on the verse states: "Even if it appears to you [*marin be-eynekha*][44] that they are telling you that right is left and left is right, listen to them."

This view of the *Sifre*, however, seems to be directly contradicted by an interpretation of the verse offered in *Yerushalmi Horayot.* "One might think that if they tell you that right is left and left is right, you must listen to them. Therefore, the verse tells us to go to the left or to the right, until they tell you that right is right and left is left."

This position taken by the *Yerushalmi* would, in turn, seem to be corroborated by the law set down in the *Gemara* in *Bavli Horayot* 2b, codified by the Rambam (*Hilkhot Sheggagot* 13:5) and cited by the Ramban (*Sefer ha-Mitzvot*, critical notes on Rambam's *Shoresh* 1), that if a sage or a student capable of issuing a ruling *(talmid she-higia le-horaah)* is convinced that the Great Court erred in a particular ruling he is forbidden to follow that ruling on the basis of its being a positive commandment to obey the charges of the Sages *(mitzvah lishmo'a divrei hakhamim).*

This apparent or real contradiction between the *Sifre* on the one hand and the *Yerushalmi Horayot* and the various other supporting sources on the other is needless to say a well-known and much discussed subject.[45] One can, of course, assume that the

---

[44]The text of the Gra is *"nirin be-einekha"*; the *Pesikta Zutarta* reads *domeh be-einekha.*

[45]For recent discussions of the problem, see Rav Menahem Kasher,

sources are simply contradictory.[46] If one assumes, however, that

---

Torah Sheleimah, vol. 17 (New York: American Biblical Encyclopedia Society, 1956), 293–94; Menahem Elon, *Ha-Mishpat ha-Ivri*, vol. 1 (Jerusalem: Magnes, 1973), 225–27; Michael Z. Nehorai, *Bein Yediah le-Emunah* (Jerusalem: Division of Education, Division for Torah Culture, 1982); Yitzhak A. Twersky, "Sanhedrin Mevarim o Mehavim Halakhah," in *Beit Yosef Shaul*, vol. 3 (New York: Rabbi Isaac Elchanan Theological Seminary, 1989), 269–76; Yaakov Ariel, "Lo Tasur mi-Kol asher Yorukha," *Tehumin* 11 (1990): 24–30; and, Jose Faur, *Iyyunim be-Mishneh Torah le-ha-Rambam* (Jerusalem: Mossad ha-Rav Kook, 1978), 21–23. For two important earlier discussions by a halakhic giant who combined both traditional and modern rabbinic scholarship, see Rav David Tzevi Hoffman, *The Great Court*, trans. from the German by Paul Forcheimer (New York: Feldheim, 1977), 110–17; and *Melamed le-Ho'il*, vol. 3, no. 82 (Frankfort: Hermon, 1926), 127–28. Both Faur and Rav Hoffman, in both of his essays, provide the reader with very rich guidance to the primary sources. Two thoughtful and learned essays by Avi Sagie (Schweitzer) that touch on this issue, though it is not their main concern, are "Iyyun be-Shenei Modelim shel Musag ha-Emet ha-Hilkhatit u-Mashma'utam," in *Higayyon*, ed. M. Koppel and E. Merzbach (Jerusalem: Bar-Ilan, 1989), 69–90, and "Baayat ha-Hakhraah ha-Hilkhatit ve-ha-Emet ha-Hilkhatit," *Dine Israel* 15 (1989–90): 1–38. A more homiletic treatment of the problem, with, however, an interesting range of primary sources, may be found in Y. Nahshoni "Afilu Omrim Lekha al Yamin she-Hu Semol," in *Hagut be-Parshiyot ha-Torah*, vol. 2 (Bnei Brak, 1984), 773–77.

[46]See Rav Hoffman, *Melamed le-Ho'il*; and Elon, *Ha-Mishpat ha-Ivri*, 226 n. 19. Rav Hoffman argues that the root of the debate is exegetical in nature, Professor Elon, that it is more ideological in character. Obviously, these two approaches need not be mutually exclusive, in other words, one may claim, for example, that the dispute at its deepest level is ideological, but that on a more formal level it expresses itself in the varying ways in which the verse is interpreted. It is striking that while Rav Hoffmam in his earlier study, *The Great Court*, tries to harmonize the *Sifre* and the *Yerushalmi*, in his later study in *Melamed le-Ho'il* he argues that all attempts at harmonization are strained and that the sources are in disagreement.

the sources are not contradictory, then there are a number of different ways of reconciling them. Perhaps they are talking about different persons, different measures of conviction, different types of rulings, or different stages in issuing a particular ruling. For example, the *Sifre* may be speaking about someone who is not a scholar or a student capable of issuing a ruling, where the *Yerushalmi Horayot* (and obviously the *Bavli*) is speaking only of a scholar or a student capable of issuing a ruling;[47] or, the *Sifre* may be speaking about someone who *believes* that the court has erred—note the use of the phrase *"marin be-eynekha"* (it appears to you)—where the *Yerushalmi* is speaking of one who is absolutely certain the court has erred;[48] or, again, the *Sifre* may be speaking of an error in judgment *(ta'ut be-shikul ha-daat)*, and the *Yerushalmi* of an error involving the oversight of an explicit authoritative precedent *(ta'ut bi-devar mishnah)*[49]—to put this another way, the *Sifre* may be referring to an error in *dinim mufla'im* where the *Yerushalmi* may be concerned with an error in a *guf torah*;[50] finally, it may be that the *Yerushalmi* is speaking of the time period immediately following upon the ruling, when the sage who is convinced the court erred must disregard its ruling, where the *Sifre* is referring to a situation in

---

[47]See Nehorai, *Bein Yediah le-Emunah*, 15.

[48]See the sources cited in Hoffman, *The Great Court*, and also *Ha-Ketav ve-ha-Kabbalah*, and *Torah Temimah* on Deuteronomy 17:11.

[49]This is the way that Twersky, "Sanhedrin Mevarim," 274, understands the Ramban's resolution (*Sefer ha-Mitzvot, Shoresh* 1) of the contradiction. But see n. 51. For recent discussions of the difference between *ta'ut be-shikul ha-daat* and *ta'ut bi-devar mishnah*, based on an analysis of the medieval sources, see Joel Roth, *The Halakhic Process* (New York: Jewish Theological Seminary, 1986), 90–103; and Rabbi Michael Rosensweig, "*Eilu ve-Eilu Divrei Elohim Hayyim*: Halakhic Pluralism and Theories of Controversy," in this volume. In general, there is a significant and suggestive overlap between the subjects treated in Rabbi Rosensweig's important paper and the issues treated in this section of this chapter.

[50]This is the way Faur, *Iyyunim be-Mishneh Torah*, 22–23, understands the Rambam's implicit resolution of the problem.

which the sage brings his arguments to the court after the ruling is issued, and the court, after discussing the arguments, rejects them and maintains its original position.[51] Nor are these varying possi-

---

[51]This would seem to be the way the Ramban (*Sefer ha-Mitzvot*, critical notes on the Rambam's *Shoresh* 1) resolves the contradiction. It should be noted that the Ramban does not specifically discuss the *Yerushalmi Horayot* but rather focuses on the *Gemara* at the beginning of *Bavli Horayot*. Nevertheless, one may safely assume—as do most later scholars who discuss the Ramban—that the Ramban would claim that the *Yerushalmi* is referring to the same situation as the *Bavli*. See, for example, the excellent analysis of the *Hasdei David*, vol. 2 (Livorno, 1790), 102:2; Rav Hoffman, *The Great Court*, 113–14; Maharitz Hayyot, "Maamar Lo Tasur," in *Torat Neviim*, 98; and Yaakov Ariel, "Lo Tasur," 20–21.

Twersky (see note 49) claims that the Ramban's distinction is equivalent to a distinction between *ta'ut be-shikul ha-daat* and *ta'ut bi-devar mishnah*. As Twersky argues: "Before the sage came to the Sanhedrin, he believed that the Great Court erred *bi-devar mishnah*—i.e., were they to hear his arguments they would reverse their decision and concur with his view. Therefore, he is obliged to act in accordance with his view against the Sanhedrin. However, once he came before them and 'they rejected his arguments, etc.' there is no possibility that the ruling of the Sanhedrin was an error *bi-devar mishnah*, but [there is only the possibility] of an error *be-shikul ha-daat*" (p. 274). It would follow, however, from Twersky's argument that if the sage, to begin with, before he came to the Sanhedrin, felt that it had committed an error *be-shikul ha-daat* in permitting that which is forbidden, he would be permitted to act in accordance with its ruling and would not be obliged to present his arguments before the Sanhedrin. But there are no grounds for assuming that this is the Ramban's view. Rather, the Ramban seems to suggest that if the sage believes the Sanhedrin erred in permitting that which is forbidden, whether the error be one of *devar mishnah* or of *shikul ha-daat*, he is not permitted to act in accordance with its ruling and must present his arguments before it. Only *after* he presents his arguments and the court rejects them may he then act in accordance with its ruling and submit to its authority, even if he still believes that it erred *be-shikul ha-daat*. (See *Hasdei David* on this last matter.) The point of the Ramban seems to be

bilities exclusive of one another. In fact, they may be cumulative, in other words, a person is forbidden to obey the ruling of a Great Court which he believes is erroneous only if (1) he is a sage or a student who is capable of issuing a ruling, (2) he is *convinced* the ruling is erroneous, (3) he is convinced that it is an error *bi-devar mishnah* or *be-guf torah*, and (4) he has not as yet presented his arguments concerning the erroneous nature of the ruling to the Great Court.[52]

Let us, however, for the purposes of this discussion, put the *Yerushalmi* and *Bavli Horayot* to the side and focus on the *Sifre*, seeking to trace its fortunes.

As we saw, the injunction in the *Sifre* is not stated in absolute terms. Its use of the phrase "even if it appears to you" leaves open the possibility, noted above, that one who does not merely believe but is convinced that the court's ruling is erroneous is not obliged— indeed, is not permitted—to follow that ruling. However, Rashi, in his Commentary on Deuteronomy 17:11, rephrases the *Sifre* in a more categorical manner. "Even if they tell you that right is left and left is right."[53]

---

that a qualified scholar must submit to the ruling of the Great Court, even if he believes that ruling to be in error, only if that ruling has been issued *after consideration of all the relevant evidence, precedents, and arguments.* Only such a ruling can be authoritative. Obviously, under such circumstances, the error, if it be such, can only be an error *be-shikul ha-daat.* This view of the Ramban is followed by the *Sefer ha-Hinukh,* negative commandment, no. 508 (Chavel ed., 631–32). See, as well, Maharitz Hayyot, "Maamar Lo Tasur," 99–102.

[52] But see the previous note, where we have argued that according to the Ramban, even if a sage believed the ruling of the Great Court permitting that which is forbidden to be an error *be-shikul ha-daat* he would still not be allowed to act on its ruling and would be obliged to present his arguments against its ruling before the Court for its consideration.

[53] Already the Ramban in his comment on Deuteronomy 17:11 differentiated between *leshon Rashi* and *leshon Sifre*. Cf., however, *Shir ha-Shirim Rabbah* 1:18 (Dunsky ed., 19) for the reading *"afilu she-yomru lekha."*

This substitution of "they tell you" (omar lekha) for "it appears to you" (marin be-eyenekha) would seem to indicate that even if one is convinced the court's ruling is erroneous, one is still obliged to heed it.

Why? Why would one have to heed the ruling of the Great Court even if one is convinced the ruling is mistaken. The Ramban, in his *Commentary on the Torah* on this verse, picks up on Rashi's reformulation of the *Sifre* and offers two varying, perhaps conflicting, explanations.

> The import is that even if you think that they are wrong, and the matter is as obvious to you as your ability to distinguish between right and left, follow their commandments. And do not say, "How can I eat *helev* or how can I kill this innocent person?" but say, "Thus was I commanded by the Lord who enjoined the commandments, that I should perform all His commandments in accordance with all that they who stand before Him in the place that He shall choose shall teach me to do. And it is on the basis of their understanding of its meaning that He gave me the Torah, even if they are mistaken." . . . And the need for this commandment is very great. For the Torah was given to us in written form, and it is known that not all views will be in agreement regarding newly arising matters. Thus, disputes will multiply and the [one] Torah will be become many *Torot*. Scripture, therefore, set down the law that we are to obey the Great Court that stands before God in the place He shall choose in all that they tell us concerning the interpretation of the Torah. . . . For it is in accordance with their understanding that He gave them the Torah, even if in your eyes [their ruling] seems to exchange right for left.

The Ramban in this explanation—in essence, the same explanation he offers in his *Sefer ha-Mitzvot*[54]—is making two points.

_____

[54]*Sefer ha-Mitzvot*, critical notes on the Rambam's *Shoresh* 1. The

First, the Divine Lawgiver has determined that the Sages' interpretation of the Law becomes the Law. Second, the reason for this determination is to ensure uniformity of halakhic practice, so that "the [one] Torah" should not "become many *Torot*." There is, however, a certain ambiguity here regarding the question of error. At one point the Ramban seems to grant the possibility of error, but deems it irrelevant.[55] The overall thrust of his statement, however, is to make the very issues of truth and falsehood, error and infallibility inapplicable. For the meaning of the scriptural text is indeterminate and only achieves determinate meaning via the interpretation of the Sages.[56]

Ramban uses almost exactly the same language in *Sefer ha-Mitzvot* as he does in his Commentary. There are slight differences in wording between the two passages, most probably of no significance. But see the next note.

[55]"And it is on the basis of their understanding of its meaning that He gave me the Torah, *even if they are mistaken*." The Ramban in *Sefer ha-Mitzvot* words this slightly differently, *perhaps* weakening the idea of error.

[56]This seems to be the import of the conclusion of the Ramban's statement. It is in the light of this contention of the Ramban that we understand his citation of the famous story in *Rosh ha-Shanah* 25a about the debate between Rabban Gamliel and Rabbi Joshua. Just as the Great Court's determination of a particular day as the new month doesn't simply affirm an already existing reality but *constitutes* that day as the new month, so, in an analogous manner, the Great Court's understanding of the meaning of a verse is similarly constitutive. For a different understanding of why the Ramban cites this story, see Twersky, "Sanhedrin Mevarim," 274. Cf., as well, R. Yitzhak Hutner, *Pahad Yitzhak: Pesah* (New York: Gur Aryeh, 1970), 64–65 (31:2).

Precisely the ambiguity in the Ramban discussed in the text has allowed Avi Sagie to state that according to the Ramban, "there can be a conflict between the divine truth and the human truth of the Sages, but God revealed His will that [in such cases] the human truth prevail," while, at the same time, it has permitted Aaron Kirschenbaum to argue "that according to the Ramban there is no objective 'right'. The 'right' is what the Sages declare to be 'right'." See Sagie, "Iyyun be-Shenei Modelim," 79

The Ramban, however, continues:

> And certainly [you must follow their rulings] for you ought to
> think that they are telling you regarding the right that it is
> right; for God's spirit is upon "the ministers of His Sanctuary"
> (Ezekiel 45:4) and "He does not abandon His pious ones
> [*hasidav*]; they are preserved forever" (Psalms 37:28) from error
> and stumbling.[57]

---

and 88 n. 34; and Kirschenbaum, "Dinei ha-Yosher be-Mishpat ha-Ivri,"
Daat 13 (Summer 1984): 50. (Again, the chapter by Rabbi Michael
Rosensweig in this volume sheds much light on this issue.)

It should be noted that this comment of the Ramban was extraordi-
narily influential and formed the basis of almost all subsequent discussions
of the *Sifre* and Rashi. See, for example, *Sefer ha-Hinukh*, negative commandment, no. 508 (Chavel ed., 671); *Derashot ha-Ran*, no. 11 (Feldman
edition, 198); Mizrachi; *Hasdei David*; Maharitz Hayyot; Rav Hoffman,
The Great Court. (For the last three sources cited, see above, n. 51.)

[57]It is worth emphasizing that the Ramban does *not* cite this reason in
his *Sefer ha-Mitzvot*. It has not been noted, to my knowledge, that the
Ramban is basically structuring his comment on Deuteronomy 17:11 as an
explanation and an expansion of Rashi's comment. In the first part of his
comment the Ramban explains the reason for obeying the Great Court
"even if—citing Rashi—they tell you that right is left and left is right." He
then proceeds in this second part of his comment to explain Rashi's
enigmatic statement "and certainly if they tell you that right is right and
left is left." *Peshita! Mai ka mashma lan?!* According to the Ramban, this
second statement of Rashi does not refer to a second situation, but to *a
second reason* for submitting to the authority of the Great Court even when
one thinks that it has erred in its ruling; in other words, in the Ramban's
view, Rashi's statement *"ve-kol she-ken she-omer lekha"* means *ve-kol she-ken
she-yesh lekha lahshov she-omrim lekha."* It is not surprising, then, that the
Ramban in the *Sefer ha-Mitzvot*, where he is explaining the *Sifre* and not
Rashi, leaves out the suggestion of divine protection from error put
forward in his commentary. (That this notion of divine protection from
error is to be found only in the Ramban's commentary and not in his *Sefer
ha-Mitzvot* has been pointed out by Gerald Blidstein. See Blidstein,

According to this explanation, the concept of error in interpretation is meaningful, but the Sages are divinely prevented from erring. Here, then, we have a view approaching, though by no means identical with, that of *Daas Torah*.

A view similar to this second explanation of the Ramban is offered by Judah Halevi in the *Kuzari* (3:41).

> The Biblical injunction "you shall not add to the word which I command you, nor shall you take away from it" (Deuteronomy 4:2) means the following: You shall not add to the word which the priests and judges in the place God shall choose have agreed to.[58] For they receive aid from the divine

---

"Masoret ve-Samkhut Mosdit le-Raayon Torah she-be-al Peh be-Mishnat ha-Rambam," *Daat* 16 [Winter 1988]: 21 n. 37. We cannot, however, agree with Professor Blidstein's explanation of this shift.)

Despite the fact that—if our argument is right—the Ramban in putting forward the notion of divine protection from error is not so much speaking in his own name as in Rashi's, this view, like the first part of his comment, has been very influential. See, for example, *Siftei Hakhamim*; and see the sources cited in Piekarz, *Hasidut Polin*, 83–87.

[58]This view of Halevi that *Bal Tosif* applies to the individual and not the Great Court may be found as well in the *Guide* 3:41 (Pines ed., 563), and, in particular, *Hiddushei ha-Rashba* on *Rosh ha-Shanah* 16a, s.v. *lamah toke'in*. This statement of the Rashba has been much discussed by the *aharonim* (see *Pnei Yehoshua*, *Keren Orah*, etc.) and in general is identified with him. However, in light of the earlier statements in the *Kuzari* and the *Guide* we may say that the innovation of the Rashba is to take a well-known Spanish view that up until his time was only to be found in "aggadic," philosophical contexts, and to put it forward as a strictly halakhic claim. (That the Rashba is drawing upon an earlier view has already been noted by Professor Blidstein. See "Maimonides on 'Oral Law,'" *The Jewish Law Annual* 1 [1978]: 114 n. 15; and "Masoret ve-Samkhut Mosdit," 13 n. 9. Blidstein, however, has the Rashba drawing upon the *Kuzari* and overlooks his immediate source in the *Guide*.) For the standard medieval explanation of *Bal Tosif*, see Rambam, "Introduction" to the *Mishneh Torah*; *Hilkhot Mamrim* 2:9; *Hassagot* of the Rabad, ad. loc.;

presence. And since their number is very great it is impossible that they should agree to something which contradicts the Torah. Nor can they err since their wisdom is very great.

It should be immediately noted that both the Ramban and Halevi limit this halakhic infallibility specifically to the Great Court functioning in the temple precincts in the presence of God. And, in general, the special grant of authority contained in Deuteronomy 17:11 is, according to the view of many authorities, limited to the Great Court.[59]

At the same time attempts were made through the centuries to extend the authority attaching to the Great Court to other institutions or individuals, attempts which, if put into practice, were more often than not bitterly opposed. The Gaon and contemporary of the Rambam, R. Samuel b. Ali, head of the Yeshiva of Baghdad, for example, put forth the radical and far-reaching claim that the *yeshivah* in Baghdad was the Sanhedrin reconstituted, and the head of the *yeshivah* its Moses. R. Samuel b. Ali's statement is particularly important insofar as he attributes ultimate political and communal authority to the *yeshivah*, arguing that just as the king was subordinate to the Sanhedrin, so the *rosh golah* ought to be subordinate to the *yeshivah* and its Gaon.[60] This entire philosophy,

---

and the discussion of the *Or Sameah*, ad loc. (For a penetrating discussion of the Rambam's view, see the two articles by Blidstein referred to immediately above.)

[59]See, for example, *Responsa of the Ribash*, no. 271; and note in particular the very limited scope accorded to *lo tasur* in Maharitz Hayyot, "Maamar Lo Tasur," 102.

[60]See the excerpts from the "pastoral" letter sent by R. Samuel B. Ali to the Jewish communities in Syria published by S. Assaf in *Tarbiz* 1:2 (1930): 64–66. For other Geonic views on the halakhic authority of the Babylonian *Yeshivot* and the *Geonim*, see the sources cited in Faur, *Iyyunim be-Mishneh Torah*, 33–36; Shalom Spiegel, "Le-Parshat ha-Pulmus shel Pirkoi ben Baboi" in the Wolfson Jubilee Volume (Jerusalem: American Academy for Jewish Research, 1965), 243–74; and, most recently, Me-

as is well known, was criticized, root and branch, by the Rambam.
As the Rambam states in the *Mishneh Torah*, the injunction of *lo
tasur* is limited to the Great Court.[61] Even the *Gemara*, inasmuch as

---

nahem Ben-Sasson, "Shivrei Iggrot me-ha-Genizah: Le-Toldot Hiddush
ha-Kesharim shel Yeshivot Bavel im ha-Maarav," *Tarbiz* 56 (1987):
180–88; and idem, "Ha-Mivneh, ha-Megamot ve-ha-Tokhen shel Hibbur
Natan ha-Bavli" in *Tarbut ve-Hevrah be-Toldot Yisrael bi-Yemei ha-
Beynayyim*, ed. R. Bonfil et al. (Jerusalem: Merkaz Shazar, 1989), 159–62.

[61]*Hilkhot Mamrim* 1:2 and the list of commandments at the head of the
section. Note, however, that in the *Sefer ha-Mitzvot* the Rambam states
that the positive commandment *"al pi ha-Torah asher yorukha"* refers to the
obligation to adhere to the commands of the Great Court (positive
commandment, no. 174) but that the negative commandment, *"lo tasur,"*
refers to the prohibition against differing from the *baalei ha-kabbalah*, the
"authorized bearers of the tradition" (negative commandment, no. 32). It
is clear, however, from the "Introduction" to the *Mishneh Torah* that, for
the Rambam, Ravina, and Rav Ashi and their generation were the last of
the *baalei ha-kabbalah*. In any event, then, even according to the formulation in *Sefer ha-Mitzvot*, the prohibition of *lo tasur* is limited to dissenting
from the rulings of the talmudic sages. Note, too, that already in the list of
the commandments in the "Introduction" to the *Mishneh Torah*, the
Rambam reformulates *lo tasur* to refer to rebelling against the authority of
the [Great] Court. (The term *ha-gadol* is found in only some manuscripts.)
In general, one can see an evolution of the Rambam's conception of the
nature of *Torah she-be-al peh* in the direction of an ever more prominent
and ever more central role being accorded to the Great Court. Thus, in
the Rambam's "Introduction" to his *Commentary on the Mishnah* there is no
mention at all of the Great Court! In *Sefer ha-Mitzvot*, as we saw, the
Rambam speaks of the Great Court in positive commandment, no. 174,
but of the *baalei ha-kabbalah* in negative commandment, no. 312. It is only
in the "Introduction" to the *Mishneh Torah* and in *Hilkhot Mamrim* that
the Great Court becomes, for the Rambam, the linchpin of the entire
halakhic system. Finally, in the *Guide*, both the prohibition against
writing down the Oral Law (*Guide* 1:71) and that against adding to or
detracting from the Law (*Guide* 3:41) are interpreted as prohibitions
designed to maintain and uphold the authority of the Great Court as the

it was edited when the Great Court was no longer functioning, is authoritative only because it was accepted by all of Israel.[62] Post-talmudic sages possess no inherent authority at all.[63] The Rambam gives yet a further twist of the knife by referring to all posttalmudic sages as *Geonim*.[64] Such a definition—and this was certainly its intention—stripped the traditional *Geonim*, the heads of the Babylonian *yeshivot*, of any special status.[65] Moreover, the Rambam's radical deflation of the authority of the traditional *Geonim* was

---

central, indeed sole, halakhic decision-making body, both judicial and legislative, and to rule out such activity on the part of individuals. (Note the similarity of language between 1:71 and 3:41.) I discuss this matter in full in a forthcoming article, "The Evolution of Maimonides' Conception of the Oral Law." See, in this connection, the two articles by Blidstein cited above, n. 58.

[62]See Introduction to the *Mishneh Torah* (Lieberman ed., 11–12). For a discussion of this famous statement of the Rambam, see, Faur, *Iyyunim be-Mishneh Torah*, 42–46; Rabbi Professor Samuel Bialoblocki, "Eim le-Masoret ha-Perush ve-ha-Halakhah," in *Eim la-Masoret* (Bar-Ilan, 1971), 95–96; Rav Joseph B. Soloveitchik, "Kevi'at ha-Mo'adim al pi ha-Re'iyah ve-al pi ha-Heshbon," *Or HaMizrach* 100 (1980): 19–20; *idem*, "Shnei Sugei Masoret," in *Shi'urim le-Zekher Abba Mari*, vol. 1 (Jerusalem: Makhon Yerushalayim, 1983), 234–36.

[63]Introduction to the *Mishneh Torah* (Lieberman ed., 10–11).

[64]Ibid., 12. "All the Sages who arose after the compilation of the Talmud and studied it . . . are called Geonim. And all these Geonim who arose in the land of Israel and in the land of *Shinar* and in *Sefarad* and in *Tzarfat*. . . ." For the Rambam's attitude to the halakhic authority of the Geonim, see Faur, *Iyyunim be-Mishneh Torah*, 41–42, 45–46; Meir Havat-zelet, *Ha-Rambam ve-ha-Geonim* (New York: Sura, 1967); and Robert Brody, "Maimonides' Attitude towards the Halakhic Innovations of the Geonim," in *The Thought of Moses Maimonides: Philosophical and Legal Studies*, ed. I. Robinson et al. (Lewiston, NY: Edwin Mellen, 1990), 183–208.

[65]I am reminded, *mutatis mutandis*, of Henry Higgins's assertion, in Shaw's *Pygmalion*, that there is no difference between treating flower girls like duchesses and duchesses like flower girls.

complemented and reinforced by his attributing extensive powers to the *rosh golah*.[66]

Another, more theoretical, attempt to extend the authority ascribed to the Great Court to contemporary rabbinic scholars is to be found in the *Sefer ha-Hinukh*. Both in the positive commandment "to heed all Great Courts which will arise" (no. 492), and the negative one "not to disobey the charge of the Great Court" (no. 508), the author of the *Sefer ha-Hinukh* insists that the obligation of obedience contained in these commandments is also owed to "the outstanding sage among us in our era" (no. 492) or to "the earlier sages and the outstanding rabbinic scholars and judges of our day" (no. 508).[67]

The extension of the authority of the Great Court to contemporary institutions and individuals, it should be immediately noted, does not, of course, necessarily mean that such institutions or individuals are divinely protected from error, since, as we have

----

[66]See *Hilkhot Sanhedrin* 4:13–14; *Commentary on the Mishnah, Bekhorot* 4:4; and *Iggerot ha-Rambam*, ed. Y. Shailat, vol. 1 (Jerusalem: Maaliyot, 1988), 309. For the Rambam's view on the *Rosh Golah*, see Blidstein, *Ekronot Mediniyyim be-Mishnat ha-Rambam* (Jerusalem: Bar-Ilan, 1983), 46–48, 140–43.

[67]Note that while Rabbi Samuel b. Ali extends the authority of the Great Court to the *institution* of the *yeshivah*, the *Sefer ha-Hinukh* extends it to individual rabbinic scholars. For a suggestive, if somewhat strained, attempt to narrow the differences between the *Sefer ha-Hinukh* and the Rambam, see Yehudah ha-Levi Amihai, "Daas Torah be-Inyanim she-einam Hilkhatiyim Muvhakim," *Tehumin* 11 (1990): 24–25. The Ran states that the authority of the post-Great Court sages in the matter of explanations of the laws of the Torah derives from *"aharei rabbim le-hattot,"* while their authority in the matter of decrees or ordinances belongs to the penumbra of *lo tasur (be-derekh asmakhta)*. See *Derashot Ha-Ran*, ed. Leon Feldman, no. 12 (Jerusalem: Makhon Shalem, 1973), 213. Of course, on the basic issue as to whether the decrees or ordinances of the Sages are covered by *lo tasur* altogether, the Ran sides with the Rambam against the Ramban.

seen, it is a matter of grave debate if even the Great Court itself enjoys such protection. On the one hand, R. Samuel b. Ali almost explicitly asserts that the rulings of the *Yeshivah* are free from error.[68] On the other hand, the *Sefer ha-Hinukh* follows the view expressed by the Ramban in the *Sefer ha-Mitzvot* and in his first explanation in his *Commentary on the Torah* in holding that the reason one may not deviate from the words of the sages, even if they say that right is left and left is right, is not because of any divine grant of infallibility but in order to ensure halakhic uniformity. Indeed, the *Sefer ha-Hinukh* goes even further than the Ramban in openly admitting the possibility of error.

> The Sages have stated: " 'You shall not deviate . . . either to the right or the left'. Even if they tell you that right is left and left is right." This is to say that *even if they err about a particular matter* it is better to suffer this particular error and let everyone always be subject to their wise understanding, than to let every person act in accordance with his own understanding. For this will lead to the destruction of religion, divisions among the people, and the complete decline of the nation.[69]

---

[68]*Tarbiz* 1:2:64. *"Ki ba-zeh nishmerot datot Yisrael u-mitkayyem mah she-be-yadam me-emunatam, she-lo yitu ve-lo yatu me-ha-amitot."*

[69]*Sefer ha-Hinukh*, negative commandment, no. 508. In this connection, the *Sefer ha-Hinukh* cites the famous story of the oven of Akhnai (*Baba Metzia* 59b), understanding it to mean that even though "the truth was with R. Eliezer," the majority still prevails "whether they declare the truth or even if they err." For a similar approach, see *Derashot ha-Ran*, no. 5, second version (84–86), no. 7 (112), and no. 11 (198–99). Note that the Ran also cites the story of the oven of Akhnai and understands it the same way as does the *Sefer ha-Hinukh*. There is a problem, however, with the view of the Ran. On the one hand, the Ran states that God in revealing to Moses *dikdukei sofrim* revealed to him "all of the disputes and different opinions [that would arise] between the Jewish Sages" (85, 112). On the other hand, the Ran states that in a disagreement between the Sages, the majority view prevails "whether it conform to the truth or to its opposite"

To return, then, to the ideology of *Daas Torah*, we may say that this ideology takes as its basis the position of the *Sifre* as formulated by Rashi (ignoring the *Yerushalmi Horayot* and the various other sources which posit an obligation of dissent under certain circumstances), understands the *Sifre* in the light of the second explanation of the Ramban in his *Commentary on the Torah*,[70] and then extends this protection from error to the out-

---

(85, 112, 198–99). But, if both views were revealed to Moses, how can the Ran say that one of them is not true?! Perhaps what the Ran wishes to say is that the divine revelation of both views only means that both views are valid and legitimate interpretations of the Torah. Nevertheless, only one of the two conflicting views can be in accord with the pure, "objective" truth of the Torah. Since, however, even the view which is not "true" was also revealed and is, therefore, legitimate, if it receives the assent of the majority, it, despite its not being "true," becomes the authoritative view, for "God, may He be blessed, has given the Sages of the generation the power of [making such] determinations *(hakhraah)* in disputes between the Sages" (85, 112, 189). For the history of the interpretation of the story of the oven of Akhnai, see I. Englard, "Tanur shel Akhnai: Perushehah shel Aggadah," *Shenaton ha-Mishpat ha-Ivri* 1 (1974): 45–56 [= "Majority Decision and Individual Truth: The Interpretation of the Oven of Akhnai Aggadah," *Tradition* 11:1–2 (Spring-Summer 1975): 137–72]. Surprisingly, Professor Englard does not even touch on what would seem to be the exceptionally relevant issue of the apparent contradiction between the *Sifre* and the *Yerushalmi Horayot* on *yamin u-semol*. Indeed, a close comparison of the history of interpretation of *both* cruxes – the story of the oven of Akhnai and the apparently contradictory rulings of the *Sifre* and *Yerushalmi Horayot* – and a determination as to what extent the issues they raise overlap or diverge is an important desideratum and would, I believe, prove enlightening. In this connection, many of Rabbi Michael Rosensweig's reflections in chap. 3 of this volume are highly pertinent.

[70]It must be stated that there is a contemporary version of *Daas Torah* that does concede the possibility of authoritative scholars being in error. Thus, Rav Aryeh Tzevi Frommer, a noted hasidic and rabbinic scholar, in a sermon delivered in 1930, set forth the following conception of *Daas Torah* (cited in Piekarz, *Hasidut Polin*, 95–96):

standing sages (*gedolim*) of contemporary times.[71]

_____

> And this is a fundamental principle of *Torah she-be-al peh*, to negate
> our views [in submission] to the views of the sages of the generation,
> even in a case where we feel that the truth is with us. And even if
> they tell you that right is left, do not turn aside [*lo tasur,*] from their
> words. . . . For this power, that the world and the entire Torah will
> be in accordance with the views [*Daat*] of the sages of the generation,
> *even if the truth is not in accordance with their words*, comes to us by the
> merit and the power of *Emunat Hakhamim*, since we negate our views
> when it is proper, even if it is against our intellect. . . . And we have
> inherited this power of *Emunat Hakhamim* from *Akedat Yitzhak*; for
> our father, Yitzhak was the first who negated his views and his
> intellect in the presence of the sage of the generation [i.e., Abra-
> ham], and he transmitted this power to all future generations.

Thus, Rav Frommer, on the one hand, and the Ramban and the *Sefer
ha-Hinukh*, on the other, grant the views of contemporary sages—for the
Ramban, the views of the Great Court—authoritative standing even in
cases of error. However, their rationales for granting such standing differ
radically. For the Ramban and the *Sefer ha-Hinukh*, the rationale is the
need for halakhic uniformity, whereas for Rav Frommer, it is the need to
demonstrate intellectual and religious submission, to perform an *akedah* of
the intellect, to declare *"credo quia absurdum est."* We can have no clearer
example of the concept of *Daas Torah* as an expression of the ethic of
submission! In general, we should sharply distinguish the spirit of self-
abnegation toward the views of earlier outstanding scholars found in the
views of Rav Frommer and other like-minded scholars (see Piekarz, *Hasidut
Polin*, 93–96) from the spirit of extreme deference and respect toward the
views of earlier outstanding scholars combined however with staunch and
unyielding critical independence, as found in all the halakhic writings of
the Ramban, and as given such eloquent expression in his prefaces to the
Commentary on the Torah, the *Sefer ha-Mitzvot*, and *Milhamot A-Donai*. But
see below, n. 83.

[71]Note how the Agudah ideology of *Daas Torah*, however, *first* extends
the authority of the Great Court to contemporary outstanding rabbinic
scholars and *then* seeks to institutionalize the personal charisma of these

Even this, however, does not amount to the full-blown ideology of *Daas Torah*. For *Daas Torah* not only extends the disputed divine protection from error granted to the Great Court to the *gedolim* of a particular generation, it further argues that this protection not only covers halakhic *pesak* but also communal policy, indeed, communal policy in particular.[72] If anything, exponents of the ideology of *Daas Torah*, when it concerns traditional halakhic *pesak*, do espouse a form of halakhic pluralism and acknowledge the legitimacy and perhaps even the desirability of debate and dissent. It is only on the broad communal hashkafic issues that the notion of *Daas Torah*, with all of its aura and weight, is invoked. As we have already noted, this should be seen as an attempt to delegitimate dissent on these issues and to create an appearance of consensus where in fact there is no consensus.

That the ideology of *Daas Torah*, then, has a basis in and constitutes an extension of certain traditional sources regarding *lo tasur . . . yamin u-semol* is clear; that it very carefully ignores other

---

scholars in the organizational form of the *Moetzes Gedolei ha-Torah*. Of course this ideology, in practice, sometimes works in reverse, in other words, a scholar, *ipso facto*, becomes a *"gadol"* by being appointed to the *Moetzes Gedolei ha-Torah*. For, were he not a true *gadol*, how could he be a member of that august body?

[72]In this respect, the view of Rabbi Samuel b. Ali provides the clearest medieval precedent for the notion of *Daas Torah* inasmuch as it ascribes general political power and communal supremacy as well as halakhic authority to the Babylonian *yeshivot*. Nevertheless, in traditional circles, it is the views of the *Ramban* and the *Sefer ha-Hinukh* that are generally cited in support of *Daas Torah*. See, for example, the many essays in *Ve-Zarah ha-Shemesh* (above, n. 28). These essays, unfortunately, do not address the many problems involved in using the Ramban and the *Sefer ha-Hinukh* as precedents for the concept of *Daas Torah*. But, then, most of these essays originated as addresses delivered at the various founding conventions and conclaves of *Degel ha-Torah*. One, in all fairness, ought not, then, to expect too much of essays which, to begin with, were primarily intended to serve as theologicopolitical pep talks.

sources and is a problematic extension of even the sources it relies upon is equally clear.

Let us turn to the second traditional source cited in support of *Daas Torah*, namely, *Emunat Hakhamim*. Here it is possible to be briefer.[73]

The term *Emunat Hakhamim* appears only once in rabbinic literature, in *Perek Kinyan Torah* of *Avot*. It would seem to be more of an aggadic concept than a halakhic concept and its meaning is very obscure. To base, then, the ideology of *Daas Torah* on *Emunat Hakhamim* amounts to what Schopenhauer—fairly or unfairly—said about the ontological argument: It amounts to smuggling an idea into a particular concept and then proceeding to discover it therein.

First, it is not even clear if *Emunat Hakhamim* means "faith in the Sages." Already the Midrash Shmuel, in one of his explanations, suggests that *Emunat Hakhamim* means the "faith *of* the Sages," that is, a faith based on tradition passed down through the generations going back to Moses. A similar explanation has been offered independently by Rabbi Norman Lamm, who notes that the term used is *Emunat Hakhamim*, not *Emunah be-Hakhamim*. For Rabbi Lamm, *Emunat Hakhamim* means "a wise man's faith," that is "a sophisticated faith as opposed to a primitive, naive, simplistic faith." An even more innovative explanation along similar lines has been set forth by Professor Eliezer Goldman, who suggests translating *Emunat Hakhamim* as the "faithfulness of the Sages" or "trustworthiness of the Sages."[74]

---

[73]For my discussion of *Emunat Hakhamim* I am greatly indebted to written comments on the original draft of this chapter which Rabbi Norman Lamm kindly made available to me. All my references to Rabbi Lamm are to those comments. On the subject in general, see Simha Friedman, "Emunat Hakhamim be-Mishor ha-Hevrati u-be-Baayot Tzibbur—Atgar Raayoni o Hanhagah Operativit," in *Sefer ha-Zikkaron le-Mordecai Veizer* (Kevutzat Yavneh, 1981), 136–59.

[74]I remember coming across this explanation in one of Professor Goldman's essays but have not been able to locate the exact source.

Even if we accept the traditional explanation that *Emunat Hakhamim* means "faith *in* the Sages," the precise import of the term is still obscure. Many commentators take it to be referring to the acceptance of the fundamental authority of the Sages of the Mishnah and *Gemara* in the realm of *Torah she-be'al peh*, "so that one should not act like a Sadducee."[75] An explanation that approaches the notion of *Daas Torah* is that suggested by the Meiri. "*Emunat Hakhamim*: that is to say that one should believe the Sages of the

---

[75]See, for example, *Mahzor Vitri* and Maharal, *Derekh Hayyim*. (For further discussion of the Maharal's view, see Piekarz, *Hasidut Polin*, 84.) Rabbi Lamm elaborates: "What *Emunat Hakhamim* means, therefore, is that Torah is 'acquired' if there is an implicit faith that the *masorah* of the *Hakhamim*—the tradition as handed down by the Tannaim and Amoraim—is legitimate and uncorrupted . . . and, therefore, of an obligatory character upon all of Israel."

It should be noted that many commentators, R. Yitzhak Abohab, for example, understand *Emunat Hakhamim* to include the authority of the Sages in matters of *aggadah*. See the references in Friedman, "Emunat Hakhamim," 4–7. But, of course, the authority of the sages in the realm of *aggadah* is a subject of serious debate among *Rishonim* and *Aharonim*. For the views and a representative sample of *Rishonim* who deny the authority of the sages in this realm, see Friedman, "Emunat Hakhamim," 15–25; and Marc Saperstein, *Decoding the Rabbis* (Cambridge, MA: Harvard University Press, 1980), chap. 1. To their lists we must now, in light of recent scholarship, unequivocally add the Ramban. See Bernard Septimus, "Open Rebuke and Concealed Love: Nahmanides and the Andalusian Tradition," in *Rabbi Moses Nahmanides (Ramban): Explorations in his Religious and Literary Virtuosity*, ed. Isadore Twersky (Cambridge, MA: Harvard University Press, 1983), 17–22; and Marvin Fox, "Nahmanides on the Status of Aggadot: Perspectives on the Disputation at Barcelona, 1263," *Journal of Jewish Studies* 40:1 (1989): 95–109. For *Aharonim*, see above, n. 36. To Rav Hirsch and Rav Hoffman, mentioned in that note, we also ought to add the Maharitz Hayyot. See his *Mavo ha-Talmud*, chaps. 17–32. In any event, the question of the authority of the sages in matters of *aggadah* is not quite the same as the question of *Daas Torah*, though the two issues are obviously related.

Torah in whatever they say, even in matters which one's intellect does not grasp." Of course, this refers to a person who does not grasp or understand what the sages are saying, someone who is in the process of *acquiring* Torah. It does not refer to an obligation on the part of a knowledgeable rabbi to suppress his own considered view of a matter in obedience to the supposed *Daas Torah* of *Gedolim*. This may be how Rabbi Bernard Weinberger understands *Emunat Hakhamim*, but his interpretation should by no means be confused with that of the Meiri. Interestingly enough, when the greatest rabbinic scholar of the Meiri's day, the Rashba, issued a ban against the study of philosophy by anyone under the age of 25, the Meiri did not submit himself to the *"Daas Torah"* of the Rashba, but opposed the ban openly and forthrightly.[76] For that matter, the Rashba himself did not appeal to any notion of *Daas Torah*, but issued the ban in the name of and as the rabbinic head of the Jewish community of Barcelona, and the ban was signed by both the rabbinic and lay leaders of the community.[77]

As has been suggested by Gershon Bacon,[78] Norman Lamm, and above all, Mendel Piekarz,[79] the concept of *Emunat Hakhamim* becomes central in hasidic ideology where, shifted away from the traditional rav, it becomes transmuted into belief in the *tzaddik*. The *tzaddik*'s word governs all the affairs of the community and all the personal affairs of the members of the community, and belief in

---

[76]See the letter of the Meiri to R. Abba Mari of Lunel in Simon B. Joseph's "Hoshen Mishpat" published by David Kaufmann in *Jubelschrift zum Neunzigsten Geburtstag des Dr. L. Zunz* (Berlin, 1884), 150–72. (Significant excerpts from the Meiri's letter may be found in B.Z. Dinur, *Yisrael ba-Golah*, vol. 2, bk. 4 [Jerusalem: Dvir, 1969], 259–61.)

[77]See *Responsa of the Rashba*, vol. 1, nos. 515–517; for an annotated, critical edition of these three responsa, see chaps. 99–101 of *Sefer Minhat Kenaot* by R. Abba Mari of Lunel, in *Teshuvot ha-Rashba*, pt. 1, vol. 2, ed. Hayyim Z. Dimitrovsky (Jerusalem: Mossad ha-Rav Kook, 1990), 722–38.

[78]See Bacon, *Agudath Israel in Poland*, 59–60; "Daat Torah ve-Havlei Mashiah," 502–3.

[79]Piekarz, *Hasidut Polin*, 81–83.

the *tzaddik* is a religious value per se. In the twentieth century the roles of the Lithuanian rav and, even more so, the Lithuanian *rosh yeshivah*, perhaps as a result of the breakdown of the traditional Jewish community, begin to resemble those of the hasidic rebbes, and belief in the *tzaddik*, suitably modified and now projected onto both rav and, again, even more so, *rosh yeshivah*, appears in the garb of *Daas Torah*.[80] However, the mitnagdic proponents of *Daas Torah* have concealed its immediate origins in the hasidic concept of the *tzaddik* and instead have directly linked it with the notion of *Emunat Hakhamim*.[81] Once again, it need not be said that this

---

[80]The connection between the breakdown of traditional communal structures and the rise of a quasi-hasidic notion of *Emunat Hakhamim* in mitnagdic circles comes to light, interestingly enough, in the following statement of Rabbi Yosef Avraham Wolf in "Le-Kayyeym Nefesh Ahat mi-Yisrael," in *Ha-Tekufah u-Baayotehah*, 10. "In a generation in which the structure of the holy communities with their rabbis at their head is no longer to be found . . . we have no support except *Emunat Hakhamim*. And in matters of healing as well, we teach that any matter of healing, be it healing of the soul or of the body, should be decided by the righteous sages that God has planted in our generation. And many sick people have been saved solely as a result of the counsel of the sages. They advise who is the proper doctor, what is the proper hospital . . . and, above all, their blessings and prayers have saved many."

[81]Another possible source for the notion of *Daas Torah* may be the *Musar* movement. See above, n. 6, for Rav Yisrael Salanter's view on *Daas Torah*. Of particular interest is a statement attributed to Rav Natan Tzevi Finkel, the Alter of Slobodka, that a view of a *Rishon* prefaced by *nireh li* (it appears to me) carries more weight than a view of his grounded in an earlier source. For while the latter rests or falls on that one specific prooftext, the *nireh li* is supported by the entire vast Torah knowledge and Torah personality of that *Rishon*. Recently, Tamar Ross, in an important essay, "Tenuat ha-Musar ve-ha-Baayah ha-Hermeneutit be-Talmud To-rah," *Tarbiz* 59 (1989–90): 191–214, has linked the use of the notion of *Daas Torah* in the writings of several major *Musar* figures, most prominently R. Joseph Bloch, to their attempted solutions to the problem of how to overcome the distortions of personal bias in the study of Torah

"strong" reading (or, better, creative misreading) of *Emunat Hak-hamim* fits in perfectly with the ethic of submission of the rejectionist Orthodox. And, also once again, we see that the attempt to ground the ideology of *Daas Torah* in traditional sources is, perhaps, a bit more problematic than Rav Dessler and other proponents of that ideology would have us believe.[82]

We therefore feel justified in concluding this section with the clear-cut and definitive pronouncement of the noted rabbinic scholar, Professor Ephraim Urbach. "*Daat Torah* ideology has never been based upon authoritative halakhic sources, and, as far as I know, recourse has never been made to it in halakhic debate."[83]

---

while avoiding the opposite hazards posed by academic detachment. In Ross's analysis, it turns out that the notion of *Daas Torah* is a key element in these *Musar* figures developing a hermeneutical approach to Torah that is both traditionalist and, at the same time, creative and relative. See n. 84, below.

[82] Another statement that has been cited in support of the ideology of *Daas Torah* is the comment of the Ramban in his *Hiddushim* on *Baba Batra* 12a, s.v. *Mi-yom she-harav.* Compare *Derashot ha-Ran*, no. 12 (214). However, as Rabbi Shubert Spero has shown, the Ramban's statement cannot be made to bear this weight. See Shubert Spero, "Daas Torah," 18–19. In general, one may say that the major thrust of traditional rabbinic scholarship and doctrine, from the *Derashot ha-Ran* through the justifiably famous preface to the *Ketzot Ha-Hoshen* down to Rav Moshe Feinstein's impressive preface to *Iggerot Mosheh*, is that scholars study and decide matters of law, not with any superhuman powers, but with their very fallible human intellects *(sekhel enoshi).* [For a somewhat different emphasis, see *Responsa of the Hatam Sofer*, vol. 1 *(Orah Hayyim)*, no. 208.] Of course, precisely this grave and daunting responsibility resting upon the shoulders of the scholar-*posek*, the charge of interpreting and applying the revealed word of God with one's own limited human abilities— demands of him, as Rav Moshe emphasizes, the utmost in both piety and intellectual rigor.

[83] "The History of Polish Jews after World War I as Reflected in the Traditional Literature," in *The Jews in Poland Between Two World Wars*,

THE OUTLOOK FOR *DAAS TORAH*

What of *Daas Torah* today? And what of its future prospects? I would argue that the ideology of *Daas Torah* today may, at least in part, be a victim of its own success and, more important, a victim of the success of traditional Orthodoxy.

What has been observed in recent years is the emergence of multiple and conflicting claims made by various competing groups and factions and their leaders within traditional Orthodoxy to be the possessors of true *Daas Torah*. Such a development, however, renders the notion that a *Daas Torah* viewpoint on a particular issue is the *sole* legitimate Torah viewpoint on that issue both tenuous and implausible.

---

ed. Yisrael Gutman et al. (Hanover, NH: University Press of New England, 1989), 229.

One apparently strictly halakhic subject where the notion of *Daas Torah* was invoked was the question of the permissibility of machine *matzot*. Both Rav Henoch Levin and Rav Tzevi Frommer defended the prohibition imposed on machine *matzot* by Rav Shlomo Kluger, the Sochaczewer Rebbe and others on the basis of *Daas Torah*. See Piekarz, *Hasidut Polin*, 94–96. It is exceptionally significant, however, that both Rabbis Levin and Frommer invoke the concept of *Daas Torah* not in their halakhic *teshuvot*, but rather in *derashot* they delivered on *Shabbat ha-Gadol*, in other words, in an aggadic context. Indeed, there is a striking contrast between the posture of extreme self abnegation assumed by Rav Frommer in his discussion of *Daas Torah* in his *derashah* (see above, n. 70) and the spirit of respect balanced with critical independence manifested in his *teshuvot*. Thus, as Professor Urbach has noted (241–42), Rav Frommer in *Responsa Eretz ha-Tzevi*, no. 103, takes issue—of course in a highly respectful manner—with the view of his own teacher, the Sochaczewer Rebbe, on the important issue of the inheritance of the post of rabbi. We can have no better example of the radical difference between the spirit of servility underlying the whole notion of *Daas Torah* and the spirit of critical indendence and debate animating the realm of halakhic *pesak!*

There would seem to be at least two reasons for the proliferation of clashing *Daas Torah* viewpoints and pronouncements.

First. The last few years have seen, particularly in Israel, mounting dissension among the various groups making up the traditionalist Orthodox *(haredi)* community. Of course, one can offer all types of specific and local reasons for the emergence of this often vicious feuding and internecine conflict. Without discounting particular triggers, I would argue that, in large measure, this fission and fragmentation should be seen as a result of traditionalist Orthodoxy's success and its new-found sense of triumphalism. Of course, there have always been divisions and tensions among the various camps comprising traditionalist Orthodoxy. However, when traditionalist Orthodoxy felt beset by the onslaught of modernity, when it was on the defensive and fighting what often seemed to be a rearguard holding action, all camps felt the need to band together, at least to a certain extent. Today, the traditionalist Orthodox—and with good reason—feel that the crisis is over, not only that the dire threat posed by modernity to their community has passed but that they have emerged victorious from their encounter, their battle with the modern world. This being the case, the external pressure has dissipated and the natural internal divisions reappear. What follows from this is that, given the popularity of *Daas Torah*, each warring traditionalist group, not surprisingly, invokes *Daas Torah* on behalf of its own position and against the positions of its rivals.

Second. Generally, as I have argued, the *Daas Torah* viewpoint on any given issue was that viewpoint which took a more rejectionist stance toward modernity and its values. Until recently, it was a fairly simple matter to identify this viewpoint. Whether the issue at hand turned on cooperation with the non-Orthodox, secular studies, or Zionism, to name but a few examples, the more rejectionist and, consequently, the supposedly more *"frum"* viewpoint was easy to determine. However, now *Daas Torah* is being invoked on both sides of a new issue, the question of the return of the territories, where such a determination becomes immeasurably more difficult.

For, pray tell, which is the more "modern" and less *"frum"* position and which the less "modern" and more *"frum"* position on the question of the territories: the "dovish" *Daas Torah* viewpoint of Rav Shach and his followers or the "hawkish" *Daas Torah* viewpoint expressed by various hasidic leaders? For, in truth, each side can and does — with some justification — claim that *its* position is the more "traditional," the more *frum*, the less — heaven forfend! — modern one, and, hence, that its position should be seen as an expression of "true" *Daas Torah*. For the firm adherent of any one of these groups there is, of course, no problem. But what is the bewildered onlooker to make of it all?

Thus, as a result of the proliferation of conflicting *Daas Torah* viewpoints, of conflicting *Deot Torah*, if we may coin a phrase, the concept of *Daas Torah* as the expression of the sole legitimate, authentic Torah viewpoint would seem to be in trouble. Nevertheless, it would be premature to predict an early demise for *Daas Torah*, or, indeed, any demise at all. For *Daas Torah*, as we have seen, is, before anything else, the quintessential expression of the traditionalist Orthodox ethic of submission. And this ethic continues to thrive and flourish in all circles of traditionalist Orthodoxy. Thus, the continued strength and vigor of this ethic make it likely that *gedolim* will continue to issue *Daas Torah* pronouncements and that demands to submit to the superior wisdom and insight of these *gedolim*, and thereby demonstrate true *Emunat Hakhamim*, will continue to be made, and, more important, will continue to be heeded. The career of *Daas Torah*, therefore, despite all its problems, is by no means over.

I have not, in this discussion, set forth what I consider to be the correct view (or views) of rabbinic authority, particularly as it bears on issues of communal policy. It is clear from what I have said that I consider the concept of *Daas Torah* to be highly problematic. I would like to make it equally clear that I believe that rabbinic authorities ought to play an important role in matters of communal policy. But I am not ready to provide answers to such questions as the exact nature of their authority or the proper relationship between rabbinic and lay leadership. My own tentative impression is that a thorough historical and halakhic study will reveal that there were different, oftentimes conflicting, notions of rabbinic authority in force in different communities and eras, and that the picture that will emerge will be a very rich and complex one. Certainly, it is beyond the scope of this chapter to even begin to sketch such a picture.

If, then, this discussion ends on a note of incompleteness, I can only say, on my behalf, that it is always easier to be a critic than to offer positive alternatives. Of course, it is oftentimes very important to be just such a critic.[84]

---

[84]Just as I had completed this chapter and was about to send it to the editor of this volume, I came across Mendel Piekarz's recently published and very important work, *Hasidut Polin* (see n. 6, above). In it, Piekarz clearly shows that the concept of *Daas Torah* originated in hasidic circles in the late nineteenth century in response to the decline of tradition and the rise of secularism in Jewish life. In light of this study, I now suspect that I followed Bacon too closely in situating the development of the concept of *Daas Torah* within the context of the history of Agudas Yisrael and its rise as a political party. Considered together, Piekarz's discussion of hasidic theology, Bacon's treatment of agudist ideology, Ross's analysis of musarist hermeneutics (see n. 81, above), and the *haredi* placards in *Torat Rebbe Amram* seem to tell the following story. *Daas Torah*, in its modern sense, originated in hasidic circles in the late nineteenth century. It soon spread to mitnagdic circles, taking root first in the extremist *haredi* community of Jerusalem (see n. 15). Gradually it entered the more mainstream separatist Orthodox circles of Agudas Yisrael, *beginning* in the interwar period, but only coming fully into its own and achieving complete dominance in the postwar era. (The *Musar* movement appears to have played a secondary and supporting role in this entire process.) Perhaps, then, the success of *Daas Torah* within the mitnagdic "*yeshivah*" world should be seen as one example among many of the "Hasidicization" of that world. While Piekarz's study, then, requires modification of my historical overview, fundamentally it only reinforces my central contention that the concept of *Daas Torah* is first and foremost an expression of the ethic of

submission. See especially in this regard his chap. 3, "*Emunat Hakhamim* and Absolute Obedience to *Daas Torah*," in which it becomes clear that *Daas Torah* is viewed, in hasidic sources, as a reenactment of the *Akedah*, whereby the individual sacrifices his intellect on the altar of blind obedience to the words of the sages (see also chap. 2). The one weak spot in Piekarz is his discussion of the classical roots of the concept of *Daas Torah*. Unfortunately, quoting only very selectively from the Ramban's *Commentary on the Torah* and thus ignoring, among other important discussions, the Ramban's significant comments in *Sefer ha-Mitzvot*, Piekarz misleadingly gives us to understand that *Daas Torah* is well grounded in traditional sources.

One final general point. While Piekarz, Bacon, and Ross focus on different ideological processes and movements in their accounts of the development of the notion of *Daas Torah*, their accounts are more complementary than contradictory, inasmuch as they share one critical element in common. For in all three accounts the notion of *Daas Torah* arises as a response to the varying challenges that the modern world poses to the authority of the rabbinic tradition. In Piekarz's account, the concept of *Daas Torah* is put forward as part of the hasidic attempt to affirm the essential heteronomy of the halakhic tradition in light of the dangers that the modern emphasis on autonomy poses to the binding authority of rabbinic law. In Bacon's account, the concept of *Daas Torah* emerges as part of the attempt to bolster the political and communal authority of the spokesmen of the rabbinic tradition in light of the ideological and political challenges posed to those spokesmen by secular Jewish movements and parties. Finally, in Ross' account, *Daas Torah* serves as a key element in developing an approach to the study of Torah that would guarantee the validity of traditional rabbinic interpretation of the law in light of the skeptical challenge posed by the hermeneutic revolution. Precisely these manifold challenges to the authority of the rabbinic tradition, then, led many of the defenders and exponents of that tradition to make extreme and far-reaching theoretical claims on its behalf and, even more important, on their own behalf as the authorized representatives of that tradition. In sociological terms: "Status anxiety . . . increases the assertiveness of status claims" (*International Encyclopedia of the Social Sciences*, vol. 15 [1968], 253). See my essay, "Rabbi Isaac Hutner's 'Daas Torah' Perspective on the Holocaust," 248 n. 5.

A HISTORICAL EPILOGUE[85]

On January 17, 1944, the Belzer Rebbe, Rav Aaron Rokeah, together with his brother Rav Mordecai—after having escaped in May 1943, from the ghetto of Bochnia in Western Galicia to Hungary—left Budapest for the land of Israel, using immigration certificates reserved for veteran Zionists. One day earlier, Rav Mordecai, "with the approval and as the agent of his brother," delivered a major farewell sermon "in the great hall of the *Kahal Yereim* of Budapest," in the presence of "a large audience of thousands of Jews together with great rabbinic scholars and the leaders and prominent men of the city and country." This sermon was printed as a special brochure, *ha-Derekh*, on February 7, 1944, and was reprinted about a month later, "since the first printing has sold out in a few days and from all camps and quarters requests are forthcoming for *ha-Derekh*." At about the same time as the second printing, an abridged version of the sermon was published under the title *Matzmiah Yeshuah (The Flowering of Redemption)*, for as the publisher stated, "Its content befits its name, for this entire farewell address is filled with promises for the future and encouragement for the present. . . . And we, believers the children of believers, are certain that the promises of the *tzaddik*, the *gadol ha-dor* [the Belzer Rebbe], will be fulfilled for us; and certainly it has been revealed to him from heaven that the end of our troubles is nigh."

In the sermon, Rav Mordecai deals with the concern raised by "many people of weak hope and faith" that the Nazi destruction of Polish and Galician Jewry as well as the Jewry of other lands

---

[85]All the primary sources cited in the epilogue are taken from the last chapter of Piekarz, *Hasidut Polin*, 373–434. We have, however, retold this harrowing story in our own way and for our own purposes. For an important recent study that partially overlaps with Piekarz, see Menahem Friedman, "The Haredim and the Holocaust," *Jerusalem Quarterly* 53 (Winter 1990): 86–115. Friedman's article, among other things, clearly delineates the various stages in the historical development and emergence of the current "official" *Daas Torah* view regarding the Holocaust.

disproved the anti-Zionist policies of the hasidic and nonhasidic separatist Orthodox leaders and proved the Zionists to be correct. "For had our leaders, the *Gedolei Yisrael* and *tzaddikei ha-dor*, adopted another approach, and had they anticipated the evil times that have befallen the world and taken care for the future and survival of the nation *as did others*, and had they occupied themselves with its salvation, then certainly many would have been spared extinction and the sword of the destroyer."

Rav Mordecai admits that on the surface this argument would seem to be borne out by the historical events. However, he claims, it is precisely this apparent substantiation of the Zionist argument that is, in truth, a divine trial sent by God to test the faith of the believer. For, historically, there have been two types of Jewish leadership: the true leadership of the *Gedolei Yisrael* and *tzaddikei ha-dor* and the false leadership of the "priests of Baal," its present incarnation being the secular [and religious?] Zionist leaders. To criticize, then, in any way, the wisdom or policies of the true leaders and to imply that the false leaders, on a particular issue, may have been more farseeing, is to side with the priests of Baal and to desecrate the sancta of Israel. Rav Mordecai, therefore, condemns those heretics and even those who are "simply led astray," all of whom "criticize the *tzaddikei ha-dor* in a time of trouble." Rather, "we have naught to do but rely on our Father in heaven and to strengthen our belief in Him, may He be blessed, and our belief in the *tzaddikim*."

In this part of the sermon, then, Rav Mordecai, as Rav Dessler would do at a later date, used the doctrine of *Daas Torah*—in his case a hasidic version of the doctrine—to defend the *Gedolim* and *tzaddikim* against the accusation that, as a result of their anti-Zionist policies, they had not done enough to encourage Jewish emigration from Europe to the land of Israel.

Of particular interest, however, is the next part of Rav Mordecai's sermon, the part containing "the promises of the *tzaddik*" to which the publisher of *Matzmiah Yeshuah* referred. Here, in a passage of twenty-two lines, a passage which because of its importance appeared in the second printing in boldface, Rav Mordecai responds to the accusation that he and his brother were abandoning their flock in a time of trouble. Already in October 1943, Rav Yissacher Teichtel, writing in Budapest, described in his work *Eym ha-Banim Semeihah* "the fear and dread that hangs over us when all the *Admorim* of our country are attempting to flee to the land of Israel for fear of the danger of the oppressor; and they do not take into account the fact that by so acting they are causing the spirits of the Jews to sink, when they hear the multitude murmuring: 'The Rebbes are fleeing and what will be with us?' "

This is how Rav Mordacai responded:

I wish to inform and enlighten you concerning the murmurings of many who are afraid and seized with trembling and . . . worried about the future. They are saying that perhaps, heaven forbid, some danger is hanging over the land and that my brother, the *tzaddik* of the generation, Shlit"a sees the future and for that reason is traveling to the land of Israel, for it is there that God ordained the blessing, "And I will give peace in the land" [Leviticus 26:6]. He, therefore, is going to a place of rest and tranquility and has left us, heaven forbid, to sorrow. What will be our end? Who will protect us? Who will save us? Who will pray for us and intercede on our behalf? Therefore, it is my obligation to let you know, my dear colleagues, sages of Hungary, the truth, that whoever is close to and a member of the circle of my brother . . . Shlit"a knows for certain that he is not going in flight or running away in haste, as if he wished to flee from here. Rather his entire longing and desire are to ascend to the holy land, which is sanctified with ten levels of holiness. And I know that for a long time he has been yearning greatly for the land of Israel. His heart's desire and the yearning of his holy soul are to ascend to the city of God, there to arouse [God's] mercy and grace on the entire community that they should know no more sorrow, and the remaining camp will be spared, and soon there will be fulfilled, "I will cut off the horns of the wicked, but the horns of the righteous will be exalted" [Psalms 75:11]. And this is alluded to in the verse, "And he saw the resting place that it was good and the land that it was delightful" [Genesis 49:15]. It would seem that the intention [of the verse] is, "And he saw the resting place" [menuhah,] the tzaddik sees that rest and tranquility will descend upon the inhabitants of this land [i.e., Hungary], "that it was good" [ki tov,] that the tzaddik sees that good, and all good, and only good and grace [ki tov, ve-kol tov, ve-akh tov ve-hesed] will befall our Jewish brethren, the inhabitants of this land [i.e., Hungary], "and the land," the reason why the tzaddik desires to ascend to and settle in the land is "for it is delightful," for it is there that the supernal delight dwells.

On March 19, 1944, just over two months after the farewell sermon in which the tzaddik had foreseen that "good, and all good, and only good . . . will befall our Jewish brethren, the inhabitants of this land," and one month after the abridged version of the sermon, Matzmiah Yeshuah, was printed, one month after the publisher of the abridged version stated, "We, believers the children of believers, are certain that the promises of the tzaddik and gadol ha-dor will be fulfilled for us," the Germans occupied Hungary. On May 14, less than four months after the farewell sermon, the mass deportations of Hungarian Jews to the extermination camps began. Toward the end of May, Rebbetzin Hayya Halberstam, the widow of Rav Avraham Halberstam, the Admor of Stropkov, was deported from Kashau to Auschwitz. There she and her son were murdered on May 25. Shortly before her death, a SonderKommando, who himself later perished, recorded her last words.

I see the end of Hungarian Jewry. The government had permitted large sections of the Jewish community to flee. The people asked the advice of the Admorim and they always reassured them. The Belzer Rebbe said that Hungary would only endure anxiety. And now the bitter hour has come, when the Jews can no longer save themselves. Indeed, heaven concealed [this fate] from them, but they, themselves, fled at the last moment to the land of Israel. They saved their own lives but left the people as sheep for slaughter. *Ribbono shel olam!* In the last moments of my life I set my plea before You that You pardon them for this great *hillul ha-shem*.

In 1967, two hasidic writers, Rabbis Bezalel Landau and Nathan Ortner, in their book *ha-rav ha-kadosh Mi-Belz*, reprinted the entire farewell sermon of Rav Mordecai, *with the exception of this entire twenty-two-line passage*. In place of this passage, they included the following comment. "Here the Gaon and Tzaddik, the Rav of Bilgoray [Rav Mordecai], explained the desire of his brother, the holy Gaon, to ascend to the land of Israel, based on the verse, 'And he saw the resting place that it was good and the land that it was delightful.' "

This convenient omission has allowed the "authorized" hasidic historians of the Belzer dynasty to write how the Rebbe and his brother "on more than one occasion warned the Jews of Hungary not to deceive themselves with illusions and not to be at ease regarding their situation. The Polish experience demonstrated that the Nazi horror was just as dangerous in its time of downfall as it was in its time of triumph." Indeed, on one occasion Rav Mordecai, according to one hasidic historian, even warned a delegation representing a Hungarian Orthodox community: "Know that the Germans are right behind us and any day we must be afraid of a German invasion." However, this historian continues, "The Jews of Hungary did not wish to understand and refused to engage in an accounting of their future."

Indeed, the career of *Daas Torah* is by no means over.

2

Subjectivity in Rabbinic Decision-Making

Aaron Kirschenbaum

The following examination of the subjective element in *pesak* will focus mainly on the "civil law" component of the *halakhah* (*Hoshen Mishpat* and, to a lesser degree, *Even ha-Ezer*). As shall be shown, however, many of the observations are equally valid regarding the "religious" *halakhah* (*issur ve-heter: Even ha-Ezer, Orah Hayyim,* and *Yoreh De'ah*).

Using the *legal* concept of "equity," the inner mechanism of the law that makes for flexibility in its interpretation and application, we wish to show (1) the central role of the rabbis in mediating between formalism and flexibility in the *halakhah*, (2) the presence of subjectivity in their equitable activity, and (3) the crucial forma-

---

This chapter is a reworking of some of the ideas I developed in my *Equity in Jewish Law* (2 vols.; New York: Yeshiva University Press and Ktav Publishing House, 1991), which should be consulted for elaboration of details.

tive component of Torah itself in the creation and development of
the subjectivity of the rabbis.

EQUITY

Similar to other legal systems, ancient and modern, religious and
secular, Jewish law had to—and still must—negotiate the tension
between its static rules and the dynamic flow of events. The rules
are characterized by an encompassing generality, whereas each
event—the specific circumstances, the individuals involved, the
conditions of the times—is informed with individuality, sometimes
even uniqueness. Thus, the glory of the law—its sublime generality—is its very undoing. For in its passion for uniformity and
stability, the law enlists the aid of formalism. Its indifference to
persons may produce heartlessness; its impartiality, injustice; its
rigid consistency, absurdity.

The major method whereby the law accomplishes the negotia-
tion between the static and the dynamic, the general and the
individual, the adherence to the formal law and the need for
flexibility is *equity*.

Aristotle defines equity as follows: "This is the essential nature of
the equitable: *it is a rectification of law where law is defective because
of its generality*."[1]

In the course of developing this definition of equity, Aristotle
makes a number of points:

1. A law is always a general statement.
2. In order to make a general statement, the law takes into
   consideration the majority of cases—consideration of all cases
   would render the formulation of a general statement impossible.
3. Thus the law is not unaware of the inadequacy of its generalization.

---

[1]Aristotle, *Nicomachean Ethics*, 1137625. Emphasis added.

4. This does not imply that the law is wrong, for the inadequacy—the error inherent in the generalization—is not in the law nor in the lawgiver, but in the special nature of the case.

We find equity, that inner mechanism whereby the law modifies itself in order to remain faithful to itself, at three levels of halakhic activity: (1) the procedural (judicial) level; (2) the interpretive (juristic) level; and (3) the legislative level. Before we can discuss these levels we must examine Jewish legal development in light of the fundamental Jewish theological doctrine of divine revelation.

EQUITY IN LIGHT OF HALAKHIC THEOLOGY

The existence of an "inner mechanism whereby the law modifies itself" must be understood against the background of the theological doctrine of the divine origin of the Law. If the Torah is the revealed will of God—the eternal, omnipotent, and omniscient God—how are we to understand the legitimacy of any change that takes place therein?

A typological analysis of the divine Revelation of the Law yields three views of the nature of the Sinaitic act of codification. These three types have great significance for an understanding of the role of equity in Jewish law.

The three types have been denominated: (1) the conservative approach; (2) the explicative approach; and (3) the accumulative approach.

The Conservative Approach

The conservative approach views the Law (Oral as well as Written) that was promulgated at Sinai as exhaustive. All subsequent halakhic activity of substance—except, probably, *takkanot*, which are, after all, "mere" amendments (I say "probably" since even *takkanot* are bound by biblical rules, guidelines, and values)—is nothing more than discovery. All interpretation and decision-making are the uncovering of that which was always there. Novelty is an illusion, so that any novel interpretation, even one offered by a student, was already revealed to Moses at Sinai. Thus, equitable activity – at the juristic, interpretative, and (probably also) legislative levels – is an exercise in bringing out into the open that which was transmitted to Moses originally.

The point of departure for the conservative approach is a passage in the Siphra, a halakhic *midrash* on Leviticus 25:1, the biblical section dealing with the laws of *shemittah*, the Sabbatical Year:

> *And the Lord spoke unto Moses at Mount Sinai* – What do the words *at Mount Sinai* come to teach us? Was not the entire Torah given at Sinai? Scripture wishes to teach us that just as all the rules of *shemittah* – its principles, details and minutiae – were revealed at Sinai, so the rules of all the Commandments – their principles, details and minutiae – were all given at Sinai.[2]

In the Introduction to his *Commentary on the Mishnah*, Maimonides took these words of the Siphra literally. Indeed Maimonides is a classic exponent of the conservative approach.[3]

The Explicative Approach

The explicative approach is made up of two different but related views. According to the first view, authorized human agencies – the ancient Sanhedrin, rabbinical synods and courts of posttalmudic times, individual scholars and decisors – loyal to tradition and following the received rules of interpretation, have the power to explicate the true intention of the divine Legislator. According to

---

[2] Cf. Ephraim E. Urbach, *The Sages – Their Concepts and Beliefs* (Jerusalem: Magnes, 1975), 304.

[3] Cf. Abraham Joshua Heschel, *Theology of Ancient Judaism* (London: Soncino Press, 1965), 2:98–99 (Hebrew).

the second explicative view, these authorized human agencies have the power to make decisions that are legitimate and halakhically binding even if they do not in fact comport with the original Sinaitic intent. Equity, in the eyes of this approach, is the development of principles and ideas latent in the scriptural code. The first view of the explicative approach was summarized succinctly by R. Joseph Albo in the following manner:

> The written Torah cannot be perfect unless accompanied by this oral interpretation, which is called the Oral Law.
>
> This is why the Rabbis say, God made a covenant with Israel only for the sake of the Oral Law. This is because the Written Law cannot be understood except with the Oral Law, and also because the law of God cannot be perfect so as to be adequate for all times, because the ever new details of human relations, their customs and their acts, are too numerous to be embraced in a book. Therefore Moses was given orally certain general principles, only briefly alluded to in the Torah, by means of which the wise men in every generation may work out the details as they appear.[4]

The second explicative view was expressed briefly by Nahmanides thus: "One must say, 'The Lord who enjoined the commandments commanded that I perform all His commandments in accordance with all that [the Sages] . . . teach me to do. He gave me the Torah as taught by them, *even if they were to err.*' "[5]

Indeed, one commentator expounds an interesting combination of the conservative approach and the explicative one. Discussing the controversies between Bet Shammai and Bet Hillel, the

---

[4]R. Joseph Albo, *Sefer Ha-Ikkarim: Book of Principles*, ed. Isaac Husik (Philadelphia: Jewish Publication Society of America, 5706–1946), vol. 3, chaps. 23, 203. Cf. *Tanhuma*, "Noah" 3.

[5][Ramban] *Commentary on the Torah* (trans. C.B. Chavel), Deuteronomy 17:11 (emphasis added). Similarly, *Sefer ha-Hinukh*, 496.

Talmud declares that two (conflicting) opinions represent *eilu ve-eilu divrei Elohim hayyim* (the words of the Living God). This declaration served "the rabbis of France," as reported by *Ritva* (R. Yom Tov b. Abraham of Seville), as the basis for their explanation of the nature of the Sinaitic promulgation of the Law. The Revelation

> did not consist of the communication of precisely formulated legal rules. Instead, law was communicated as a series of options—a range of permissible outcomes for every case that requires a decision. The halakhic process consists of selecting the most appropriate option. The final decision in any case is not preordained but left to the Sages of each generation to whom the question is addressed. They must determine the law based on their opinion regarding the requirements of the times they live in. In so deciding, they are not innovating laws, but selecting among options included in the original Revelation.[6]

The Accumulative Approach

According to the accumulative approach, subsequent to the divine Revelation at Sinai the Torah was given to man not only to obey but to carry on. A kind of ongoing revelation takes place whereby the authorized human agencies—made up of men possessing the requisite scholarship, piety, and integrity—make Torah law. They do so by interpreting the biblical, talmudical, and medieval heritage (to which they have subjugated every fiber of their being) anew. Juristic, interpretative, and legislative activity of an equitable nature is a significant area of halakhic creativity.

The accumulative approach found its expression chiefly in the writings of the mystics. On the phrase, *ve-lo yassaf* (Deuteronomy 5:19), Rashi had written, "We render this in the Targum by *ve-lo*

---

[6]Jeffry T. Roth, "Responding to Dissent in Jewish Law: Suppression Versus Self-Restraint," *Rutgers Law Review* 40 (1987): 33 and n. 6.

passak, 'And it did not cease,' for His voice is strong and goes on continuously." Rashi's comment evoked the following remarks of R. Meir ibn Gabbai of the sixteenth century (Turkey–*Eretz* Israel):

> And not only did the Prophets receive their prophecy from Sinai, the Sages who arose in each generation also received theirs from Sinai. Thus Scripture declares, *These words the Lord spoke unto all your assembly . . . with a great voice, "ve-lo yassaf," and it did not cease*, which the Rabbis explained to mean that all innovations in interpretation which the Sages introduced throughout all the generations were received from that Voice at Sinai. . . . This is the basic idea: that all future insights had already been included in that heavenly Voice, and the Lord of the universe so desires that they be made manifest by mortals.[7]

In order to understand how these three views regarding the nature of the Sinaitic act of codification manifested themselves in Jewish legal philosophy and in the *halakhah* itself, we must study (1) the role of *hazal* in Jewish law and legal development and (2) their equitable activity which made for a significant source of flexibility in the Law.

---

[7] R. Meir ibn Gabbai, *Sefer Avodat ha-Kodesh* (Jerusalem: Lewin-Epstein, 1973), 170b. Roth, ibid., nn. 150–51, also cites R. Solomon Luria (Maharshal), *Yam Shel Shelomoh, Baba Kamma*, at beg. of Introduction, referring to the talmudic interpretation of Ecclesiastes 12:11 as found in *Hagigah* 3b.

For most of the foregoing I am indebted to my friend Prof. Yohanan Silman of Bar-Ilan University who was kind enough to share these ideas with me, which were subsequently published in Hebrew in *The Bar-Ilan Annual* 22–23 (1987): 261–86. These ideas have profound implications for an understanding of the Jewish views of prophecy; cf. Ephraim A. Urbach, "Halachah and Prophecy," *Tarbiz* 18 (1946): 1–27 (Hebrew). They are, however, beyond the scope of our study.

THE SOURCES OF JEWISH LAW AND THE ROLE OF THE RABBIS

Who are the carriers of divine Revelation in this world of ours—whichever of the three concepts of the nature of the Sinaitic act of codification we accept? Indeed, who presides over that inner mechanism whereby sacred law develops, whereby it modifies itself in order to remain faithful to itself, and whereby it enters the human arena and is applied to living human beings? In order to answer these questions, we turn to the role of the rabbis in halakhic jurisprudence.

In his definitive introduction to Jewish law, Justice Menahem Elon of the Israeli Supreme Court has given a most admirable description of the legal sources of the *halakhah*, that is, the sources of Jewish law and the recognized means of creating norms that are halakhically binding. His exposition may be summarized as follows.[8]

The sources of Jewish law are divided into two types, the static and the dynamic. The ultimate legal principle *(Grundnorm)* is the rule that the Torah, the Five Books of Moses, is of binding authority for the Jewish legal system. Parallel to this Written Torah is the Oral Tradition, which Jewish theology traces back to what Moses received from God. These, the components of the Sinaitic Revelation, are the static and immutable bases upon which the entire *halakhah* is built.

The dynamic sources of law—whereby the provisions of Scripture and of the Oral Tradition are developed, modified, abrogated,

---

[8]Menachem Elon, *Jewish Law: History, Sources, Principles* (Jerusalem: Magnes Press, 1973), chaps. 6, 8–24 (Hebrew). An English summary may be found in the *Encyclopaedia Judaica*, s.v. "Mishpat Ivri," "Interpretation," "Takkanot," "Minhag," "Maaseh and Precedent," "Sevarah." These have been collected in: *Principles of Jewish Law*, ed. M. Elon (Jerusalem: Keter, 1975), 5–15, 57–120. A nineteenth-century rabbinic scholar was perhaps the first to undertake a systematic analysis of the topic; cf. R. Zvi Hirsch Chajes, *The Student's Guide Through the Talmud*, trans. J. Schacter, 2nd ed. (New York: Philipp Feldheim, 1960).

or adapted to new situations, and whereby new statutes and ordinances, normative rules and regulations are created—are five.

1. *Midrash*, the exegesis, investigation, and *interpretation* principally of sacred Scripture and, to a lesser extent, of other authoritative texts. Interpretation may be creative (productive of new provisions) or integrative (validating practices that have come down as part of the Oral Tradition and bringing them into line with sacred Scripture). Methods of interpretation are highly developed; the most significant are the Thirteen Hermeneutical Rules of Rabbi Ishmael (*middot she-ha-Torah nidreshet ba-hen*).

2. *Takkanah* and *gezerah*, *positive and precautionary enactments*, directives enacted by legal authorities—halakhic scholars and public bodies—that, after Scripture, constitute the body of secondary legislation.

3. *Minhag*, legal norms derived from *custom* and usage.

4. *Maaseh*, legal norms derived from *an act* performed by a halakhic scholar in the form of a judgment rendered, or in the form of his conduct in a particular case.

5. *Sevara*, legal norms derived from the *natural reason* of the halakhic scholars. (*Sevara* may also refer to the logic employed by the scholars in the course of adjudication and interpretation of the law.) All of Jewish positive law, derived from almost all the above-mentioned legal sources, is divided by the Talmud into two broad categories: *divrei Torah*, or *de'oraita* (biblical law) and *divrei Soferim*, or *de-rabbanan* (rabbinic law). Both these expressions connote degrees of sanctity and entail practical differences in application, modification, and amendment.[9] This description of the legal sources of the *halakhah* may serve as a convenient basis for an understanding of the creative role of the Jewish legal authorities, the rabbis, the halakhic scholars, in the development, application, and perpetuation of Jewish law.

---

[9]See Chajes, *The Student's Guide*, chaps. 1–14: *Talmudic Encyclopaedia*, s.v. "divrei soferim," "gezerah"; Elon, *Encyclopaedia Judaica*, s.v. "Mishpat Ivri," 113–15 [= *Principles*, 9–10].

The transmission of the Oral Tradition from generation to generation was accomplished on two levels: in practice, by the masses of law-abiding Israelites; and both in theory and in practice, by the rabbinical judicial elite. The interpretation of sacred Scripture, whether creative or integrative, was the function of the rabbis. Interpretation was, it is true, not limitless, neither free nor unfettered. Rules of interpretation, inherited as part of the Oral Tradition, were regarded as divine in origin. Moreover, all interpretation—certainly interpretation that was integrative in nature—was rendered in a manner calculated to justify or to conform to hallowed tradition. Nevertheless, the vital role of the rabbis in authoritative interpretation is undeniable.

Takkanot were enactments adopted to cope with new situations. They were invariably introduced in order to promote, inculcate, or preserve sacred biblical values, or to lay down precautionary measures to prevent possible violations of biblical prohibitions. A significant rule of law decrees that the ultimate validity of a *takkanah* depended upon popular ratification, in other words, its acceptance by the people. Nevertheless, the role of the rabbinical authorities was central. Either the rabbinical courts themselves initiated the *takkanah*, or, if initiated by the lay leaders of the community, its validity depended upon the ratification of *hakham ha-ir*, the local rabbinic authority.

Moreover, the validity of a customary practice depended upon the rabbinical authorities. They could convert it into formal law by embodying it in a *takkanah*, by recognizing its validity as part of a judicial decision, or by upholding it with the simple declaration that it was a *minhag kasher* (an acceptable practice, a valid custom). The opposite declaration on the part of a halakhic scholar, to the effect that the practice is *minhag shtut* (a foolish practice), reduced the custom to superstition and nonsense.

And, finally, *maaseh* and *sevara* were respectively the acts and the application of the natural reason of the scholars, the rabbis, the halakhic leaders.

Thus Jewish law, with regard to its sources, is essentially aristocratic, that is, rabbinic, not democratic, not emanating from the sovereignty of the people. This is equally true with regard to the administration of the law. Halakhic adjudication and halakhic interpretation in their traditional, classical forms have invariably been in the hands of rabbinical judges and rabbinical scholars.

In view of the vital role of the rabbis, we are justified in calling Jewish law *divrei Soferim* (rabbinic law). Indeed, the *halakhah* of *lo tasur*—Thou shalt not turn aside from the sentence which they [the rabbis] shall teach thee (Deuteronomy 17:11),[10]—and the theology of *Emunat Hakhamim* (faith in the sages) enunciated by the aggadic addition to the *Sayings of the Fathers*,[11] take on fuller meaning: Jewish law without the rabbis—their erudition, their devotion, and their ethical sensitivity—is inconceivable.

If, however, we have referred to these rabbis as the "aristocracy" of Torah, Jewish history would regard such a reference as a distortion. For historically the legal authorities of the Jewish people had their origins in all segments of the population: prophets, *kohanim* (priests), Levites, and lay Israelites; rich, middle-class, and poor; urban and rural; pedigreed and humble. Their common denominator was their religiomoral excellence. Thus, although there is an aristocracy of scholarship, piety, integrity, and commitment, its *roots* are undoubtedly democratic.

TWO AREAS[12] OF HALAKHIC EQUITY

At the Judicial (Procedural) Level

Aristotle's description of equity continues as follows:

> When therefore the law lays down a general rule, and thereafter a case arises which is an exception to the rule, it is then

---

[10]Elon, *Jewish Law*, 394ff.; *Encyclopaedia Judaica*, s.v. "Authority, Rabbinical," *idem*, *Principles*, 53–57.

[11]M. *Avot* 6:6

[12]We omit, for the purposes of our study of subjectivity in rabbinic decision-making, the legislative level of halakhic equitable activity and the provisions enacted and decisions made under such rubrics as *horaat shaah*; *et laasot*; *le-migdar milta*; *dinei melekh*.

right, where the law's pronouncement because of its absoluteness is defective and erroneous, to rectify the defect by deciding as the lawgiver would himself decide if he were present
on the occasion, and would have enacted if he had been
cognizant of the case in question. Hence, while the equitable
is just . . ., it is not superior to absolute justice but only to the
error due to its absolute statement.[13]

The Aristotelian exposition of the concept of equity finds its
fullest expression in Jewish literature in the homiletical commentary of R. Isaac Arama on the Pentateuch.[14] To illustrate the
understanding of R. Isaac *Baal ha-Akedah* of the workings of the
halakhah, we make reference to the case of Mari bar Isak as
adjudicated by R. Hisda.[15]

There came a brother to Mari bar Isak from [the town of] Be
Hozai, saying to him, "Divide [my father's estate] with me."
"I do not know you," he replied.
So they went to R. Hisda.
R. Hisda said to the plaintiff, "He [Mari] may be speaking
the truth to you, for it is written, *And Joseph knew his brethren,
but they recognized him not* (Genesis 42:8), which teaches that
he had gone forth without a beard and now appeared before
them with one. (So Mari may not recognize you, too, even if
you are his brother.) Go then," he continued, "and produce
witnesses that you are his brother."
"I have witnesses," he replied, "but they are afraid of him
because he is a man of violence."
Thereupon R. Hisda turned to Mari, "Go you and bring
witnesses that he is not your brother."

---

[13] Aristotle, *Nicomachean Ethics*.
[14] *Akedat Yitzhak*, Yitro (ed. H. Pollack, Pressburg; rep. Jerusalem,
1961), para. 4.
[15] *Baba Metzia* 39b; *Ketubot* 27b.

"Is that the Law?!" he exclaimed. "The onus of proof lies on the claimant!"

"Thus do I judge in your case," retorted R. Hisda, "and for all other men of violence of your like."

A plain reading of the account yields a bold departure on the part of the judge from the established rules of procedure. A violent defendant may easily stifle all the testimony that is to his disadvantage. Thus, R. Hisda did not hesitate suspending the basic rule that places the burden of proof on the shoulders of the plaintiff and placed it upon the defendant himself. After all, elementary justice requires that the formal rules of procedure not be abused by men of violence for their own benefit.

Did R. Hisda, then, deviate from the law or did he fulfill it? The answer is: he did both. He deviated from the letter of the law—in its general formulation—but he did not deviate from the law proper. The law as required in the particular circumstances achieved its proper fulfillment. Thus, when Mari b. Isak objected, "Is that the Law?!" the judge retorted, "Thus do I judge in your case"—without answering, "Yes." For it was indeed a deviation from the formal wording which holds that "the onus of proof lies on the claimant." In other words, regarding a properly qualified tribunal of halakhic judges, "The blessed Lord has permitted them and has empowered them to set the Torah law straight and to *correct it* [emph. added-Ed.] at their discretion in a specific matter."[16]

This doctrine of the "correction" of the Law was rejected by

---

[16]Don Isaac Abarbanel, *Commentary* to Deuteronomy 17:11. Abarbanel was a colleague of R. Isaac Arama and followed his school of thought. Both R. Arama and the Abarbanel would undoubtedly *not* agree to the phrase used by students of jurisprudence in describing equity as providing solutions for problems "the legislator did not foresee." They both, however, make explicit reference to "the correction of (Torah) law," a correction necessitated not by any defect in the Legislator but by the intrinsic defectiveness of the (Torah) law due to the generality and absoluteness of its formulation.

Maimonides. His *Guide* offers the classic expression of the idea that law is general in character[17]:

> Among the things that you likewise ought to know is the fact that the Torah, the Law of Scripture, does not pay attention to the isolated case. The Torah was not given with a view to things that are rare. For in everything that it wishes to bring out . . . it is directed only toward the things that occur in the majority of cases and pays no attention to what happens rarely or to damage occurring to the unique human being because of the way of determination and because of the legal character of governance. . . . In view of this consideration, it also will not be possible that the laws be dependent on changes in the circumstances of the individuals and of the times, as is the case with regard to medical treatment, which is particularized for every individual in conformity with his present temperament. On the contrary, governance of the Torah ought to be absolute and universal, including everyone, even if it is suitable for certain individuals and not suitable for others; for if it were made to fit individuals, the whole would be corrupted and *natata devareikha le'shiurin*, "you would make out of it something that varies." For this reason, matters that are primarily intended in the Torah ought not to be dependent on time or place; but the decrees ought to be absolute and universal.

Thus Maimonides expounds the idea that the Torah, the Law, pays no heed to the isolated case, cannot be dependent on changes in the circumstances of the individuals and of the times; its decrees are absolute and universal. As a result, the rare case or the unusual circumstance may not be covered by the Torah in its generality, and the individual involved may be done an injustice.[18]

---

[17]Moses Maimonides, *The Guide of the Perplexed*, ed. and trans. S. Pines (Chicago: University of Chicago Press, 1963), 3:34.

[18]See further: *Responsa Rambam*, ed. Blau, no. 252, p. 460, and, more directly to the point, no. 224, p. 398f.

The Maimonidean expressions connoting generality are *la-rov, al derekh ha-rov* (according to the majority of cases). In a most learned article, the late Professor E. S. Rosenthal has shown the Aristotelian roots of the Maimonidean formulation, which he translates as "for the most part."[19] It is Professor Rosenthal's contention, however, that the Aristotelian roots of the Maimonidean formulation produced nothing more than the concept of the generality, absoluteness, and occasional callousness of the law. With the (Aristotelian) idea of the correction of the (divine) law, bringing it in line with the just, the upright, and the good, Maimonides, the Jewish theologian, parts company. Torah law suffers no exceptions. Divine law—heteronomous—brooks no correction by man and his autonomous ethic.[20]

There thus exists a significant chasm between Maimonides' interpretation of the law and that of R. Isaac Arama,[21] which is best understood by another look at the Mari bar Isak case as adjudicated by R. Hisda. Although civil procedure regularly places the burden of proof on the plaintiff, R. Hisda accepted the allegation of the plaintiff that his witnesses were afraid to testify against Mari bar Isak. The judge therefore ruled that the burden of proof was to be shifted onto the shoulders of the defendant.

How did Maimonides react to R. Hisda's judicial conduct? He

---

[19]E. S. Rosenthal, "Al Derekh Harov," *Perakim* 1 (1967–1968): 183–224; 2 (1969–1970): 381–83.

[20]Rosenthal, ibid., 1:199–204.

[21]After expounding his (Aristotelian) interpretation of the process of "correcting" general Torah law in the name of the Torah and rendering the decision that is appropriate for the individual (or minority) situation, R. Isaac Arama himself states: "However, in chapter 34 of the same part, *i.e.*, Part II, he [Maimonides] appears to have been discussing the laws of the Torah as being just in a general way [but] not [necessarily] when it comes to specific details. Ponder over his position, for what we have written is correct; the perfection of the divine Torah demands that it be as we have written." The influence of R. Arama on subsequent generations is easily discernable; see, for example, R. Joshua b. Alexander Hakohen Falk (Poland, 1555–1614), *Derishah, Hoshen Mishpat* 1:2.

simply codified it and included it among all the other rules of procedure and evidence![22] He took no cognizance of its exceptional character and made no mention of the deviation involved. The conclusion is inescapable: Maimonides neither regarded it as exceptional nor viewed it as a deviation from the law. R. Hisda is perceived as simply applying a law that was there all the time. In a similar fashion Maimonides formulated equitable rules of procedure, that is, neither as "corrections" of more general ones nor as relaxations of more formal ones, but rather as rules of procedure pure and simple.[23]

It would seem to me, therefore, that the divergences between Maimonides and R. Arama regarding equity in Jewish law may be summarized as follows: Maimonides appears to emphasize the general nature of law and the tendency of that general nature to create hardships—even injustices—in certain individual cases. Such cases undoubtedly exist, for the law does not easily bend to adapt itself to exceptional circumstances. R. Arama appears to place greater emphasis on those instances where the law does depart from the general norm in its desire to achieve greater justice, in other words, the justice appropriate to the facts of the particular case.

Thus, whereas R. Arama perceived R. Hisda to be "correcting" the law because of its general nature, Maimonides understood R. Hisda to be merely explaining the law as it is in itself: R. Hisda was correcting not the law but the unreflective impression the literal and superficial wording of the law gives. According to R. Arama, R. Hisda deviated from the law in its generalized form; according to Maimonides, he merely *appears* to have deviated from the law.

According to R. Arama, equity in adjudication and equity in legislation have this in common: they are both the product of the deliberate attempt of the Rabbis to have the everyday administra-

---

[22]Judges, "Evidence" 13:12.
[23]Ibid., 24:1.

tion of the *halakhah* conform to the true meaning and the true intent of the divine Legislator.[24] According to Maimonides, rabbinic legislation creates new provisions in the law; rabbinic adjudication creates nothing new. In other words, reading Maimonides one gets the feeling that equity in legal interpretation and in decision-making is essentially achieved by the halakhic authority unawares.[25] On the other hand, R. Arama and his school conceive equity as being accomplished consciously, knowingly, and deliberately. R. Arama, of course, is closer to equity as it is understood in legal history: the deliberate modification of the letter of the law in order to achieve that which is perceived as its true, deeper meaning. We thus have arrived at a Jewish medieval anticipation, albeit inchoate, of the classic, modern, jurisprudential debate as to judge-made law and judge-discovered law.[26]

The Babylonian Talmud reports R. Hiyya, the son of R. Difti, to have declared that the judge who dispenses justice in accordance with the true intent of the law *(ha-dan din emet la-amito)* becomes thereby a partner of the Holy One, blessed be He, in His act of

---

[24]Cf. the comparison made by Benjamin Cardozo of the task of the judge with that of the legislator. Each of them is "legislating within the limits of his competence. No doubt the limits for the judge are narrower. He legislates only between gaps. He fills the open space in the law. . . . [His] action [is] creative. The law which is the resulting product is not found, but made. The process, being legislative, demands the legislator's wisdom." See further Anthony D'Amato, "Judicial Legislation," *Cardozo Law Review* 1 (1979): 63–97.

[25]Cf. Rosenthal, "Ve-shuv al Derekh ha-rov," *Perakim* 1:234, last paragraph.

[26]The debate in Jewish legal literature is a most limited one. The overwhelmingly dominant view (from *Sifre* to Leviticus 25:1 to Y. Blaser, *Ohr Yisrael* 89b–90a) is that the law has always been there waiting "to be discovered." This doctrine has been succinctly expressed by the famous declaration, "Even that which a distinguished student may yet expound in the presence of his teacher has already been declared to Moses at Sinai"; *Pe'ah* 2:4; cf. *Megillah* 19b.

creation.[27] But what did R. Hiyya wish to convey by the expression "in accordance with the true intent of the law"? Those who followed the Arama doctrine of equity interpreted R. Hiyya's statement accordingly, perceiving that

> the Rabbis were referring to a judge who dispenses the justice appropriate to the particular place and to the particular time, so that the decision be in accordance with the true intent of the law. Such judgment is to the exclusion of decisions rendered without deviation from the strict law of the Torah, for sometimes a judge must decide *lifnim mishurat ha-din*, above and beyond the requirements of the formal law, in accordance with the needs of the time and the circumstances.[28]

Thus, according to the followers of R. Arama, the "true" intent of the law is the accommodation of this formal rule of Scripture to the needs of the individual case.

At the Juristic (Interpretive) Level

In instances where a law lends itself to two interpretations, one of which comports favorably with equity whereas the other is indifferent or antagonistic to the principles of equity, the former interpretation, the one which agrees with equity, is adopted.

A careful analysis of the discussion of *hazal* regarding the identification of the *lulav* with the biblical "branches of palm trees" and of the *hadas* with the biblical "boughs of a thick tree,"[29] and of Rashi's commentary on the laws of *Yibum*,[30] introduces the equitable principle "ways of pleasantness" (from Proverbs 3:17, *Derakheha darkhei no'am ve-khol netivotehah shalom*, [Her ways (i.e., the

---

[27]*Shabbat* 10a.

[28]R. Joshua Falk, *Derishah, Hoshen Mishpat* 1:2.

[29]*Sukkah* 32a–b.

[30]Rashi, s.v. "derakheha"; *Yevamot* 87b.

ways of the Torah) are ways of pleasantness, and all her paths are peace]) as a guideline in interpretation. According to this principle, where a verse or a *halakhah* lends itself to a number of possible interpretations, it is the interpretation that comports well with the image of the Torah as consisting of ways of pleasantness that is to be adopted.

There are a number of instances, however, where the "pleasantness" Jewish law is supposed to foster and the concomitant "unpleasantness" it purposes to avoid are not quite obvious. Let us examine how *no'am*, "pleasantness," appears to the eyes of Jewish decision-makers. We consider a few cases.

R. Samuel b. Moses de Medina, the Maharashdam of sixteenth-century Salonika, was asked to decide the basis upon which public officials, such as the rabbi and cantor, were to be chosen. Two principles were proposed: *rov minyan*, a quantitative majority of the members of the community, or *rov binyan*, a qualitative majority. The qualitative majority is made up of the aristocracy of wealth and of learning; the preponderance, apparently, is that of wealth.

After proving to his own satisfaction that even the Talmud gives preference to a qualitative majority—only where there are no significant qualitative differences does the simple quantitative majority rule obtain—the Maharashdam adds:

> In sum, Heaven forbid that we should accept the popular notion of strict majority rule regardless who the majority is. True justice would suffer. Imagine a town or a community consisting of one hundred people, ten of them distinguished and affluent and ninety of them belonging to the lower classes. Should the ninety wish to elect a pastor fit for them, then the ten aristocrats would have to submit to the authority of that same pastor, no matter who he might be. Heaven forbid! This is certainly not the way of pleasantness.[31]

---

[31]*Responsa Maharashdam, Orah Hayyim* 37; *Hoshen Mishpat* 421.

A case may be made for the preference of a benevolent despotism or an enlightened aristocracy over a democracy based upon the undifferentiated masses. On the other hand, one could conceive of another rabbinical authority waxing indignant at an opposing possibility. He might just as easily exclaim, "Should the ten wish to elect a pastor fit for them, then the ninety plain citizens would have to submit to the authority of that same pastor, no matter who he might be."[32] Whatever the case may be, however, the reasoning outlining the advantages of one system over the other does not fall into the very obvious types of pleasantness enumerated above.

In another case, the Maharashdam utilizes *darkhei no'am* as the basis for supporting monopolistic interests.[33] We are at present concerned with neither the appeal to talmudic legal precedent nor the merits of the holders of the particular monopoly under attack. We limit ourselves to the observation that the benefits often accruing to the public from competition in manufacture and sales in a free market cast some doubt as to the appropriateness of ways of pleasantness as contributing to the *ratio decidendi* on behalf of monopoly.

A century earlier than that of the Maharashdam, R. Joseph Colon, invoking the principle of *darkhei no'am*, had made a value judgment in favor of collectivistic – as opposed to individualistic – agreements and arrangements.[34]

Jacob ibn Zur invalidated a codicil, drawn up in a perfectly legal manner, in which a man promised his wife that upon his death

---

[32]Cf. e.g., *Responsa Eliyahu Mizrahi* 53, and R. Menahem Mendel Krochmal, *Responsa Zemah Zedek* 2. On the substantive issue of majority rule in the body politic of a community, see M. Elon, "Authority and Power in the Jewish Community: A Chapter in Jewish Public Law," *Shenaton ha-Mishpat ha-Ivri* 3–4 (1976–1977): 10–11, 21–27, and the references therein cited.

[33]*Responsa Maharashdam, Hoshen Mishpat* 259.

[34]*Responsa Maharik* 181; cf. Eliezer Goldman, "Ha-Mussar ha-Dat ve-ha-halakhah," *Deoth* 22 (1963): 71–72.

all his property would be turned over to her. The rabbi upheld the claims of the children to a share in the property. Logic and justice, he declared, dictate the conclusion that the man had not intended to disinherit his children. "Heaven forbid that our holy Torah whose ways are ways of pleasantness should agree to it. We have no doubt that the husband himself, when he wrote his instructions, did not imagine that she would take all and deprive his children of everything."[35]

Logic, justice, and *pleasantness* are undoubtedly tinged here with subjectivity.

Should a convert to Judaism die heirless and intestate, his property is free for all. This is the law as codified on the basis of the Talmud itself.[36]

The Rosh was asked by his son, R. Yehiel, the following question: In the event that the estate of a convert, upon his death, was plundered by neighbors, who is supposed to cover the funeral expenses? The reply: The Maharam Rothenberg has laid down the principle that there is no lien on a man's property, hence no attachment can be made thereto to cover the outlay for his funeral.[37] Now, if a creditor has seized part of the estate in collection of the money due to him, surely he need not return that money in order for the funeral expenses of the deceased to be paid. Similarly, if people plundered the estate, they cannot be compelled to return what they have taken to cover the funeral expenses. Hence, the costs of the burial of the indigent convert must be covered out of the community fund.[38]

---

[35]*Responsa Mishpat u-Tzedakah be-Yaakov* 1:52; cf. Eliezer Bashan, "Derakheha Darkhei Noam: A Study of the Responsa of the Oriental and North African Sages from 1391 to the 17th Century" (Hebrew), *Deoth* 48 (1980): 175 n. 17.

[36]Cf., e.g., M. *Baba Batra* 3:3; *Baba Batra* 149a; Maimonides Acquisition, "Original Acquisition and Gifts" 1:6; Tur and *Shulhan Arukh, Hoshen Mishpat* 275:1.

[37]*Responsa Maharam Rothenberg*, vol. 4 (Prague), 176.

[38]*Responsa Rosh* 15:3.

This responsum, duly codified in the classical codes,[39] evoked the opposition of R. Joel Sirkes (Bah) on the grounds both of legal theory and of human decency. A man's estate, maintains the Bah, is mortgaged to, among other things, the costs of his own funeral. But beyond that, it is simply a scandal that will lead to contention if some plunder his property and others are charged for his burial: *Her ways are ways of pleasantness, and all her paths are peace.*[40]

R. Shabtai Kohen (Shakh)[41] makes mention of the Bah's opposition, but dismisses his legal argument as unconvincing. The moral argument of the Bah he ignores. The Bah's "scandal" did not move him, as it evidently had not disturbed the Rosh and the classical codifiers who preceded him.

Having come this far, we are inevitably confronted with the element of clear-cut subjectivity in applying *darkhei no'am* as a principle of equitable interpretation in the *halakhah.* Above and beyond the general debate regarding all legal systems as to the extent to which the judge "finds" the law and the extent to which the judge "makes" the law, the standard of "pleasantness" as a built-in control over excessive legalism and formalism necessarily carries with it a degree of subjectivity that cannot be denied even by the staunchest upholders of the "law-finding" school.

RABBINIC SUBJECTIVISM AND LOYALTY TO FORMAL RULES

Many studies have contributed to the description of how the *halakhah* has coped with the tension between the demands of justice appropriate to a particular case and the legal rules in the official texts. The justice of the case is strongly affected by "outside"

---

[39]Tur and *Shulhan Arukh, Hoshen Mishpat* 275:2.
[40]Bah, *Hoshen Mishpat* 275.
[41]Shakh, *Hoshen Mishpat* 275:1.

realities. Economic factors, social and cultural context—forces often emanating from outside the spiritual world of the Jew—powerfully influence the views of the halakhic authorities, even their conceptions of what constitutes the "justice" and "fairness" that formalism must not be allowed to thwart. Indeed, in periods when the boundaries between the Jewish and non-Jewish worlds are partially blurred, the influence of the cultural and intellectual milieu of the latter on the former may sometimes be discerned.[42] The accommodation to these outside influences of the inner world of the Jew took various forms: *minhag* (custom), *takkanah* (enactment), *pesak* (court decision), *perush* (interpretation).[43] Sometimes it resulted in combinations of these forms, as, for example, where *takkanah*, *pesak*, or *perush* confirm *minhag*, or where *perush* results in *pesak*, or where *minhag* culminates in *takkanah*.

But just as "outside" forces affect the views of the halakhic authority as to what constitutes the just solution to the problem before him, so his subjective makeup[44] affects the manner in which he perceives the relevance and weight of the various social, economic, and intellectual aspects of that problem.[45] Instinctively

---

[42]Cf. Marvin Fox, "Judaism, Secularism and Textual Interpretation," *Modern Jewish Ethics*, ed. M. Fox (Columbus, OH: Ohio State University Press, 1975), 3–26.

[43]"[The] process of exegesis and interpretation is the most important device that Jewish tradition used in order to be able to stand simultaneously in the classical tradition of Judaism and in the contemporary world"; Fox, ibid., 4.

[44]I distinguish between "subjectivity," which refers to personal characteristics of mind, and "bias," which carries the connotation of a predisposition of mind that does not allow it to respond impartially to the matter at hand.

[45]Prof. Yohanan Silman has been kind enough to call my attention to R. Moses b. Isaac Noah of Poznan (early 17th century), *Lehem Mishneh* to *Avot* 33b. Not able to find the book itself, I quote Prof. Silman's translation: "Disputes are necessary throughout the Torah, for no one person can grasp all sides of it. If the root of his soul is in God's strict

sensing this, the Jewish traditional community has consistently insisted that its halakhic decision-makers be men of impeccable honesty, intense personal piety, and profound faith, *so that even the subjective element in their decisions may be confidently accepted as reflecting the "true" intent of the divine Legislator and His successors.*[46] In addition, touches of humility, reverence for one's teachers, and the fear of tampering with hallowed tradition all combined to buttress the conservative elements of decision-making.

Jewish legal activity is a most complex blending of objective and subjective elements. The citation of precedents and the strict scientific deduction of conclusions from authoritative texts (typical of formal rationality) are ever-present. Traditional halakhists read authoritative texts with great care, analyze them with consummate acumen, approach formal rules with the utmost reverence, and are ever-faithful to the rules of halakhic jurisprudence.[47] Nevertheless, despite the loyalty to the same formal rules, precedents, and authoritative texts, halakhists come up with varying interpretations and conflicting decisions. The subjective feelings, the personal wisdom, and the general orientation of the judge-rabbi-interpreter inevitably play a significant role in decision-making.

R. Israel Salanter, addressing himself to this phenomenon in the application of Torah law, has given us a clear abstract formulation of the key role of "soul-forces" *(kohot ha-nefesh)* in the understanding and application of Torah law.

---

justice *(middat ha-din)*, then he will always lean towards stringent rulings — declaring impure, forbidden and guilty, so that his opponent must provide innovative interpretations *(hiddushim)* in the opposite direction, based on the root of *his* soul, to permit things." See also M. Silberg, *In Inner Harmony* (Hebrew) (Jerusalem: Magnes, 1981), 151–59.

[46]Cf. A. Kirschenbaum, "Rabbi Moshe Feinstein's Responsa: A Major Halachic Event," *Judaism* 15 (1966): 367. For a mystical expression of this idea, see R. Aaron Halevi *(HaR'ah)* of Barcelona, *Berakhot* 48, ed. Bamberger-Blau (New York, 1957), 179.

[47]S. Graineman, *Kovetz Iggerot me-Et . . . Hazon Ish* (Bnei Berak, n.d.), 1:33.

Man, inasmuch as he is man, even though it is within his capacity and power to strip [*le-hafshit*] his intellect from the arousal of his soul-forces until these soul-forces are quiescent and resting (unaroused, so that they do not breach the intellectual faculty and pervert it), nonetheless man is human, his soul-forces are in him, it is not within his power to separate them [*le-hafrisham*] from his intellect. Thus it is not within man's capacity to arrive at the True Intellect [*sekhel amitti*] whole, separated [*ha-mufrash*] and disembodied [*ha-muvdal*] from soul-forces, and the Torah is given to man to be adjudicated according to human intellect (it being purified as much as possible; see *Bekhorot* 17b: "Divine Law said: Do it, and in whatever way you are able to do it, it will be satisfactory"). . . .[48]

The complexity of the blending, however, is more profound. The legalistic, logical approach that strives for an internally consistent comprehension, classification, and application of legal propositions is itself conditioned by the subjective modes of perception of the rabbinic scholar. But the subjective feelings and modes of perception of the decision-maker are themselves the creations of the halakhic training he received and the religious Torah values in which he has been steeped throughout his life.[49]

The recognition of this profound blending of sacred text, authoritative tradition, and subjective creativity prompted an exclamation by one of the leading *Amoraim* of the Babylonian Talmud. "Rava observed: How dull-witted are those people who

---

[48]Recorded in R. Isaac Blaser, *Ohr Yisrael*, chap. 30, Note (London, 1951), 80–98. Translation taken from: Hillel Goldberg, *Israel Salanter: Text, Structure, Idea* (New York: Ktav, 1982), 119.

[49][Rabbi Abraham Isaiah Karelitz,] *Hazon Ish al Inyanei Emunah u-Vitahon* 3:1, 10, 16, 24; *Makkot* 22b.

stand up in deference to the Scroll of the Torah but do not stand up in deference to a great Torah personage. . . ."[50] Scripture with all its sanctity is nevertheless mere words. The authentic *talmid hakham* embodies the living Word. This interplay of the subjective and objective elements of the law is inevitable and legitimate.[51] Thus the decision to adhere to the formal law or to depart therefrom is the prerogative of the halakhist, and it depends upon his perception of the various external factors interacting with his subjective views of *tzedek* (justice), *yosher* (fairness), *no'am* (pleasantness), as well as *hesed* (beneficence), *tov* (goodness), and *shalom* (peace and good will).[52]

---

[50]These observations are, of course, not original. Except for our religious emphasis, analysts of judicial thinking (e.g., Cardozo in his *The Nature of the Judicial Process*) have already observed the complex interaction of judicial subjectivism with loyalty and adherence to the formal rules; see A. Kirschenbaum, "Rabbi Moshe Feinstein's Responsa," n. 14.

[51]Is the *posek* aware of the subjective elements of his *pesak*? Most probably not. It is the nature of an authentic decision-maker of integrity to be faithful to the authoritative texts. We, as outsiders, would say, "to be faithful to the authoritative texts *as best he can*"; and, upon reflection, the *posek* would agree.

See in this connection E. E. Urbach, *The Tosaphists: Their History, Writings and Methods* (Hebrew) (Jerusalem: Bialik Institute, 1968), 571–72. Cf. R. Dworkin, *Taking Rights Seriously* (Cambridge, MA: Harvard University Press, 1977), 86ff. The similarity between our presentation of rabbinical jurisprudence and Dworkin's formulation of Anglo-American jurisprudence is most striking—and very illuminating.

[52]Is the freedom of conscience granted to the learned halakhist also granted to the unlearned layman? Undoubtedly not. Cf. the stimulating statement by Nachum L. Rabinovitch, "Halakhah and Other Systems of Ethics: Attitudes and Interactions," *Modern Jewish Ethics*, 89–102, certain stray remarks (e.g., 94) notwithstanding. On the other hand, however, the legitimacy of *minhag*—the practice and usage of law-abiding and self-sacrificing *kelal Yisrael*—even when it deviates from the formal rules, can also not be denied. Anyone familiar with the literature of the *halakhah* can

FOUR CONCLUDING NOTES

Issur ve-Heter

The individual case and its specific demands is forever being weighed against the universality of the rule and its general requirements in the process known as *horaah* (the rendering of halakhic decisions). Invariably used in the area of *issur ve-heter* (ritual practices), the expression serves to describe the role of the rabbi as *posek* (mentor) and authoritative guide in matters of religious observances. The rabbi-teacher resembles the rabbi-judge when, applying the general directive to the particular case at hand, he appears to be modifying—even negating—the rule insofar as he deviates from its literal meaning and external form. The *heter* (dispensation), which is a product of *horaah*, parallels the equitable decision in the judicial process, for both are regarded as having rendered that decision which reflects the deeper meaning of the rule and the authentic intention of the Legislator.

The Parameters

What are the parameters of subjectivity and innovation? Does everything "go"?

Dr. Louis Jacobs has written a book, *Tree of Life*, in which he catalogues innumerable changes in the *halakhah*—drastic modifications as well as moderate adjustments. These changes are so varied—in subject matter, in geographic distribution, in historical periods—that one is at a loss to delineate the precise parameters of halakhic development. Perhaps the following observation will be helpful in shedding light on the common denominator of all historic *pesak*.

Jonathan Sacks, in chapter 4 of this volume,[53] has brought to

---

testify to the untold instances where great halakhic scholars have defended such practices respectfully and with great acumen.

[53]See Jonathan Sacks, "Creativity and Innovation in *Halakhah*," in this volume.

our attention Ronald Dworkin's felicitous analogy of the judicial process to a chain novel, in which a number of novelists write a book sequentially, each contributing a chapter. Each *posek, le-havdil*, renders his *pesak* – in form and in content – as an addition to the traditional corpus of the *halakhah* in such a manner as to preserve the coherence of Jewish law as a whole. Interpreting the authoritative texts already received and creating a new addendum, the *posek* inevitably regards himself, in deciding the *she'elah* (halakhic query) before him,

> as a partner in a complex chain enterprise of which these innumerable decisions, structures, conventions and practices are the history; it is his job to continue that history into the future, through what he does on the day. He *must* interpret what has gone before because he has a responsibility to advance the enterprise in hand rather than strike out in some new direction of his own. So he must determine, according to his own judgement, what the earlier decisions come to, what the point or the theme of the practice so far, taken as a whole, really is.[54]

The *Posek*

Who, then, is this *posek* in the hands of whom halakhic decision-making is entrusted, to whose discretion it falls to interpret and to apply the *halakhah* to new conditions and in new situations, whose subjectivity, in short, is trusted? A man of consummate learning and acute analytical prowess, "who hath poured water on the hands" of a halakhic master? Yes. A man of piety and impeccable honesty totally committed to the faith? Yes.[55] But there is more.

---

[54]Ronald Dworkin, *A Matter of Principle* (Oxford: Clarendon Press, 1986).

[55]In this connection I have written elsewhere: "Thus, paradoxically, it has been the men who have committed themselves most completely to the Halachah who have been the rulers over it – applied, modified and

To attempt an ultimate answer to the question of what constitutes a recognized, revered *posek* whose decisions are followed in the twentieth century is to be faced with the unknown and imponderable. From a sociological perspective, we may say that a *posek* is that man (or those men) to whom *kelal Yisrael* gravitates for halakhic guidance. Indeed, in a sense, it is the corpus of the law-abiding citizenry of the Jewish people who decides. From a theological perspective, as believers and the children of believers we aver that it is that man (or those men) whom the *hashgahah* has selected to lead His Chosen People in its desire to fulfill His Word.[56]

Halakhic Evolution

We have noted the subjectivity of the rabbinical decision-maker vis-à-vis the why, the when, and the where of formalism and flexibility, conservation and innovation in the *halakhah*. But above and beyond his role as an agent of change, to what extent has subjectivity been a factor in the *evolution* of *halakhah?* In other words, to what extent does the subjective element of *pesak* contribute to the development of the *halakhah* in a particular, well-defined direction?

At this point it seems appropriate to refer to the central thesis of Jonathan Sacks's treatment of creativity and innovation in *halakhah*. Speaking of what led to the formation of rabbinic Judaism, he points out that the series of changes were "radical indeed."

> They led to the substitution of prayer for sacrifice, the sage for the prophet, and the synagogue for the temple. There was a move from an agricultural to a money-based conception of welfare and charity. There was a shift from a national-

---

reinterpreted precedent, so that supposedly fixed laws appear to be overruled, suspended, or even abrogated" ("Rabbi Moshe Feinstein's Responsa," 367).

[56]Cf. Maimonides' third opinion concerning prophecy, which "is the opinion of our Law and the foundation of our doctrine" (*Guide* 2:32).

historical to an ethical-covenantal sense of collective responsibility. . . .

An Orthodox scholar will see them as . . . an absolute
determination on the part of the sages to conserve and
preserve the institutions of the covenant in an utterly transformed world.[57]

I believe that an Orthodox scholar—and a non-Orthodox one as
well—would severely qualify Dr. Sacks's description of the role of
the sages—the earliest *Tannaim*, I take it—in bringing about these
transformations. A number of innovations he mentions have their
beginnings in sacred Scripture itself. This is important, for innovation based on *nevuah* and *Ruah ha-Kodesh* is, in the Orthodox view,
of a different kind from that which chapter 4 purports to be dealing
with. Moreover, it is well-nigh impossible to distinguish those later
innovations, which were based on received tradition, *Torah she-
be-al peh*, from those of the sage who acts as the essential force in the
creation of new *halakhah*.

Dr. Sacks's metahalakhic pronouncements that "they were
changes intended to establish *that nothing has changed*" and that the
halakhah, to be sure, "changes. But it changes not merely *despite* the
fact that Torah does not change, but *in order to ensure* that Torah
does not change"[58] are refreshing formulations of the doctrine of
Emunat Hakhamim. They are of little help, however, in our attempt
to analyze the history and development of Jewish law.

We do, however, possess the essential authoritative talmudic
texts which served as bases for the radical changes in medieval
Judaism. These changes were occasioned by (1) the breakdown of
the relatively centralized authority and geographic contiguity of
pre-European communities, which was accompanied by (2) the
geographic uprooting of masses of Jews and their transformation
from orientals, (3) the impact of Christianity and Islam, (4) feudal

---

[57]Sacks, "Creativity and Innovation," 141–142.
[58]Sacks, "Creativity and Innovation," 140. Emphasis by Dr. Sacks.

society and the medieval guilds, (5) the Industrial Revolution, and (6) the French Revolution and the movement for emancipation.

Comparing the texts with posttalmudic Judaism we are left with a truism that does not tell us very much. The great catalyst of halakhic development—halakhic creativity and innovation wherein the subjective component of *pesak* is maximal—is, of course, what always has been, that is, societal change. The great challenges to traditional life—new economic conditions, new socio-cultural phenomena, new threats to Jewish physical survival, and the like—are the forces that move *halakhah* by pressuring the authorities to respond to them. It therefore appears to this author that the development of the *halakhah* in a well-defined direction is impossible, for the catalysts of change, the ever-present challenges, themselves never develop in a well-defined direction. And this is equally true of the challenges of today and the questions of to-morrow—in medicine and bioethics, in technology and communication, in economic conglomerates and computer science, in ecology and space travel, in secular statehood and the status of woman, we find just some of the forces that will influence *halakhah* in ways and directions impossible today to predict.

3

Eilu ve-Eilu Divrei Elohim Hayyim: Halakhic Pluralism and Theories of Controversy

Michael Rosensweig

HALAKHIC PLURALISM: METHODOLOGICAL CONSIDERATIONS

The theme of pluralism, as it relates to the value of controversy and to the legitimacy and precise status of conflicting opinions, is fundamental to law and obviously constitutes a crucial conceptual and pragmatic challenge for any legal system. With respect to *halakhah*, however, there are additional elements and dimensions to consider, which further complicate an already elaborate issue. *Halakhah* is, after all, a uniquely divine system of law predicated on the interaction of two superficially dissonant motifs—an ontologically independent *devar ha-Shem*, on the one hand, and, on the other, the almost autonomous human capacity and obligation to interpret that *devar ha-Shem* along with the responsibility that this measure of autonomy entails. Thus, the topic of halakhic controversy and pluralism assumes even greater prominence than one

93

might have anticipated in reflecting the essential character of *halakhah* as an effective legal system.

From one perspective, an analysis of this topic is important because it enables us to formulate the halakhic attitude and policy toward the issue of dissent as well as the dissenting, even rejected, minority view. It affords us the opportunity to evaluate its role and to assess what it contributes to the overall system, as well as to define the necessary parameters which limit its significance, without which *halakhah* as a unifying and authoritative legal system would be jeopardized.

There is, however, an additional contemporary dimension to this issue which increases the urgency for its proper investigation. We live in an era in which extravagant claims march under the banner of religious pluralism. In part this is due to the present connotations of the term, which conjure up the image of standards watered down by unrestricted and uncritical flexibility. Primarily, however, this phenomenon can be traced to the bold assertions of the Conservative and Reform movements whose justification of halakhic deviation on the basis of a pluralistic perspective constitutes the perversion of a concept that in its authentic form accents the depth and intensity of a maximally demanding *halakhah* as the embodiment of *devar ha-Shem*.

The enterprise of investigating this topic is plagued by both methodological and substantive difficulties. There is no clear locus classicus in terms of the central issues. Even the talmudic passages in *Hagigah* (3b) and *Eruvin* (13b), which we shall demonstrate to be the most significant texts, are ambiguous in terms of their real implications. At the same time, the broad issues that are central to this theme pervade the philosophy of *halakhah* and therefore encompass many subtopics. Issues such as *lo ba-shamayim hi* (the Torah is not in heaven), the independence of a *posek* from previous authority and perhaps even from divine authority, and complex questions of procedure and methodology of *pesak* vis-à-vis the pursuit of halakhic truth border and sometimes overlap our theme and thus complicate the picture considerably.

The philosophical and epistemological difficulties suggested by the very concept of multiple truths—an apparent oxymoron— constitutes another dimension of the problem. This can be illustrated by what I believe to be a fundamental misconception: the association of our concept of *eilu ve-eilu divrei Elohim hayyim* (both positions of a debate represent the word of the living God) with the so-called medieval Double Truth Doctrine of the Averroist school with respect to conflicts of faith and reason. First, it should be noted that there is considerable doubt that such a theory ever existed. Etienne Gilson and others have pointed out that such an attribution first appears in 1277 in the introduction to a church document, authored by Bishop Stephen Tempiers of Paris, that condemned heterodox ideologies. It is likely that rather than representing a true and justifiable doctrine, this view was attributed to the Averroists by their religious critics, who suspected them of covering up their heresy by cynically and insincerely clinging to faith while truly being committed to reason. In fact, Averoists merely asserted that despite their authentic belief in the teachings of faith, they were forced to acknowledge that reason revealed a different set of conclusions, and they were unwilling to brand logical philosophical analysis a waste of time in spite of this dilemma.[1] Be this as it may, this theory of Double Truths fundamentally acknowledges the absolute dichotomy between two distinct spheres—religion and reason. This approach cannot serve as a model for the concept of *eilu ve-eilu*, which refers to multiple truths all of which are legitimate expressions of the divine spiritual domain.[2]

---

[1]A convenient summary of different approaches and orientations regarding the Double Truth theory can be found in *The Encyclopedia of Philosophy* (New York: Macmillan and Free Press, 1967), 1:223–26. See also Etienne Gilson, *History of Christian Philosophy in the Middle Ages* (New York, 1955), and C. Touati, "Vérité philosophique et vérité prophétique chez Isaac Albalag," *Revue des Etudes Juives* 71 (1962): 35–47.

[2]Dr. Norman Lamm has proposed that Niels Bohr's Theory of Com-

Moreover, in attempting to evaluate the overall topic of halakhic pluralism, confusion is likely to stem from a lack of clear differentiation between different phases of the issue, each characterized by its own dynamics and range of options. These include (1) biblical exegesis and Jewish philosophy, (2) the process of *talmud torah* and the theoretical status of *heftzah shel torah* (an essence of Torah), and (3) *pesak halakhah* and the relationship between procedure, and its de facto conclusions, and the pursuit of objective halakhic truth.

I will analyze some of the possible approaches to this problem with the qualification that any attempt to achieve a comprehensive treatment would demand much more extensive elaboration on issues of authority, procedure, and methodology of *pesak* than the scope of this chapter permits.

PARSHANUT AND HASHKAFAH

In the realm of biblical exegesis (*parshanut*) and Jewish thought (*hashkafah*), diversity of opinion and of interpretation is pervasive and the perception of its legitimacy is widely acknowledged. Pluralism in these contexts poses no real difficulty inasmuch as the fundamental guidelines that regulate these disciplines and provide their religious sanction are quite clear. Moreover, there are several additional factors that are responsible for this state of affairs.

The primary focus of pluralism in these contexts is not the relationship of contradictory views but of multiple layers of meaning, since generally no absolute, mutually exclusive values or determinations are at stake. It is not only possible but even compellingly logical that events, institutions, and *mitzvot* that are perceived to be divinely inspired and spiritually invested should

---

plementarity in nuclear physics may be a more accurate analogue to the notion of legitimate epistemological and ontological pluralism. This suggestion is articulated in his recently published *Torah Umadda: The Encounter of Religious Learning and Worldly Knowledge in the Jewish Tradition* (Northvale, NJ: Jason Aronson, 1990), 232–36.

have the capacity to accomplish many functions and to symboli-
cally represent more than one single theme. Moreover, when faced
with divine (biblical) texts as opposed to human (rabbinic) ones, as
those involved in these enterprises most often are, the possibility of
multiple meanings can be taken for granted. Even when relevant,
rabbinic texts do not exert the same measure of binding authority
in areas of *parshanut* and *hashkafah* as they do in halakhic discussions. The *midrash* and *aggadot* of the Talmud are open to allegorical
interpretation and according to some halakhists even to rejection.[3]

---

[3]Obviously the precise status of *aggadot* and *midrashim* constitutes a
complex issue and one that is very much reflective of the overall orientations of the various theorists themselves. Thus, any serious analysis of the
topic would require an elaborate and comprehensive independent treatment of the sources. See Marc Saperstein, *Decoding of the Rabbis* (Cambridge, MA: Harvard University Press, 1980), 1–20, for a summary of basic
rabbinic perspectives on *aggadah*.

In connection with our specific purpose in this context, see the famous
formulations of Rav Sherira Gaon and Rav Hai Gaon as they are recorded
in S. Albeck, *Sefer ha-Eshkol* (Jerusalem, 1984), vol. 1, *Hilkhot Sefer Torah*,
157–58, and in B. Levin, *Otzar ha-Geonim—Hagigah* (Jerusalem: Hebrew
University Press, 1932), nos. 66–69, pp. 59–60.

One should note in particular the intriguing possibility advanced by R.
Hai Gaon that the stature of talmudic *aggadot* exceeds that of *aggadot*
whose origin is exclusively midrashic. Nevertheless, even talmudic *aggadot*
will not be binding if they do not conform to logic and intuition based on
the principle of *ein somhin al aggadah*. (See also *Pe'ah* 2:6.)

See also the celebrated passages in Maimonides' *Introduction to Perek
Helek*, in J. Kapah, *Perush ha-Mishnayot la-Rambam* (Jerusalem: Mossad
ha-Rav Kook, 1965), 2:136–37, where Rambam describes three basic
approaches to rabbinic *aggadah*, associating himself with the more flexible
interpretive posture. Some of the literature of the Maimonidean controversies (of 1232 and 1305) revolved around the legitimacy of this view. (See
also *Hagahot ha-Gra, Yoreh De'ah* [179:12] for an example of an emphatic
critique of Rambam's philosophic posture.)

The controversial formulations of Nahmanides in his polemic with
Pablo Christiani (Barcelona, 1263), in which he sharply downgrades the

While one must seriously consider the message of *aggadot*, they certainly do not have the force and normative weight of *halakhah*.

On the social-communal level, too, there is not the same kind of urgency for uniformity in the sphere of *hashkafah* as there is in *halakhah*, where concrete performances, mutual obligations, and objective procedures are central. With respect to the notion of a subjective inner life of the spirit, a pluralistic ideology addressing itself to individual inclinations and intuitions potentially constitutes a more valuable and effective approach to religious life.

And yet, the broad parameters of even this pluralism should not be misconstrued to be unrestricted as some would have us believe. Moses Mendelsohn's dogma of the "dogmalessness of Judaism" is clearly an unacceptable exaggeration, explicitly rejected by *Rishonim* who articulated Articles of Faith *(Ikkarim)* in whatever form, pattern, or number. Obviously, there can be no Orthodox Judaism without an absolute affirmation of certain basic concepts of God, of the commitment to a binding *halakhah* based on the concept of *Torah mi-Sinai*, and of the notion of human responsibility and accountability in the form of divine providence, reward, and punishment. Moreover, beyond adherence to official *Ikkarim*, it is evident that to be acceptable as a legitimate expression of

---

significance of *midrashim*, is also relevant to this topic. He declares, for example: *Ve-zeh ha-sefer mi she-yaamin bo tov, u-mi she-lo yaamin bo lo yazik.* and even more strikingly: *Ve-od anu korin oto haggadah rotzeh lomar . . . she-einam ela devarim she-adam maggid le-haveiro* (*Vikuah ha-Ramban* in C. Chavel, *Kitvei ha-Ramban* [Jerusalem, 1963], 308). There is a whole literature that debates the extent to which these comments should be perceived as accurately reflecting Ramban's authoritative position, or, in the alternative, should be viewed as an insincere, but strategic, response motivated by the circumstances of Jewish-Christian disputations in which *aggadot* were often used by Christian advocates to establish the authenticity of their claims. See, for example, the comments of Rabbi Chavel in *Kitvei ha-Ramban*, ad loc.; Y. Baer, "Le-Bikoret ha-Vikuchim shel R. Yechiel mi-Paris ve-shel ha-Ramban," *Tarbiz* 2:2 (1930/31); and S. Lieberman, *Shekiin* (Jerusalem, 1970), 81–83.

Judaism, a perspective must establish itself by meeting additional basic criteria. It should, for example, have visible roots in authoritative texts or in rabbinic tradition (mesorah), and it should be advocated by a religious personality of some stature.

These qualifications notwithstanding, the diversity and range of perspective in parshanut and hashkafah is impressive and wholly acceptable to Chazal. Statements like: shivim panim la-torah (there are seventy dimensions to the Torah)[4] and u-kepatish yefotzetz sela—mah patish zeh mithalek le-kamah nitzotzot, af mikra ehad yotzei le-kamah te'amim (and like a hammer that breaks the rock in pieces, i.e., just as [the rock] is split into many splinters, so also may one biblical verse convey many teachings),[5] and the view expressed by Ramban in the preamble to his commentary in the Torah, where he formulates the notion of Torah as a divine text formed by the infinite combinations of divine names, allowing it to serve as a creative exegetical source of all types of knowledge simultaneously are representative of this approach. Indeed, they provide the conceptual basis for this diversity.

We are witness to diversity of opinion not only on every page of the Mikraot Gedolot and Midrash Rabbah, but within the schemes of particular parshanim as well, as each suggestion advanced claims for itself a measure of truth. Ramban moves with facility from derekh ha-peshat to derekh ha-emet, and Rabbenu Bahyah from peshat to derash to sekhel. We encounter the same phenomenon with regard to taamei ha-mitzvot. Rambam and Ramban represent diverse approaches to this discipline and certainly to specific mitzvot. Within individual schemes, such as that promulgated by Sefer ha-Hinukh,

---

[4]Bamidbar Rabbah 13:15. Cf. Responsa of Radvaz (Venice, 1749), 3:643. Radvaz posits that the multiplicity of legitimate meanings of Torah is responsible for the text being unencumbered by nekudot and taamim, which would inhibit many possible readings, although these symbols signal the proper method of public reading—Keriat ha-Torah—and are of Sinaitic origin.

[5]Sanhedrin 34a.

we are witness to the assertion of multiple purposes and truths.[6]

This approach pervades discussions of Jewish philosophy even when positions that are developed are mutually exclusive. Debates rage on such fundamentals as the eternity of the universe, free choice, knowledge of particulars, the role of the intellect for prophecy and so on. Passionate argumentation regarding the very legitimacy of such basic orientations as philosophy, *Kabbalah*, *Hasidut*, and *Musar* characterizes this approach as does the integration into some individuals of multiple disciplines. The projection by some Jewish historians of an absolute demarcation between Jewish philosophers and kabbalists, for example, represents a distortion, as Gershon Scholem has demonstrated.[7] This misreading of Jewish intellectual history derives at least in part from a failure to fully appreciate the wide-ranging hashkafic pluralism of Judaism.

To be sure, a basic consensus and hierarchy of values and perspectives has emerged from the historical process of generations of debate—acceptance, rejection, refinement. In this sense, *hashkafah* is self-regulating as it must be. At the same time, it is evident that there is a great deal of flexibility and latitude in establishing legitimacy in this area. Clearly, diversity of opinion and multiplicity of meaning are not only acceptable but contribute to and are consistent with the attainment of the religious ideal in Judaism.

HALAKHIC PLURALISM: ONE TRUTH OUT OF MANY

Halakhic controversy, though it too is obviously very prevalent, represents a different kind of problem. The ultimate goal of a halakhic analysis is to arrive at a specific, single solution, and halakhic debates generally revolve around mutually exclusive positions, only one of which is purported to represent absolute truth.

---

[6]Introduction to *Sefer ha-Hinukh*, and *mitzvot* 95, 98.

[7]*Hakaballah be-Provence, Lectures of Gershon Scholem—1963*, ed. R. Shatz (Jerusalem: Akadamon, 1979), 5–21.

From this perspective, one can account only for the value of sincere if failed effort accorded to all but the proponent of the authentic view and for nothing more than a measure of respect for each view that may prove to be the authentic one. Yet, several talmudic sources suggest a notion of the inherent value of dissenting views and possibly even of multiple truths. Thus, the Talmud (*Eruvin* 13b) relates the following:

> For three years there was a dispute between Beth Shammai and Beth Hillel, the former asserting, "The *halakhah* is in agreement with our views" and the latter contending "The *halakhah* is in agreement with our views." Then a *bat kol* issued announcing, "The utterances of both are the words of the living God, but the *halakhah* is in agreement with the ruling of Beth Hillel."

It is particularly noteworthy that this apparent advocacy of multiple truths appears in a context whose primary concern is to establish the halakhic decision according to one particular view.

Another talmudic passage attributes the legitimate diversity of halakhic perspectives to a single act of revelation, despite the obvious logical paradox that this entails. The Talmud (*Hagigah* 3b) explains:

> "The masters of assemblies": these are the disciples of the wise, who sit in manifold assemblies and occupy themselves with the Torah, some pronouncing unclean and others pronouncing clean, some prohibiting and others permitting, some disqualifying and others declaring fit. Should a man say: How in these circumstances shall I learn Torah? Therefore the text says: "All of them are given from one Shepherd." One God gave them; one leader uttered them from the mouth of the Lord of all creation, blessed be He; for it is written: "And God spoke all these words." Also do thou make thine ear like the hopper and get thee a perceptive heart to understand the

words of those who pronounce unclean and the words of those who pronounce clean, the words of those who prohibit and the words of those who permit, the words of those who disqualify and the words of those who declare fit.

How, then, is one to evaluate this concept and these sources?

One approach might be to view statements such as these as referring to the inherent significance of the process of *talmud torah*, which necessarily includes an exchange of conflicting opinions. The author of *Netivot ha-Mishpat* articulates the view that there is considerable value in halakhic debate: it contributes to the process of *talmud torah* by identifying misconceptions, refining authentic views, and honing and sensitizing halakhic intuition. He argues:

Though halakhic errors are inherently false, they nonetheless serve an important didactic function. Indeed, one cannot successfully establish halakhic truth without some measure of initial failure. The early stages of halakhic analysis bear a similarity to a diver who is not yet capable of distinguishing worthless stones from the treasure he wishes to retrieve. More often than not, he surfaces with the former rather than the latter. However, once he has analyzed his error he emerges with an enhanced capacity to discern. The very process of failure increases his sensitivity to the nuances that distinguish precious jewels from stones, enhancing his future prospects for success. When he dives again many of the worthless stones that were initially responsible for his confusion are no longer present, having already been discarded. Those that remain are unlikely to generate further confusion inasmuch as the diver has learned to identify the differences between precious and worthless stones. Thus his initial failure contributes to his ultimate success. As the Rabbis indicate—if he had not drawn worthless objects, he would not have discovered the valuable item which they camouflaged. For this entire process there is heavenly reward.[8]

---

[8]Introduction to *Netivot ha-Mishpat* on *Hoshen Mishpat*.

These sentiments accurately reflect an ambitious view of *talmud torah* not simply as a means of attaining *pesak — le-asukei shamita aliba de-hilkhata* — but as constituting the vehicle for dialogue and encounter with *devar ha-Shem*, an intrinsically significant spiritual process and religious experience. As important as this theme is, however, it does not adequately justify the striking language and dramatic formulations that these sources contain.

One might assess the concept of *eilu ve-eilu divrei Elohim hayyim* against the background of the overall scheme developed by Netziv in his introduction to the *Sheiltot, Kidmat ha-Emek*, though Netziv himself does not fully explicate his position with respect to this concept specifically.[9] Netziv develops two distinct categories of halakhic decisions. One means of halakhic resolution is rooted primarily in intuition. Objectively, the issue remains unresolved despite the fact that a practically binding normative conduct has been established. The historical model of this kind of *pesak*, classified by Netziv as *horaah*, can be traced to the methodology of the *kohen* in his function as *posek*. From this point of view, dissenting opinions retain an absolute status as *heftzah shel torah*, with respect to which one could justifiably declare *eilu ve-eilu divrei Elohim hayyim*. The second method of *pesak*, characterized by Netziv as *hakhraah le-dorot*, derives from exhaustive and ultimately conclusive logical analysis, and is the special domain of the *shofet-mehokek* (judge-legislator) whose historical prototype was Yehudah. When a halakhic issue is resolved in this manner at a particular point in history, the dissenting position loses at least its equal status as a legitimate expression of Torah. This form of *pesak* was revealed to Moshe at Sinai as the product of a specific individual's definitive analysis — *kol mah she-talmid vatik atid le-horot ne'emar le-Mosheh mi-Sinai* (halakhic decisions that will be formulated in the future by qualified scholars were already, in fact, articulated by Moses at Sinai) — and is even occasionally designated as *hilkhata gemiri*, reflecting its absolute authority. Thus, Netziv asserts a limited histor-

---

[9]*Kidmat ha-Emek* — the introduction to Netziv's commentary on *Sheiltot de-Rav Ahai Gaon* (Jerusalem: Mossad ha-Rav Kook, 1961), 18–19.

ical double truth theory, effective only until the point of absolute logical resolution.

However, Netziv does posit that even within his second motif of decisive *pesak* there exist two basic categories of rejected opinions. Employing homiletical license, he likens minority opinions to the *nitzotzot* (sparks) and *netuim* (branches) as these are used in *Sanhedrin* (34a) and *Hagigah* (3b), respectively. Just as one cannot speak about sparks or branches without acknowledging the differences between them of size, significance, function, and purpose, one cannot speak about disputed halakhic opinions in uniform terms either. While the resolution of many halakhic debates strips the rejected position of any redeeming value, there are some minority opinions which retain a measure of *or torah* (light of Torah), although in their stated form they remain objectively inaccurate. Thus, for example, the view that a female Amonite is included in the prohibition of *lo yavo amoni u-mo'avi be-kehal ha-Shem* (Amonites and Moabites are prohibited from marrying Jews) is valueless if it is incorrect. However, R. Eliezer's assertion that one must fulfill the *mitzvah* of *Keriyat Shema* before the first third of the night has passed—*ad sof ashmorah rishonah*[10]—retains the stature of *or torah* inasmuch as it contains and highlights valuable kernels of conceptual, if not practical, truth. It establishes that *ashmorah rishonah* may be a significant halakhic time frame. More significantly, R. Eliezer dramatizes through his radical application that *be-shakhbekha u-bekumekha*, which defines the obligation, may refer to the time period when people go to sleep rather than the time during which they are asleep. This theory possibly serves as the basis of the position of the *hakhamim* who extend the obligation until midnight, though they dispute R. Eliezer's technical restriction of this concept to the period of *ashmorah rishonah*. This theme—that radical minority views have considerable conceptual and didactic value—is a common one in *halakhah*, and is especially central to the methodology of conceptual Torah study. From this perspective, the notion

---

[10]*Berakhot* 2a, 3a, 4b.

that there is value in halakhic debate and more than one absolute truth represents a limited but still meaningful principle.

It is conceivable that this view of the value of rejected opinions, of their potential contribution to a more accurate and sophisticated conceptual understanding of *halakhah*, underlies Ramo's understanding of yet another problematic talmudic text. The Talmud (*Sanhedrin* 17a) evidently establishes the capacity for inaccurate mental gymnastics as a prerequisite for judicial appointment to the *Sanhedrin*. Thus we are informed: *ein moshivin be-sanhedrin ela mi she-yode'a le-taher et ha-sheretz min ha-torah* (the ability to argue convincingly that an insect is not ritually impure is a prerequisite for judicial appointment). The Tosafists accent the apparent difficulty and comment on the dubious value of this characteristic: "R. Tam queried, What is the purpose of such meaningless mental gymnastics?"[11] Ramo, in responsum, explains:[12]

> If one is capable of logically demonstrating the ritual purity of these animals, one will perceive the Torah's ruling as a *hiddush* (revealed, but radical doctrine). This is significant because it dictates that we should limit its application as much as possible. Thus, while the blood of a *sheretz* is assigned the status of impurity as is its body, it is conceivable that the minimal measure that generates impurity with respect to the body of the *sheretz* (*ke-adasha*) does not apply to its blood. The purpose of this mental gymnastics then, is to reveal to us the innovative character of the Torah's ruling and therefore it yields important substantive results in terms of the limiting of that ruling.

Ramo thus argues that this statement does not refer to the meaningless capacity for intellectual gamesmanship, nor does it seek only to insure the appointment of judges with an impressive grasp of a

---

[11]*Tosafot, Sanhedrin* 17a, s.v. *she-yode'a le-taher et ha-sheretz.*

[12]R. Moses Isserles, *Responsa of Ramo* (Jerusalem, 1977), no. 107.

great deal of knowledge. In fact, it establishes that a measure of additional sophistication regarding the inner workings of the halakhic process, including the ability to assess the implications of nonnormative possibilities and to utilize halakhic debate to shed light on the nuances of a topic which might have some normative impact, is a necessary precondition to judicial appointment where the stakes are so high.

At the same time, if we accept the general scheme developed by Netziv, it is conceivable that even the *mitzvah* of *talmud torah* would extend only to that class of minority viewpoints that retain the status of *or torah* due to some normative, or at least conceptual, benefit that they may yet provide. This stance is certainly open to debate. In the twentieth century, for example, R. Moshe Feinstein in one of his responsa eloquently argues on the basis of *eilu ve-eilu divrei Elohim hayyim* that in the realm of *talmud torah* and for purposes of *birkhat ha-torah*, minority positions are absolutely equivalent to normative *halakhot*. He goes so far as to suggest that even God and his heavenly retinue *(mesivta de-rakia)* spend time discoursing and studying these doctrines in the context of *talmud torah*.[13]

The possibility of real multiple halakhic truths does not really emerge from Netziv's scheme. This approach is, however, implied by other sources. Rashi, for example, seems to affirm this doctrine.[14]

> When a debate revolves around the attribution of a doctrine to a particular individual, there is only room for one truth. However, when two *Amora'im* enter into a halakhic dispute, each arguing the halakhic merits of his view, each drawing upon comparisons to establish the authenticity of his perspective, there is no absolute truth and falsehood. About such

---

[13]R. Moshe Feinstein, *Iggerot Mosheh* (New York, 1982), 4:9, 24.
[14]Rashi, *Ketubot* 57a, s.v. *Ka mashma lan.*

issues one can declare that both represent the view of the living God. On some occasions one perspective will prove more authentic, and under other circumstances the other view will appear to be more compelling. The effectiveness of particular rationales shift as conditions of their application change, even if only subtly.

This more ambitious approach to our topic is explicated by Ritva, Maharshal, and Maharal—each providing his own nuances and subtleties of formulation, each requiring a conceptual underpinning to justify this difficult concept.

Ritva (Eruvin 13b) cites the inherent paradox of this theme as raised by the Tosafists.[15] The rabbis of France asked: How is it possible for conflicting views both to represent the truth? They responded as follows:

> When Moshe ascended to receive the Torah, it was demonstrated to him that every matter was subject to 49 lenient and 49 stringent approaches. When he queried about this, God responded that the scholars of each generation were given the authority to decide among these perspectives in order to establish the normative halakhah.

His response posits that a full range of halakhic options—possibly even of equal status—was revealed to Moshe and sanctioned as heftza shel torah. License was provided to the scholars of every generation to pursue what they deemed to be the most accurate pesak on the basis of accepted halakhic methodology.[16] The clear

---

[15]This view is apparently based on the formulation in Masekhet Soferim (16:6). See Sanhedrin 4:2, where an important aspect of this theme is expressed in a slightly different context.

[16]For an interesting discussion of this basic perspective see the article by Rabbi Yechiel Michal Katz, "Ve-hayei Olam Nata be-Tokheinu—Zu Torah she-be'al Peh," Sefer Yevul ha-Yovloth: The Centennial Torah Volume of Rabbi Isaac Elchanan Theological Seminary, ed. N. Alpert, A.

implication of this formulation is that for those scholars, halakhic conclusions are not arbitrary but based on rigorous analysis and, consequently, the decisions become normative for that generation.[17]

A similar perspective would emerge if one were to adopt the position that the primary thrust of the Sinaitic *mesorah* was not a detailed revelation of the multiple permutations of *halakhah*, but a revelation of general principles.[18] Man's obligation to apply halakhic principles by means of the methodology of hermeneutic principles would then account for the potential existence of many valid, yet technically mutually exclusive, solutions to the same problem.

Maharshal affirms the existence of multiple truths, possibly of equal value, and contributes a mystical-historical explanation for it. He states:[19]

> One should not be astonished by the range of debate and argumentation in matters of *halakhah*. . . . All these views are

---

Kahn, and Z. Schachter (New York: Tova Press, 1986), 346–60, and the sources cited therein.

[17]This view, combined with the notion of exclusive human responsibility for the halakhic process as reflected by the principle of *lo ba-shamayim hi* (see *Baba Metzia* 59b), represents the conceptual underpinning for the somewhat radical view of halakhic autonomy that is manifest in its independence from even divine *derashah* and interference. This doctrine is articulated by *Derashot ha-Ran*, ed. L. Feldman (Jerusalem: Shalem Institute, 1973). It is also developed in the famous introduction to the *Ketzot ha-Hoshen* on *Hoshen Mishpat* in his analysis of the concept of halakhic *hiddush*.

[18]See, for example, *Midrash Rabbah* on *Shemot*—41:6 [on *Shemot* (31:12)]: *Ve-khi kol ha-torah lamdah Mosheh? Ela kelalim limduhu ha-Kadosh Barukh Hu.* This position is very clearly formulated by R. Yosef Albo in his *Sefer ha-Ikarim* (3:2) and may represent Rambam's view as well. See Responsa of Hayyim Ya'ir Bachrach, *She'eilot u-Teshuvot Havot Ya'ir* (Jerusalem, 1973), no. 481. Cf. R. Tzevi Hirsch Chajes, *Torat ha-Neviim* (Zolkiew, 1836), chap. 4—*maamar Torah she-be'al peh.*

[19]Introduction to *Yam Shel Shlomo* on *Baba Kamma*.

in the category of *divrei Elohim hayyim* as if each was received directly from Sinai through Moshe. This is so despite the fact that Moshe never projected opposing perspectives with respect to any one issue. The Kabbalists explained that the basis for this is that each individual soul was present at Sinai and received the Torah by means of the 49 paths *(tzinorot)*. Each perceived the Torah from his own perspective in accordance with his intellectual capacity as well as the stature and unique character of his particular soul. This accounts for the discrepancy in perception inasmuch as one concluded that an object was *tamei* in the extreme, another perceived it to be absolutely *tahor*, and yet a third individual argues the ambivalent state of the object in question. All these are true and sensible views. Thus, the wise men declared that in a debate between true scholars, all positions articulated represent a form of truth.

The Jews who stood at Sinai evidently were not merely the passive recipients of the Torah. Their presence and their acceptance, as individuals, shaped the very content of the Torah at the critical historical moment it took effect. This formulation dramatizes the spiritual significance that *halakhah* ascribes to human singularity by revealing that the subjective inclinations of individuals invested their perspective of Torah with intrinsic worth. While this approach shares much in common with Ritva in terms of human input and the focus on broad principles rather than details, it significantly departs from Ritva's perspective in its accent on the historical moment of Sinaitic Revelation and with respect to the role of the recipients of the Torah in forming this pluralistic Torah and in establishing its contours.

Maharal represents yet another formulation of the legitimacy of multiple halakhic truths.[20] He advocates a doctrine of unequal yet intrinsic truths. His comparison of halakhic categories and

---

[20]Maharal of Prague, *Be'er ha-Golah* (Jerusalem, 1971), 19–20. See my article, "Personal Initiative and Creativity in Avodat Hashem," *The Torah U-Madda Journal*, ed. Jacob J. Schacter, 1 (1989): 79–83.

institutions to the human personality and its manifold complex characteristics suggests a kind of Platonic model, which presupposes the existence of an ideal halakhic status that precedes and supersedes the sum of its components. There is often no one decisive response to the issue of *taharah* or *tumah*, for example, since overall proximity to the ideal form represented by the classic case, rather than a specific combination of components, determines this status. Thus, one may speak of approximating the ideal sufficiently but not fully, and by the same token substantially but not sufficiently, and consequently, a whole hierarchy of truths would emerge. Dilution of some components and combination with competing and undermining characteristics may also contribute to the creation of a quasi-status, whose ultimate fate in the realm of practical *halakhah* is likely to be debated. Maharal's understanding of the statement in *Sandredrin* (17a) cited earlier flows from this perspective. Even technically inaccurate or flawed halakhic opinions do contribute to a more sophisticated appreciation of the depth of content of Torah, which makes the ability to justify all angles of a halakhic problem a proper condition for judicial appointment.

THE IMPACT OF MINORITY OPINIONS ON *PESAK*

Having established several formulations and theories underlying *eilu ve-eilu divrei Elohim hayyim* regarding the status of dissenting minority views as *heftza shel torah*, it is now incumbent upon us to examine the impact of these perspectives and the role of rejected minority opinions generally on the institution of *pesak*.

Whatever position one adopts on the value of debate to theoretical study, there clearly is an obligation to arrive at one practical solution based on the sincere conviction of its accuracy. The relationship of *pesak* as an enterprise dedicated to the goal of a single uniformly binding conclusion to the ambitious formulations of the theory of halakhic pluralism is complex and even double-edged. If one advances the position that there is only one authentic, or at least preferred, halakhic truth, then the stakes of *pesak* are high indeed. Halakhic decision becomes a hit-and-miss exercise in which the dissenting view stands in clear opposition to truth. If one has faith in the process that aspires to produce that truth, one cannot consider dissenting opinions legitimate fall-back positions to be possibly rehabilitated even under extraordinary circumstances. To do so would be tantamount to expressing a serious lack of faith in the effectiveness of the decision-reaching process. At the same time, if one advocates the objective validity of alternative *pesakim*, then even as they are more palatable as *devar ha-Shem*, they are, ironically perhaps, less legally significant as practicable alternatives once they have been rejected by the process of *pesak*, for under these circumstances the formal and procedural aspect of halakhic resolution dominates. *Pesak*, according to this view, need not concern itself with the risky, uncertain, and fallible task of revealing the one authentic truth, but instead focuses on establishing the best truth consistent with its own principles of resolution. In this sense, the conclusions reached are absolutely binding in the realm of normative conduct inasmuch as this view establishes *pesak* as a *din vadai* (an absolute surety). This aspect of the relationship between *pesak* and the theoretical value of alternative perspectives has been largely ignored by those who perceive of *eilu ve-eilu* in strictly modern-liberal terms, ignoring the concomitant ascendancy of pure formal procedure in these schemes.[21]

How then does *halakhah* view the right to dissent from majority *pesak*, and how does it evaluate the objective status of dissenting views? Again, the question is a complex one, since beyond the status of the minority opinion, hitherto analyzed, the resolution of these questions turns on the interaction between two competing and transcending values of *halakhah*: the pursuit of truth and toleration of multiple perspectives, on the one hand, and the pragmatic need to establish uniformity, discipline, and order— *she-lo yihiyu kishtei torot* (not to fragment the torah)[22]—to insure effectiveness, on the other. The very need for *pesak* despite *eilu*

---

[21]See n. 16 above.

[22]*Sanhedrin* 88b.

ve-eilu divrei Elohim hayyim is due to this factor, according to Maharshal, *Arukh ha-Shulhan*, and others.[23]

The status of *Zaken Mamrei* (Z.M.), the rebellious elder who disputes the *pesak* of the Great Sanhedrin, is one of the best examples of this theme of authority. Ramban explains that the need to publicize the punishment of Z.M. (*Sanhedrin* 89a) follows from the fact that he is executed not because of the severity of his offense per se but because of its destructive impact.[24] He is, after all, entitled to express his sincerely held halakhic convictions, but is put to death despite this as a result of his refusal to acquiesce, which threatens to undermine the very concept of uniform normative behavior crucial to any legal system. The fact that Z.M. is obligated to accept rabbinic authority and its procedures, even when they appear to be blatantly inaccurate — *af al yemin she-hu semol, ve-al semol she-hu yemin* (even if they declare right to be left and vice versa) — further underscores the significance of formal procedure and principles of *pesak*, which may even outweigh objective halakhic truth.[25]

---

[23]Introduction to *Yam Shel Shlomo* on *Baba Kamma*; Introduction to *Arukh ha-Shulhan* on *Hoshen Mishpat*.

[24]*Ramban al ha-Torah, Devarim* 21:18. Cf. *Perush ha-Radvaz* on Ramban *Mishneh Torah — Hilkhot Mamrim* 3:8.

[25]*Sifre* and *Ramban al ha-Torah, Devarim* 17:11. This theme is, of course, both crucial and controversial in terms of its precise parameters and therefore its wider implications. It requires extensive clarification. I have cited one formulation in this context in order to highlight a particular perspective, but it is by no means the only approach to this topic. See also *Horayot* 1:1 and Rabbi Elhanan Wasserman, *Kuntres Divrei Sofrim* — no. 4, in *Kobetz Shiurim*, vol. 2 (Tel Aviv, 1963), 106–09. One should also contrast Ramban's position with that of Abarbanel on *Devarim* 17:8 and the rationale provided by *Sefer ha-Hinukh*, no. 508. *Kli Yakar* (ad loc.) directly links the *Sifre*'s doctrine with the principle of *eilu ve-eilu divrei Elohim hayyim*. Professor Menachem Elon points to the stark contrast between *halakhah*'s view of rabbinic license of interpretation and sixteenth- and seventeenth-century English law, which, in theory, severely limited such flexibility (Menachem Elon, *Ha-Mishpat ha-Ivri* [Jerusalem: Magnes Press, 1978], 1:229 n. 24).

According to Netziv, the principle of Z.M. applies not only to the *hakhraah le-dorot* (definitive decision) of the *shofet-mehokek*, but also to the intuitive *horaat kohen,* since corrosive impact on uniform conduct and respect for rabbinic authority are the crucial components. Thus, he emphasizes the reference to both *kohen* and *shofet* in this context — *ha-ish asher yaaseh be-zadon le-bilti shemo'a el ha-kohen ve-el ha-shofet* (he who intentionally defies the *kohen* and the *shofet*).[26]

There are indications that the basic theme of Z.M. also extends to less qualified disputants and less impressive sources of authority. *Derashot ha-Ran*[27] and *Sefer ha-Hinukh*[28] argue that the basic prohibition of *lo tasur* applies to any individual who rejects rabbinic decisions. According to Maharam ibn Habib, this notion of a parallel to Z.M. applies to all judges, and is responsible for the obligation of a minority judge to join with the majority whose ruling would otherwise be ineffective due to the principle of *ein holkhin be-mamon ahar ha-rov* (majority or probability does not dictate in monetary matters), which appears to require unanimity in monetary disputes.[29]

R. Jacob Emden rejects the idea that an individual may continue to adhere to his own halakhic convictions after the principles that regulate *pesak* have discounted them.[30] He, too, points to the Z.M. parallel as the foundation for this position. However, others dispute the existence of such parallels and limit the motif of authority in favor of greater flexibility in the pursuit of truth.

The tension between the pursuit of halakhic truth and the integrity of halakhic procedure that ensures its effectiveness as a

---

[26]*Kidmat ha-Emek,* 6–7.

[27]*Derashot ha-Ran, derush* 12, 212–13. He projects the principle of *aharei rabbim le-hatot* as the basis for this, rather than *lo tasur.* See also Abarbanel on *Devarim* 17:8.

[28]*Sefer ha-Hinukh,* no. 508. He perceives this as an extension of *lo tasur.*

[29]This position is also recorded by *Kuntres ha-Sefekot* 6:2. [This work was authored by the brother of the *Ketzot ha-Hoshen* and is printed in many editions of the standard *Hoshen Mishpat* or *Ketzot ha-Hoshen.*]

[30]R. Jacob Emden, *She'alat Yaavetz* (Lemberg, 1884), no. 153.

system pervades any number of topics. These range from a proper evaluation of the story of *tanur shel akhnai* (*Baba Metzia* 59b), and its climax of *lo ba-shamayim hi*, to an issue of judicial deception discussed by *Pit'hei Teshuvah*—whether a minority judge is permitted to falsely declare himself undecided in order that he may delay the decision, possibly laying the groundwork for ultimate reversal of the majority consensus by undermining the self-sufficiency of the existing court.[31]

The complex status of minority opinions is further reflected in several halakhic contexts. As suggested earlier, the Tosafists and others were disturbed by the apparent clash between the principles of *ein holkhin be-mamon ahar ha-rov* and judicial majority rule.[32] Various solutions were proposed, two of which underscore opposing perspectives with respect to the concepts of *pesak* and objective halakhic truth.

R. Yonatan Eibschitz in his *Tumim* distinguishes between most majorities, which are not mutually exclusive of the minority, and issues of *halakhah*, which have only one absolute resolution. Thus, in his view, the minority perspective in *halakhah* is totally negated by the majority decision and consequently poses no challenge to it, even in the monetary realm. This explanation probably represents a deemphasis of halakhic pluralism.

R. Jacob Emden, in a slightly different context, proposes a different approach.[33] He argues that judicial procedure excludes any real doubt (*safek*) since the majority has the capacity to

---

[31]*Pit'hei Teshuvah*, *Hoshen Mishpat* 18:4, 8. The background to this issue is the *sugyah* in *Sanhedrin* 5b.

[32]*Tosafot*, *Baba Kamma* 27b, s.v. *ka mashma lan*, *Tosafot*, *Sanhedrin* 3b, s.v. *dinei mamonot*; *Hiddushei ha-Gra al ha-Shas*, *Baba Kamma* 27b— *ba-inyan ein holkhin be-mamon ahar ha-rov*; *Kuntres ha-Sefekot* 6:2.

[33]Rabbi Jacob Emden, *She'alat Yaavetz*, no. 157. Compare this view to the positions regarding majority rule outlined in Rabbi R. Margolies, *Margaliyot ha-Yam on Sanhedrin* (Jerusalem: Mossad ha-Rav Kook, 1977), *Sanhedrin* 40a, no. 22, 163–64.

establish — not just reveal — the law. Obviously, in the absence of real doubt one cannot be concerned with the weight of presumptive monetary rights *(hezkat mamon)* that determine *ein holkhin be-mamon ahar ha-rov.* In this formulation we observe the notion that *pesak,* devoid of the burden of revealing truth, which carries with it the potential for error, is an independent and strictly formal process. This view is consistent with a theory of halakhic pluralism.

The insight of *Kli Hemdah* represents an almost ideal balance. A judge who is overruled by the majority has a right of appeal to the Great Sanhedrin in terms only of the theoretical issue and its future application; he is denied any possibility of actually challenging and overturning the previous application of that *pesak.*[34] This safeguards the integrity of halakhic processes while, at the same time, encouraging the pursuit of maximal halakhic perfection by allowing for theoretical and future reevaluation.

Halakhists discussed a similar issue, one that took them outside the strict confines of court decision. Does an individual have the right to insist that he is convinced of the validity of a minority halakhic position and thus refuse to comply with the majority-held ruling? This question was debated by major halakhists and possibly represents a dispute between scholars of Franco-Germany and Spain. It also reflects several of the themes that are crucial to our evaluation of multiple truths in *halakhah* and of the character of halakhic decision-making. Maharik and others who distinguish between the monetary and other realms due to the factor of *hezkat mamon* certainly appear to view *pesak* as a means of resolving doubt rather than establishing conduct irrespective of halakhic truth.[35] Other halakhists reject such distinctions, possibly because of these implications.

The possibility that one might rehabilitate a previously rejected minority opinion or rely upon one in absence of definitive evidence

---

[34]*Kli Hemdah al ha-Torah — Devarim* 17:8, pp. 106–9. Cf. *Margaliyot ha-Yam, Sanhedrin* 2a, no. 51.

[35]Joseph Colon, *Responsa of Maharik* (Jerusalem, 1973), no. 14.

to the contrary is obviously linked to our topic. The *mishnayot* in *Eduyot* (1:5,6) provide us with ambiguous information:[36]

> And why do we mention an individual opinion along with the majority, though the *halakhah* follows the majority? That a Court may approve an individual view and rely on him: for a Court cannot gainsay a decision of its fellow Court unless it is greater in wisdom and number. . . . R. Yehudah said, If so why do we mention an individual view along with the majority unnecessarily? That if a person says, So I have a tradition—he will say to him, You heard it as the opinion of so-and-so.

Tosafot Sens interprets the *mishnah* as follows:[37]

> Although the minority view was not accepted when initially proposed, if a majority of the scholars of the next generation agrees to the rationale that underlies this position, it is established as the normative *halakhah*. The entire Torah was revealed to Moshe with a range of perspectives yielding opposing conclusions. He was told that the majority position prevails, but that both views retain their status as *divrei Elohim hayyim*.

According to this interpretation, the *mishnah* refers to what was previously a minority opinion but has now achieved majority backing and whose implementation is, in fact, based on the principle of majority rule. The issue thus becomes one of justifying the overturning of a previously established truth. The response of *Tosafot Sens* projects *eilu ve-eilu divrei Elohim hayyim* as a real multiple truth theory that relegates halakhic decision-making to

---

[36]See also the interpretation of *Or Zarua* (Bnei Brak, 1958), vol. 1, *Hilkhot Sheviis ve-Hadash*, no. 328, and *She'iltot de-Rav Ahai Gaon Shemot*, no. 36.

[37]*Tosafot Sens, Eduyot* 1:4.

the status of mere legal procedure, with the consequence that the principles of halakhic decision-making may themselves cause it to be overturned. This perspective effectively addresses both the motif of multiple truths and the significance of halakhic process and procedure.

The theme of halakhic pluralism is also central to an issue of codification policy that was the subject of heated debate in rabbinic circles particularly in the aftermath of the appearance of Rambam's *Mishneh Torah* in the twelfth century and the *Shulhan Arukh* in the sixteenth century. The omission of minority opinions in these works provoked a critical reaction in some circles. The brother of Maharal of Prague, R. Hayyim, justified his critique of *Shulhan Arukh* on the basis that even rejected doctrines contain inherent spiritual value, as the concept of *eilu ve-eilu divrei Elohim hayyim* provides.[38]

A passage in *Massekhet Soferim* (16:5) accurately conveys the significance of the contribution that minority opinions may offer to the halakhic process:

> R. Tanhum b. Hanilai said: If the Torah had been given as a clear-cut code, no judge would have a *locus standi* in laying down a ruling; but now a judge has a *locus standi*, for if he declares a thing to be clean there are [authorities] who declare a thing in a similar condition to be unclean, and if he decides that it is unclean there are [authorities] who declare a thing in a similar condition to be clean.

The very next section asserts that the initial revelation entailed multiple halakhic approaches and options. "R. Jannai said: The Torah which the Holy One, blessed be He, gave to Moses was delivered to him in forty-nine aspects of uncleanness and forty-nine

---

[38]Rabbi Hayyim b. Bezalel, *Vikuah Mayyim Hayyim* (Amsterdam, 1712), 5b. For a further discussion of this position see my article "Personal Initiative," 84–85.

aspects of cleanness" (16:6). The juxtaposition between these statements provides the justification for this ideal of flexibility in *pesak*.[39]

The talmudic distinction between two categories of judicial
error represents another interesting facet of halakhic pluralism. A
fundamental judicial error brought about by ignorance or misreading of basic crucial sources (*ta'ut be-devar mishnah*) invalidates
the *pesak*. However, rulings that stem from questionable evalua-
tions or improper adherence to procedures designed to establish the
hierarchy of different opinions and sources (*ta'ut be-shikul ha-daat*)
stand, though the judge may be liable and must compensate the
victim of his miscalculation. One might propose, at least according
to some *Rishonim*, that the ambivalence which characterizes our
approach to the category of *ta'ut be-shikul ha-daat*—in which the
ruling is valid and yet admits of liability—derives from its status as
a possibly legitimate expression of Torah which has been discarded
on procedural grounds. From this perspective, the details that
govern and define the two categories of error are instructive indeed.

How we define *ta'ut be-devar mishnah*, for example, should help
to determine the boundaries of legitimate halakhic debate. Thus,
the discussion among *posekim* regarding whether accepted rulings of
Geonim or *Rishonim* should be classified *devar mishnah* or *shikul
ha-daat* is very significant. The distinction advanced by some
between those geonic positions that when revealed are accepted
and those that generate opposition is also striking. At the same
time, the position of Rosh that knowledge of an error of *shikul
ha-daat* prior to the implementation of the ruling would still not
render *pesak* invalid perhaps attests to a notion of legitimate
pluralism at least of this variety.[40] Moreover, the opinion quoted in

---

[39]Cf. *Sanhedrin* 4:2.

[40]This position is disputed by Ramah. See *Tur, Hoshen Mishpat*, no. 25.
A comprehensive analysis is required of the full range of perspectives
regarding the subtle criteria that differentiates *ta'ut be-devar mishnah* from
ta'ut be-shikul ha-daat, and of the implications for the relationship of the

Or Zarua that a *ta'ut be-shikul ha-daat* that is motivated not by incorrect application of halakhic rules of resolution but by a lack of information of the positions of some *posekim* does not create any kind of liability seems to hold improper procedure alone responsible for this status, not any flaw in the pursuit of objective halakhic truth.[41]

There are, of course, significant limitations even of a pluralism grounded in equal truths. This is clearly manifest by the distinction between *ta'ut be-devar mishnah* and *ta'ut be-shikul ha-daat*, as we have just demonstrated. The parameters of *kim li*, for example, attest to this. Even those who accept the effectiveness of the claim of *kim li* impose definite limitations. Maharik believes that one can only resort to this claim when the minority opinion one seeks to rely upon has definite prominence and stature—the opinion of a Rashi or R. Tam.[42] There are *Aharonim* who require that such a position be cited by the *Shulhan Arukh* or Ramo. Some *Rishonim* demand that at least two *Posekim* adopt a position before one can declare *kim li*. A position advocated by only one authority is too idiosyncratic to be taken as a serious expression of Torah. *Kuntres ha-Sefekot* characterizes such positions as *meuta de-meuta* (extreme minority)— an unlikely candidate for halakhic truth even of the pluralistic variety. Others conclude that the precise parameters of legitimacy should be left to the intuition of the halakhic authorities involved in the particular case, since it is difficult to quantify such a concept. The broad guidelines of restriction are in any case apparent.[43]

We also encounter definite limitations upon the permissability of a minority judge to falsely claim indecision in order to block what

---

twin themes of authority and autonomy in *pesak* that issue from these perspectives. I hope to address this topic elsewhere.

[41]*Or Zarua, Sanhedrin* 5a.

[42]*Responsa of Maharik*, no. 94:6.

[43]See *Kuntres ha-Sefekot* 6:6 for a review of some of the major positions on this issue.

he believes to be an incorrect majority ruling.[44] These, too, can
serve a broader function as models of the parameters of legitimate
dispute and dissent.

Clearly, pluralism is not a blank check. There are objective
limits to a sincere interpretation of sources. The author of *Arukh
ha-Shulhan* in his introduction to *Hoshen Mishpat* emphasizes that
most halakhic debates revolve around details and the application of
principles, not the principles themselves. This is particularly true,
he argues, about those debates that are characterized as *eilu ve-eilu
divrei Elohim hayyim*. R. Moshe Feinstein in the introduction to his
Iggerot Mosheh cautions about the need for *yirat shamayim* (fear of
God, i.e., piety) and intellectual rigor to insure valid conclusions.

At the same time, in terms of the themes of tolerance and
respect for the legitimately arrived at conclusions of others with
whom we may disagree, the implications of *eilu ve-eilu divrei Elohim
hayyim* are crucial. The *Gemara* (*Baba Batra* 130b) informs us that
even a *pesak* that we reject should not be shredded for it may
represent a valid approach:

> When a legal decision of mine comes before you (in a written
> form), and you see any objection to it, do not tear it up before
> you have seen me. If I have a (valid) reason (for my decision) I
> will tell (it to) you; and if not, I will withdraw. After my death,
> you shall neither tear it up nor infer (any law) from it. "You
> shall neither tear it up" since, had I been there, it is possible
> that I might have told you the reason; (131a) "nor enter (any
> law) from it"—because a judge must be guided only by that
> which his eyes see.

R. Feinstein suggests that the underlying principle of *eilu ve-eilu
divrei Elohim hayyim* demands that we treat a rejected opinion
relating to a halakhic concept—as opposed to the *pesak* referred to
in the talmudic passage—with a full measure of reverance even if we

---

[44]*Pit'hei Teshuvah, Hoshen Mishpat* 18:4, 8.

are familiar with and still not convinced by its argument. The climate of debate between Bet Shamai and Bet Hillel as related in *Yevamot* (13b–14b) eloquently expresses this theme:

> Though these forbade what the others permitted, and these regarded as ineligible what the others declared eligible, Beth Shammai, nevertheless, did not refrain from marrying women from (the families of) Beth Hillel. Nor did Beth Hillel (refrain from marrying women) from (the families of) Beth Shammai. . . . This is to teach you that they showed love and friendship towards one another, thus putting into practice the Scriptural text, "Love ye truth and peace."

The *Gemara* in *Eruvin* (13b), the very source of *eilu ve-eilu divrei Elohim hayyim*, concludes that the *halakhah* is in accordance with Bet Hillel precisely because they displayed greater fidelity than Bet Shammai to this theme of respect.

> Since, however, "both are the words of the living God" what was it that entitled Beth Hillel to have the *halakhah* fixed in agreement with their rulings? – Because they were kindly and modest, they studied their own rulings and those of Beth Shammai, and were even so (humble) as to mention the actions of Beth Shammai before theirs.

This motif should guide us in relating to other communities and their distinctive customs and *pesakim*.

Finally, it should be stated emphatically that *eilu ve-eilu divrei Elohim hayyim* should never be used as an excuse for complacency or mediocrity. Even as we encounter equal truths we must aspire to pursue our own conviction of ideal truth culled from and on the basis of insights that we form from the wealth of legitimate perspectives before us. Our pursuit should be intensified and enhanced by these exposures. In this way, it is to be hoped that we will emerge with the concept of pluralism beautifully depicted by the *Arukh ha-Shulhan* in his introduction to *Hoshen Mishpat*:

> The debates of Tanaim and Amoraim and Geonim in fact represent the truth of the living God. All of their views have merit from a halakhic perspective. In fact, this diversity and range constitute the beauty and splendor of our holy Torah. The entire Torah is called a song whose beauty derives from the interactive diversity of its voices and instruments. One who immerses himself in the sea of Talmud will experience the joy that results from such rich variety.

Torah, then, is to be perceived as a harmonious symphony enriched by the diversity of its instruments and variations and bearing the singular message of *devar ha-Shem*.

4

Creativity and Innovation in *Halakhah*

Jonathan Sacks

I was asked to address, in this chapter, the broad subject of "Creativity and Innovation in *Halakhah*," discussing among other things the following:

1. What legitimates *hiddush be-halakhah* (halakhic innovation)?
2. How, in this context, are we to understand the idea of *lo ba-shamayim hi* (Torah is not in heaven)?
3. What is the role of precedent in *halakhah?*
4. What is the role of *horaat shaah*, halakhic rulings directed to specific emergencies or temporary conditions?

In the first half I will briefly address these topics, but I will then move on. For these, I believe, are *not* the key issues. Concentrating on the formal powers of a *posek* (halakhic decisor) to innovate is misleading. It begs wider and seminal questions, to which I can only briefly allude. In the second half I focus on a single narrow question:

123

The difference between an acceptable and an unacceptable *hiddush be-halakhah*.

WHAT LEGITIMATES *HIDDUSH BE-HALAKHAH?*

Torah does not change. *Halakhah* does. *Halakhah* changes precisely because *Torah* does not change, for *halakhah* is the application of *Torah* to a changing world. The connection between these two propositions was set out classically by Maimonides:

> God knew that the judgments of the Law will always require an extension in some cases and curtailment in others, according to the variety of places, events and circumstances. He therefore cautioned against such increase and diminution and commanded, "Do not add to it or subtract from it" (Deuteronomy 13:1), for constant changes would tend to disturb the whole system of the Law and would lead people to believe that the Law is not of Divine origin. But permission is at the same time given to the wise men of every generation—namely the *bet din ha-gadol*—to take precautions with a view to consolidating the ordinances of the Law by means of regulations in which they innovate with a view to repairing breaches. . . . In the same manner they have the power temporarily to dispense with some religious act prescribed in the Law, or to allow that which is forbidden, if exceptional circumstances and events require it. . . . By this method the Law will remain perpetually the same and will yet admit at all times and under all circumstances such temporary modifications as are indispensable.[1]

Maimonides is speaking here of the *legislative* powers of the sages, their power, for example, to enact *gezerot* (decrees) and *takkanot* (ordinances). Throughout this chapter we will be speaking only of the *interpretive* powers of a *posek*; his power to create new law not by

---

[1] Moses Maimonides, *Guide for the Perplexed* 3:41.

formal enactment but by addressing new questions, or old questions in new circumstances, often by giving a new interpretation of the sources. But the general principle remains. Halakhic innovation is essentially conservative and preservative. It aims, in the first place, at ensuring a strict identity of Torah through time, and second, at preserving Torah as law, which is to say, as the code which governs the behavior of the Jewish people.

What this means in practice is, of course, highly controversial, along two different axes. The first is: what constitutes identity? Is this to be seen in formal terms, such that identity is measured by minimal deviation from antecedent rulings? Or are we to conceive Torah, as Maimonides seems at times to do in the third book of the *Guide*, as a series of provisional enactments tending toward the realization of an ideal society? This, at any rate, is what Eliezer Berkovits refers to when he speaks of the "tension between . . . the ultimate ethos of the Law, and its institutionalisation in specific laws."[2] Closely related to this, though not identical with it, is what Emanuel Rackman refers to as "a functional approach to halakhah."[3]

The functional approach would see *halakhah* as instrumental in actualizing certain values, or achieving certain social ends. Its rulings would change as society changed but its purposes would remain constant. The Berkovits-Maimonidean approach would project *halakhah* against a larger canvas of human development, in the course of which certain institutions like sacrifices and slavery fell by the wayside, as no-longer-needed concessions to primitive religious and economic forms. The first sees the function of *halakhah* as homeostatic, maintaining an *equilibrium* of values under changing social conditions. The second sees it as *educative* and

---

[2]Eliezer Berkovits, "The Status of Woman within Judaism," in *Contemporary Jewish Ethics*, ed. Menachem Kellner (New York: Sanhedrin Press, 1978), 365.

[3]Emanuel Rackman, *One Man's Judaism* (New York: Philosophical Library, 1970), 253–61.

developmental, tending toward progressively closer approximations
of an ideal. But both see halakhic identity in terms of fidelity to an
underlying value structure, rather than to its past and concrete
actualization in the form of specific rules.

The second and possibly more interesting axis of disagreement
is: How are we to understand the idea of preserving Torah as the
law of the Jewish people? This has been a central dilemma for
halakhah in modernity; rarely, however, articulated as such. How
should Jewish law be interpreted (1) when it lacks coercive sanc-
tions, as it has done since European emancipation, and (2) when a
substantial proportion of the Jewish people identify as members of
that people without identifying with or seeing themselves as bound
by *halakhah?* Is *halakhah* to be given, under these circumstances, an
exclusive or inclusive interpretation? What is the halakhist's responsibility to the, as it were, *covenantal* dimension of Jewish law —
its role as the law of the Jewish people in its entirety? I have touched
on this question in my forthcoming book, *One People? Tradition,
Modernity and Jewish Unity*, and will say no more about it here
except to note that it is a critical question; that *how* one approaches
it will make a significant difference to whether one interprets the
sources strictly or leniently; and that it turns on the question of
how one conceives the *constituency* of a halakhic ruling.

So Maimonides' statement in the *Guide*, that the mandate for
halakhic change is so that "the Law will remain perpetually the
same" is capable of bearing widely different interpretations. What it
rules out, however, is a cluster of approaches to Jewish law that can
roughly be characterized as "Conservative." Broadly speaking,
these views hold that Jewish law evolves, not only in its detailed
actualization, but even in its ultimate conceptions of value and
purpose. It is responsive, in Robert Gordis's phrase, to "fresh ethical
insights."[4] Or — on a range of views from Zechariah Frankel to

---

[4]David Hartman seems to come *close* to this position when he writes
that "the development of the halakhah must be subjected to the scrutiny
of moral categories that are independent of the notion of halakhic

Solomon Schechter to Mordecai Kaplan to Louis Jacobs—it just evolves, imperceptibly and organically, the way a custom or culture or tradition evolves. These views embrace a wide range of opinion on what *halakhah* and halakhic authority are. But they share the assumption that history is in some sense normative. There may be, perhaps, an evolutionary continuity but not a *principled identity* between *halakhah* now and in rabbinic or Mosaic times. This view is ruled out by the Maimonidean principle that *halakhah* changes so that Torah should always remain the same.

LO BA-SHAMAYIM HI

Halakhah must be interpreted to be applied. The question thus arises as to the authority of interpretation. The talmudic account of the dispute between R. Eliezer and the sages on the *tannur shel Akhnai* (oven of Akhnai) invokes the idea of *lo ba-shamayim hi*: the Torah is "not in heaven."[5] What does this imply?

First, a sharp distinction between revelation and interpretation. The word—that is, the Torah—has been revealed. The *meaning* of the word has not been revealed. Second, there is no suprarational access to the meaning of revelation. That which is disclosed through a heavenly voice, a mystic insight, or even a prophetic visitation has no privileged status over a purely human interpretation. Third, some criterion must therefore be sought if we are to decide the law, and that criterion cannot be "truth" in the sense of identifying the intention of the Lawgiver, as it were independent of interpretation and argument. The Talmud finds such a criterion in the principle of a majority vote of the sages. The principle of *lo ba-shamayim hi* is that the Torah itself confers authority on the sages to interpret and apply its laws.

---

authority" and that "our human ethical sense" must "shape our understanding of what is demanded of us in the mitzvot" (*A Living Covenant* [New York: Free Press, 1985], 98).

[5]*Baba Metzia* 59b.

Posekim tend to invoke the principle as their warrant for *pesak* (halakhic decision-making). The question to which it serves as an answer is: How may man, with his finite and fallible understanding, dare to pronounce on what is the will of God in an undecided case? The answer lies in a distinction between "truth" and "authority." The ruling of a sage is authoritative even if we cannot be sure that it is true. Thus R. Nissim b. Gerondi writes, in explication of *lo ba-shamayim hi*:

> All of the sages saw that the view of R. Eliezer was closer to the truth [*maskim el ha-emet*] than theirs, and that the signs he produced were honest and legitimate, and that Heaven itself had decided in his favour. Nonetheless they ruled in accordance with their consensus. For since their reason was inclined to declare the oven impure even though they knew that their decision was counter to the truth, they would not agree to declare it pure. Had they declared it pure, they would have been violating the Torah, since their reason guided them to declare it impure. For the determination of the law has been entrusted to the sages of each generation and what they decide is what God has commanded.[6]

Basing himself on this and similar passages, R. Arye Leb Heller writes in the introduction to *Ketzot ha-Hoshen* that God "gave us the Torah according to the resolution of the human intellect, even though it may not be the truth." His will was that "truth spring up from the ground," the truth being decided by "the consensus of the sages" according to their understanding. In a similar vein, the late R. Moshe Feinstein wrote, in the introduction to *Iggerot Mosheh*:

> Certainly there are grounds for concern as to whether [contemporary halakhic authorities] have fathomed the true de-

---

[6]*Derashot ha-Ran*, ed. L. Feldman, 7:112.

termination of the law in the sense of "true from the perspective of Heaven" [*emet kelapei shamaya*]. But the truth which is halakhically normative [*emet le-horaah*] is governed by the principle of *lo ba-shamayim hi,* meaning: that which seems to the sage to be so after he has searched the halakhic literature to determine the law to the best of his ability, with due gravity and the fear of Heaven. The ruling that then appears to him to be correct is halakhically normative [*emet le-horaah*] and he is obliged to rule accordingly even if, in fact, it is "revealed before Heaven" that the correct interpretation is otherwise.[7]

Thus far the rule of "not in Heaven," a principle much beloved of those who argue for halakhic innovation, flexibility, and creativity. However its import is, I believe, precisely the reverse of that usually attributed to it. For *lo ba-shamayim hi* is—if I may be forgiven for using such terminology—an assertion of a "Catholic" as against a "Protestant" view of divine law. By it, interpretive authority is vested in the *ecclesia,* the community of the sages, as against the individual in lonely confrontation with the divine word.

To be sure, R. Feinstein speaks about the individual *posek,* for we lack a *bet din ha-gadol.* But had a sage acted in accordance with his logic at a time when a *bet din ha-gadol* was in existence, he would have been a *zaken mamrei,* "a rebellious elder." *Lo ba-shamayim hi* is not an intrinsically revolutionary doctrine; if anything it is a conservative one. It may have relevance in contemporary halakhic discourse, for example to counter any quasi-oracular interpretation of the concept of *daat Torah.* But it places *pesak* firmly in the context of interpretation and consensus, what Stanley Fish calls "the authority of interpretive communities,"[8] and excludes "intuition" or "autonomy" or "subjectivity" as halakhically determinative. Nor

---

[7]*Iggerot Mosheh, Orah Hayyim,* vol. 1, introduction.

[8]Stanley Fish, *Is There a Text in This Class?* (Cambridge and London: Harvard University Press, 1980).

is Eliezer Berkovits's inference correct, that "the result is not objective truth but pragmatic validity."[9] "Not in heaven" may entail that the idea of "absolute" truth is inapplicable to *halakhah*, but it does not exclude "objectivity." Nor is there any suggestion that *halakhah* is to be determined on "pragmatic" grounds. In short: *lo ba-shamayim hi*, along with the rabbinic insistence that "prophets may not innovate," is precisely directed *against* a revolutionary by-passing of text, precedent, and consensus in the name of a "heavenly voice."

EIN LO LA-DAYYAN AND THE FORCE OF PRECEDENT

Far more relevant to the subject at hand is the rule of *ein lo la-dayyan ella mah she-einav ro'ot*: a judge must rule on the basis of what his eyes see.[10] The general effect of this dictum is to preserve an area of judicial discretion, as against an overly stringent view of the binding force of halakhic precedent. As understood by *Rishonim* and *Aharonim*, it generally implied that a *posek* was entitled, perhaps bound, to base his decisions on a fresh consideration of the sources as opposed to an uncritical acceptance on the rulings of his predecessors. In particular it was invoked by those opposed to the process of halakhic codification. It was raised by critics of the project of the *Mishneh Torah*, and later of the *Shulhan Arukh*. A codifier, it was argued, could not bind the hands of his successors. An area of judicial discretion remained, even on matters ruled on in the codes, for "a judge must rule on the basis of what his eyes see."

We recall several powerful statements to this effect. There was the forceful argument of R. Avraham ben ha-Rambam:

> The general principle is this: I maintain that a judge who in his rulings exclusively follows that which is written and explicit is

---

[9]Eliezer Berkovits, *Not in Heaven* (New York: Ktav, 1983), 48.
[10]*Niddah* 20b, *Sanhedrin* 6b, *Baba Batra* 130b.

weak and timid. For such a course results in the abandonment of the rule *ein lo la-dayyan ella mah she-einav ro'ot*. This is not as it ought to be. Rather, the matters which are written are the foundation [*ikkar*], and the judge or decision-maker must carefully weigh each individual case that comes before him in the light of analogous cases, drawing out detailed prescriptions [*anafim*] from those foundations. For the many cases which encompass only some of the laws were not recorded in the Talmud for nothing, but were also not intended to dictate the decision in accordance with what is mentioned there. Instead they were intended to endow the sage who has heard them many times with the capacity to weigh up matters rationally and acquire a sound approach in rendering decisions.[11]

There are, in short, matters which require judicial discretion: the more so, the more the judge attends to the individual features of the case before him. No less significant is the statement of the Maharal which focuses on the obligation of the *posek* to rule on the basis of his understanding of the sources, and not to rely on halakhic codes:

It is more fitting and correct that one should determine the law for himself directly on the basis of the Talmud, even though there is a danger that he will not follow the true path and not decide the law as it should be in truth. Nonetheless, the sage has only to consider what his intellect apprehends and understands from the Talmud, and if his understanding and wisdom mislead him, he is still beloved by God when he decides in accordance with the mind's dictates, for *ein lo la-dayyan ella mah she-einav ro'ot*. Such a person is superior to one who rules from a code without knowing the reasons for the decision, who walks like a blind man on the way.[12]

---

[11]*Teshuvot R. Avraham ben ha-Rambam*, 97.
[12]Maharal, *Netivot Olam, Netiv ha-Torah*, 15. I owe this source to my

A similar statement is to be found in the Maharsha,[13] and the point is powerfully reaffirmed by R. Moshe Feinstein.[14]

How far this rule applies and with what constraints is beyond the scope of this chapter.[15] To some extent it turns on what is

---

teacher, R. Nachum Rabinovitch (see his "Halakhah and Other Systems of Ethics: Attitudes and Interactions," in *Modern Jewish Ethics*, ed. Marvin Fox [Columbus, OH: Ohio State University Press, 1975], 97). On the basis of this and other sources, R. Rabinovitch makes a powerful case for the place of autonomy in the halakhic system. "The process of halakhic decision is not meant to release us from the struggle of conscience or the toil of the intellect that must be involved in any decision if it is to be a worthwhile spiritual experience." Despite the many cases where there is little room for individual variation, "there are still situations . . . where the ultimate decision must be the individual's alone, taken in the privacy and loneliness of his own conscience, where the immediacy and ethical awareness of the demands of love and justice are such that only the individual himself can confront the storms within his heart and determine which demands shall prevail."

[13]*Hiddushei Halakhot ve-Aggadot* to *Sotah* 22a.

[14]*Iggerot Mosheh, Yoreh De'ah* 1:101. R. Feinstein defends the right of a contemporary *posek* to rule contrary to other *Aharonim* when there is clear proof for his position.

[15]Joel Roth has summarized the sources in *The Halakhic Process: A Systemic Analysis*, 81–113, as has Eliezer Berkovits in *Ha-Halakhah Kochah ve-Tafkidah*, 156–98. Roth's book, however—an attempt to present a coherent Conservative position on *halakhah*—contains a remarkable, if obscure, disclaimer. He speaks of "a third group of contemporary Jews," evidently those who stand between Orthodoxy and Reform, "who are committed both to the halakhic system and to the affirmation not only of the acceptability of extralegal data within that system, but also of the terminology *and methodology* that those data imply." What this means is not clear. Apparently it implies that *halakhah* may have to be rewritten in terms of new sociological, cultural, and intellectual "realities." The question then arises for Roth: what shall the halakhist of this "third group" do with the weight of halakhic precedent which opposes such innovation? For while his argument—cryptic and contestable as it is—might justify a

considered a *devar mishnah* (a settled, authoritative, and binding precedent); what is a matter for *shikkul ha-daat* (weighing out), where more than one view is present in the literature and where the *posek* rules against majority practice; and what is a matter of *sevara be-alma* (general reason), where alternatives may be equally available. There is more than one view on these questions, and more than one style of *pesak*. Some *posekim* feel freer than others to move directly to an analysis of talmudic sources. They vary in the degree to which they feel bound by the literature of the *Aharonim*.[16] They vary too on the degree to which they accept apparently conflicting sources at face value.

To some extent, also, it turns on the nature of the issue involved. The rule of *ein lo la-dayyan* preserves a measure of judicial

---

"Conservative" halakhic *opinion*, it would never justify a "Conservative" halakhic *ruling*, since the opinion would always be in a minority when weighed against the rest of the halakhic literature. Roth is thus forced to a further dramatic proposition. An argument between a Conservative authority and an Orthodox one cannot be construed as a legitimate halakhic argument since "the disagreement is about the very nature and systemic functioning of the halakhic system." In such a case one cannot say *eilu ve-eilu divrei Elohim hayyim* (both these and these are the words of the living God), since either *halakhah* operates the way a Conservative theorist says it does, or it does not. Here, there can be no conjoint truths. "Thus, the Jew holding the third view must react to the class of the committed [i.e., the Orthodox] in the same way as he reacts to those who find the system irrelevant. *He must disregard their opinions*" (309–10). The revolutionary character of these two propositions—that contemporary sociology is in some way normative, and that all halakhic precedent that does not concede the point may be dismissed—is itself the clearest indication of the constraints surrounding halakhic innovation. For nothing in Roth's long and detailed study provides the slightest halakhic warrant for either assertion.

[16]See, for example, R. J. Schwartz, *Maaneh le-Iggerot*, 123, who takes issue with R. Feinstein on the scope of *ein lo la-dayan* in relation to precedent.

autonomy. But in some cases that autonomy is not available. Issues relating to personal status, for example, require consensus if the law is not to collapse altogether. It is this, one would suspect, that has proved the stumbling block in the many attempts to alleviate the position of women in relation to divorce. With increased mobility this is beginning to prove a problem even in one of the few areas where halakhic codes themselves prescribe autonomy to a *bet din* to rule in accordance with individual judgment: *gerut* (conversion).[17] A *bet din* which maintains a restrictive policy on conversion may find its efforts frustrated by the availability of Jewish courts of law in other countries which use less demanding criteria. In extremis, this may result in a conversion of limited geographical validity. The trauma and controversy created by one such case recently in Britain revealed how unacceptable such a policy is, and I have yet to see a reasoned halakhic justification for it.

In short, how far a halakhist may innovate will depend on how far he can establish that the case in hand is one in which legitimate alternatives are present in the literature and how far he can reconcile apparently conflicting rulings. The halakhist may well feel, even having achieved what he regards as a correct analysis of the sources, that his argument has the status of *halakhah* but not yet *halakhah le-maaseh* (to be implemented in practice). It is a defensible ruling, but not yet one which ought to be acted on. He may defer that final judgment until a consensus has been reached, or until his analysis has been supported by a given number of eminent *posekim*. His reservations may relate either to *principle* or *policy*. He may, that is to say, have doubts as to whether he has read the sources correctly or at least defensibly. Or he may, even if he is sure that the ruling is one that *may* be acted on, have doubts as to whether it *ought* to be acted on. For its acceptance may have halakhically undesirable consequences.

Ronald Dworkin, a philosopher of law to whose work we will turn shortly, argues that judges must attend to matters of principle

---

[17]*Ha-kol lefi re'ot einei bet din. Bet Yosef, Yoreh De'ah,* 268.

only. Issues of policy are the proper concern, not of judges but of legislators. At present, however, given the lack of formal legislative powers within *halakhah* in the absence of a *bet din ha-gadol*, *posekim* are of necessity legislators also, and must responsibly attend to the consequences of their rulings.

No purely formal analysis, then, of *ein lo la-dayyan* and its related concepts will allow us to delineate the actual, as opposed to potential, scope of halakhic innovation. It is here that disciplines such as the history and sociology of *halakhah* are of great interest; though it must not be forgotten that both are descriptive rather than normative disciplines. Neither is part of the halakhic process per se.

HORAAT SHAAH

Ein lo la-dayyan and related concepts are concerned with the scope of judicial autonomy as against the force of precedent. Another set of concepts, which include *horaat shaah* (a temporary decision), *le-migdar milta* (to improve a particular matter), *laasot seyag la-Torah* (to create a protective boundary for the Torah), and *eit laasot la-Shem* (a time to act for God), concern the relationship of *halakhah* to time: specifically to unusual circumstances. Here policy overrides principle. An act or rule that could not normally be mandated is permitted on consequentialist grounds. In exceptional circumstances, the consequences of temporarily suspending a rule are overwhelmingly more beneficial within the terms of the halakhic system than those of maintaining it. In such cases, its temporary suspension may be justified. These are the cases to which *horaot shaah* are directed.

One way of understanding the logic of *horaat shaah* is this. In the *Guide*, Maimonides maintains two apparently contradictory propositions. On the one hand he argues that Torah law is to be understood against its historical background. The Torah makes concessions, as in the case of sacrifices, to the religious and cultural circumstance of the Israelites in the wilderness. This would suggest that Torah law should evolve over time. On the other hand, Torah law does *not* evolve. Maimonides' view as to why this is so is not wholly clear. It may be simply the will of God that there should be one and only one revelation. It may be that it is a condition of a perfect law that it should be "definite, unconditional, and general." A law that varied according to time and place would "be imperfect in its totality, each principle being left indefinite."[18] Or it may be, alternatively, that "constant changes would tend to disturb the whole system of the Law and would lead people to believe that the Law is not of Divine origin."[19] Change might lead not only to a loss of certainty as to what the law is, but also to a certain secularization of the law.[20]

Be this as it may, Maimonides reconciles the two positions by drawing a contrast between law and medicine. Medicine is directed to the individual. Law is directed to society as a whole. Law is essentially universal, a point emphasized more recently by Kant and R. M. Hare. The project of searching for reasons for the commandments—Maimonides' concern at this point—must therefore be constructed in a strict form of what would nowadays be called rule consequentialism. The Torah consists of rules that optimize

---

[18]Maimonides, *Guide* 3:34. R. Yosef Albo disagrees with this proposition (*Ikkarim* 3:13–14).

[19]Maimonides, *Guide* 3:41.

[20]The last point is directed, not to the possibility that the Torah might have delegated authority to the sages to change its own primary legislation (*de-oraita*) and not merely to create secondary legislation (*de-rabbanan*). In effect, this would make God the source of legislative authority only, and not of substantive legislation.

To understand Maimonides' point, we have only to consider the role of the monarchy in a parliamentary democracy such as Great Britain. The sovereign may be the source of legislative authority, but in a purely formal sense. God, Maimonides seems to be arguing, would be marginalized in religious consciousness as such a monarch is marginalized in political consciousness. To put it slightly differently, were a human court to have the power of primary legislation, God would be *transcendent*, not *immanent*, in relation to the commands.

consequences as a whole, considered *sub specie aeternitatis*. Its laws, even if primarily intelligible against a particular historical background, maximize benefits over time: the time in question being the whole of human history from Sinai to the messianic age and beyond. For they are universal and eternal, and it is only in the light of this universality and eternity that they are to be understood.

These rules do not take into account exceptional cases. It "necessarily follows that there should exist individuals whom this governance of the Law does not make perfect." Any rule that maximizes consequences over time, may fail to maximize consequences in particular cases.[21]

The general logic of *horaat shaah* is to provide room for exceptional cases: a limited and necessarily circumscribed intrusion of act consequentialism into a system of universal rules. The normal circumstances under which *horaat shaah* arise are ones in which the system of rules itself is under threat. The point is made most clearly in Resh Lakish's remark that "there are times when the suspension of Torah may be its foundation."[22]

The subject of *horaat shaah* has been extensively dealt with elsewhere[23] and here I would make only two general observations. First, it seems to me that the range of purposes for which a *horaat*

---

[21]The most striking instance of this is the law of the *mamzer* (bastard), where the privation of the individual child is outweighed by the overall consequence of a law that attaches the utmost severity to adultery. This, presumably, is why the halakhic tradition—deeply sensitive to the apparent injustice of a child who suffered for its parents' sin—tended to seek *individual* remedies where possible, rather than a *global* remedy. Perhaps, to be sure, there *is* no global remedy. But the search for individual, case by case, solutions preserves the rule while mitigating its consequences in particular cases. Conservative critics of the law of *mamzerut* often fail to make this elementary distinction between rule- and act-consequentialism.

[22]*Menahot* 99a–b.

[23]See Marahatz Chajes, *Torat ha-Neviim*, chaps. 3–6, *Kol Kitvei Maharatz Chajes* 1:23–43; *Encyclopaedia Talmudit* 8:512–527; Berkovits, *Ha-Halakhah Kohah ve-Tafkidah*, 75–83.

shaah may be issued is significantly different from the rest of rabbinic law. Rabbinic law is frequently justified by reference to a set of value considerations: *she-lo le-vayesh mi she-ein lo* (not to shame whoever has not the means), *mipnei takkanat ha-shavim* (for the benefit of repentant sinners), *hasah torah al mamonam shel Yisrael* (the Torah cares for the possessions of Israel), *kedei she-lo linol delet mipnei lovim* (not to shut the door in front of borrowers), *shakdu hakhamim al takkanot benot Yisrael* (the sages were concerned for the sake of the women of Israel), and so on. *Horaat shaah* is, I suspect, never undertaken in pursuit of such values. Its sole justification is the protection of the law itself. Consider, for example, Maimonides' famous definition of the scope of *horaat shaah:*

> The court may inflict flagellation and other punishments, even in cases where such penalties are not warranted by the law if, in its opinion, *religion will thereby be strengthened and safeguarded and the people will be restrained from disregarding the words of the Torah.* It must not, however, establish the measure to which it resorts as a law binding upon succeeding generations, declaring, "This is the law."
>
> So too if, *in order to bring back the multitudes to religion and save them from general religious laxity,* the court deems it necessary to set aside temporarily a positive or a negative command, it may do so, taking into account the need of the hour. Even as a physician will amputate the hand or the foot of a patient in order to save his life, so the court may advocate, when an emergency arises, the temporary disregard of some of the commandments, that the commandments as a whole be preserved. This is in keeping with what the early sages said: "Desecrate on his account one Sabbath that he be able to observe many Sabbaths."[24]

Horaat shaah never possesses independent logic. It is always justified by consequences, but those consequences are assessed by only one criterion: the keeping of *mitzvot.*

---

[24]*Mishneh Torah, Mamrim* 2:4.

Second, *horaat shaah* is, on its own logic, the exception that proves the rule. The time-and-place-specific nature of the suspension of halakhic norms is itself testimony to the unboundedness of those norms by space and time. The point was well made by R. Moshe Feinstein in a responsum on the Women's Liberation movement. The exemption of women from *mitzvot asei she-ha-zeman gerama* (time-bound positive commandments) is, he suggests, to free women to occupy themselves in raising children, "the most precious activity in the eyes of God and the Torah." Therefore, "even were the conditions of life to change for women generally, and even for wealthy women at all times, even if it were possible to entrust the raising of children to others as it is in our country, neither biblical nor rabbinic law would change."[25] R. Feinstein's point, as I understand it, is that *halakhah* is constructed in terms of norms that obtain generally across space and time. Predictably, then, there will be exceptions. There will be individuals ("wealthy women") at *all* times, and particular societies (contemporary America) at *some* times, to which the norms do not apply. This does not affect the law, which is predicated on that which is normal across human history and society considered as a whole.

HALAKHAH AND HISTORY

By now, my restlessness with this way of looking at halakhic "creativity and innovation" should be clear. A formal analysis of the powers of a *posek* or *bet din* to reinterpret the sources, overturn precedent, or temporarily suspend extant legislation, rabbinic or biblical, will at best address only the *how*, not the *why*, of halakhic change. Even the how it will address only partially, for halakhic change is a far more subtle process. A well-founded halakhic ruling may not receive the endorsement of other major halakhists. Even if it does, it may simply fail to become general practice. In the other

---

[25]*Iggerot Mosheh, Orah Hayyim*, vol. 4, no. 49.

direction, practice may precede *halakhah*, and eventually win its approval.

Yet, it is our belief that these complex processes are not simply random—the mere "history" of an "evolving religious civilization." At the heart of the halakhic enterprise is the faith that *halakhah* is that which binds the Jewish people to God in an immutable covenant. *Halakhah* is the translation of the metahistorical word of God into the shifting history of the human situation. Just as *halakhah* takes the absolutely nonempirical God into the absolutely empirical human frame of reference, so it takes eternity into history. To be sure, it changes. But it changes not merely *despite* the fact that Torah does not change, but *in order to ensure* that Torah does not change.

Halakhah is, in short, the Jewish protest against history. No one saw this more clearly than Saadia Gaon. The legal-metaphysical arguments for the eternity of Jewish law, debated by Maimonides and Albo, were not his concern. Instead, in *Emunot ve-Deot*, he argued the definitive relationship between Jewish law and the Jewish people: our people, the children of Israel, are a people only by virtue of their laws. Therefore Jewish law was eternal *because the Jewish people was eternal.*[26]

Nature, said Maimonides, is a series of cycles of growth and decline. So, for some historians, is history, whether we focus on nations or civilizations or economic classes. We are familiar with this imagery from *midrash*: it is how some rabbis understood Jacob's dream, of the ladder of time on which the angels of other civilizations climbed and descended. Judaism is—as Nietzsche saw so clearly—a negation of nature and history, an attempt to construct an unchanging order within the very flux of time. There is no Shabbat in nature;[27] no *tzibbur* (Jewish community) in his-

---

[26]*Emunot ve-Deot* 3:7.

[27]On this see R. Soloveitchik's *Ish ha-Halakhah*, and Cynthia Ozick's moving essay, "On Living in the Gentile World," in *Modern Jewish Thought*, ed. Nahum Glatzer (New York: Schocken, 1977), 167–74.

tory.[28] The concept of *kenesset Yisrael* (assembly of Israel) is that of the strict identity of the Jewish people over time, an identity predicated not on nature or history but on law.

On Pesach, *we* are slaves in Egypt; *we* experience the exodus. On Tisha be'Av *we* endure the grief and suffering of all Jews throughout history, from the generation condemned to die in the wilderness, through those who saw the Temples destroyed, to the Spanish exiles and those who awaited death in Auschwitz. Jewish consciousness, as Hayyim Yerushalmi has noted, is constructed in terms of *memory*, not *history*. History is what happened to *others*. Memory is what happened to *us*. And this as it were aggadic consciousness is born out of the halakhic axioms that Jewish identity is constructed out of Jewish law, and Jewish law is built out of rules that apply across space and time.

Now this cuts sharply across the historicism of modern consciousness. Whether history is evolution toward utopia or progress toward the abyss, it is for us a real and determinative category. We find it easy to see the distance, hard to sense the kinship, between ours and previous generations. Historicism has affected most postenlightenment scholarship in most disciplines, and it has profoundly influenced all modern forms of Jewish identity. The most poignant example is the contemporary Conservative movement in America in its effort to combine historical consciousness with *halakhah*. It cannot be done. The story of why it cannot be done is for another occasion. But we will analyze a single example below.

This is one of the many reasons why *halakhah* is in conflict with modern consciousness. But there is a second problem, no less profound, for Orthodoxy itself. The series of historical changes which led to the formation of rabbinic Judaism were radical indeed. They led to the substitution of prayer for sacrifice, the sage for the prophet, and the synagogue for the temple. There was a move from an agricultural to a money-based conception of welfare and charity.

---

[28]I refer here to the idea, explored by the Rogatchover, of *tzibbur* as an unchanging entity. See *Mefane'ah Tzsefunot*, p. 1.

There was a shift from a national-historical to an ethical-covenantal sense of collective responsibility.

A non-Orthodox scholar will see these as changes, *simpliciter*. An Orthodox scholar will see them as the opposite: an absolute determination on the part of the sages to conserve and preserve the institutions of the covenant in an utterly transformed world. They were changes intended to establish *that nothing had changed*. There were no prophets to rebuke the people; therefore, every Jew, under the command of *hokhe'ah tokhiah* (rebuking one's fellow) was a prophet. There was no national entity to define a collective fate; therefore, *kol Yisrael arevin zeh ba-zeh* (all Jews are responsible for one another). Judaism had lost what Peter Berger calls its "plausibility structure," its objectification in a historical and societal environment; therefore, each Jew through sustained *talmud torah* would construct that environment in his consciousness. The radical transformations involved in the passage from biblical to rabbinic Judaism are all intended to create a Jewish world in which nothing changes, however sharply external circumstance does.

The transformations of Jewish modernity – emancipation and its social and intellectual implications – have been no less profound. But there were deep disagreements as to what would constitute continuing the covenant in such a way as to maintain a *strict identity with the Jewish past*. That story I have told elsewhere,[29] but it includes such seminal figures as the Hatam Sofer, Samson Raphael Hirsch, Rav Avraham Kook, R. Hayyim Hirschensohn, and R. Isaac Reines. Was emancipation a lessening, continuation, or deepening of *galut* (exile)? Was Jewish segregation from general culture in the Middle Ages an aberration or an ideal? What was the role of secular action in bringing about the independent sovereignty of Israel? To what extent is Israel still *galut*? In an age where Jews identify as Jews but not through *halakhah*, should such Jews be, as far as possible, included or excluded by the halakhic system?

---

[29]See, for example, my book, *Arguments for the Sake of Heaven* (Northvale, NJ: Jason Aronson, 1991).

Approaches to these and similar questions, more than any other factor, have been decisive in the halakhic process for the past two centuries.

The overarching halakhic issues have not been formal ones. They have not, for the most part, surfaced in the detailed argumentation of responsa, though they can be glimpsed from time to time. We remain in a kind of metahalakhic limbo, for these basic questions have not yet been resolved within Orthodoxy itself. We share a determination to create a Jewish world in which there is strict identity with the past. But that involves an interpretation of the past. More than one interpretation is possible. And we have not yet reached consensus.

This has given a *horaat shaah* character to a vast range of modern rulings, from Samson Raphael Hirsch's *Torah im derekh eretz* to the opposition to secular culture among disciples of the Hatam Sofer, from the Hafetz Hayyim's permissive ruling about Torah education for girls to prohibitive rulings about women's prayer groups. Each, that is to say, has been constructed or perceived as a response to crisis, and whether we rule *le-kulah* or *le-humrah* (permissively or strictly) depends on our general orientation to crisis: whether it is best met by accommodation or resistance. For Judaism *is* in a process of redefinition and we have not yet reached agreement on what is aberrant and what normative in either the Jewish past or the Jewish present.

Our approach to *halakhah* cannot be dissociated from the broadest questions of the interpretation of history and society, and any attempt to do so will miss the salient issues. To take one simple example, compare R. Hershel Schachter's responsum on women's prayer groups with that, *le-havdil bein hayyim le-hayyim*, of R. Yechiel Weinberg on *bat hayil*. On strictly formal grounds, which is the more innovative? In broader terms, which is the more conservative, the more concerned with creating a *seyag la-Torah*? These questions are hard to answer, and curiously irrelevant. Both *posekim* are concerned above all to secure Jewish continuity, the one by permitting, the other by prohibiting, new forms of women's

religious self-expression. One sees change as a means of conservation, the other as a symbol of disintegration. Each is conscious of an
emergency: the "times are out of joint." Each, then, has given us a
horaat shaah. But in opposite directions. A "No" can be as innovative as a "Yes." And it is not "creativity" or "innovation" that should
be our concern, but rather a deep soul searching as to what the God
wants of us at this hour, in this place, to secure the eternity of
Jewish law, which is the eternity of the Jewish people.

WHAT CONSTITUTES CREATIVITY IN HALAKHAH?

Moving away, then, from these broad and open-ended reflections,
can we suggest a characterization of what halakhic creativity might
be?

Creativity in *halakhah* cannot be creativity in the sense applied
to the arts, say, or technology. For there creativity relates to the
production of something new and essentially unpredictable. An
invention cannot be predicted; neither can a novel; for to have
predicted it would already have been to have created it.[30] *Halakhah*,
with its necessary association of fidelity to revelation and the
history of its interpretation, cannot be open-endedly unpredictable
in quite this way.

Halakhah might be described as creative in the quite different
sense in which one speaks of "creative solutions" to practical
problems. Here the outcome is fully specifiable in advance. Origi-
nality lies in simply solving the problem given the practical constraints. Paradigms of halakhic creativity, on this model, would be
the formal mechanisms by which, for example, one drafted a
prenuptial agreement such that a woman could be reasonably sure
of obtaining a *get* (divorce document) if she wished to terminate her
marriage.

---

[30]See the intriguing analysis in Alasdair MacIntyre, *After Virtue* (London: Duckworth, 1981), 84–102.

This narrow view of creativity assumes that a desired legal outcome can be specified independently of the formal argumentation and procedures by which that outcome is halakhically vindicated and achieved. In some cases, doubtless, that is true. But not, surely, all; and not in the most interesting ones. There is a close kinship between the narrow view and Blu Greenberg's famous aphorism: where there is a rabbinic will, there is a halakhic way. I doubt whether this is true. But the converse is certainly false. For where there is a halakhic way, there is not necessarily a rabbinic will. The significant question is: where *is* there a rabbinic will? The processes of deciding which outcome is halakhically *desirable* and which is halakhically *warranted* often cannot be sharply distinguished in the way the narrow view assumes.

Creativity in *halakhah* is therefore normally something more than devising novel means to predetermined ends, and something less than shaping entirely new worlds of legal signification. It may of course be either of these things. The development of the practice of selling *hametz* might be taken as an example of the first. The institution of *tefillah* (prayer)—on Ramban's view that the obligation was created rather than regulated by rabbinic law—would stand as an example of the second.

But even these examples are less clear-cut than they seem. The development of *mekhirat hametz* was more than a series of formal means to an end already predetermined in rabbinic law. It subtly changed the nature of Pesach, even if it drew on a prior understanding of the implication of *lo yera'eh lekha* (i.e., the prohibition of owning *hametz*), just as *heter iska* changed economic relationships between Jews. In the other direction, even if prayer was created as a halakhically significant activity by rabbinic law, it was certainly not created as a human activity. Rabban Yohanan ben Zakkai took the view that *tumah* (impurity) and *taharah* (purity) are states wholly created by divine decree. Revelation may therefore create legal worlds *ex nihilo. Halakhah*—the application of revelation—does not.

Halakhic creativity is thus a complex process in which the will and the way, ends and means, the underlying values and the formal structures of the law are both in play, each shaping and in turn shaped by the other.

THE NEW AND RENEWAL

Within the rabbinic tradition there are two apparently sharply conflicting views on innovation in Torah. On the one hand, the new is forbidden. *Eleh ha-mitzvot: she-ein navi rashai le-hadesh davar me-atah.*[31] A prophet may not innovate. Neither may a sage. *Afilu mah she-talmid vatik atid le-horot lifnei rabbo kevar ne'emar le-Mosheh be-Sinai* (even that which a senior disciple will later teach in the presence of his master has already been revealed to Moses at Sinai).[32] All innovation is merely apparent and was already revealed to Moses at Sinai. The new is simply a disclosure of the old. If true, it is not new. If new, it is not true.

On the other hand, there is the rabbinic delight in innovation: *hiddush. Iy efshar le-bet ha-midrash be-lo hiddush* (there can be no house of study without innovation).[33] The process of study is essentially tied to an idea of the new. "These words which I command you today" means "they should not be in your eyes like an antiquated ordinance which no one attends, but as one newly given which everyone runs to meet."[34] We recall the remarkable paean to *hiddushei Torah* contained in the *Zohar*: "We have learned: at that moment when a word of Torah is made new [*mit'hadesh*] in the mouth of man, the word ascends and stands before the Holy One blessed be He, who takes it and kisses it and crowns it with seventy decorated and engraved crowns."[35] The second part of R. Soloveitchik's *Ish ha-Halakhah* is a kind of prose-poem to this idea. "Halakhic man is a man who longs to create, to bring into being

---

[31]*Megillah* 2b.

[32]*Pe'ah* 2:6.

[33]*Hagigah* 3a.

[34]Deuteronomy 6:6, *Sifre* and Rashi ad loc.

[35]*Zohar* 1, 4b; Tishby, *Mishnat ha-Zohar* 2:404.

something new, something original. . . . The dream of creation is the central idea in the halakhic consciousness."[36]

The tension between these two approaches is mitigated once we translate *hiddush* as renewal rather than innovation. An interpretive *hiddush* is one that discloses new meanings in an old text, or new patterns and configurations linking texts, or new alignments that resolve apparent contradictions, or new conceptualities that allow us to clarify the nature of a disagreement. A *hiddush* renews by revealing a consistency, shape, or applicability in the antecedent literature that we had not noticed before. It rescues the text from oldness or fragmentation.

These remarks suggest a way of characterizing the process of *pesak halakhah*. In most cases, of course, it is uncontroversially the application of rules and precedent to the case under consideration. But necessarily, given the constantly changing social, economic, historical, and technological environment, not all cases can be so resolved. There may be no rule or precedent covering the case at hand. There may be legitimate room for doubt as to whether the precedent covered this kind of situation, ostensibly similar but contextually different. Or there may be scope for disagreement as to how the case is to be characterized and which rules or precedents are relevant to it. Legal theorists call these "hard cases." This is not to say that there are agreed criteria for deciding what is a hard case and what is not. Whether or not a case is hard will often be part of the argument over how to decide it.

To my mind the most persuasive description of what is involved in judicially deciding a hard case—persuasive in that I find it most germane to *pesak*—is that given by Ronald Dworkin, who draws a strong analogy between a judge and a literary critic.[37] Both are engaged in an essentially interpretive activity. Dworkin suggests,

---

[36]R. Joseph Soloveitchik, *Halakhic Man*, trans. Lawrence Kaplan (Philadelphia: Jewish Publication Society, 1983), 99.

[37]Ronald Dworkin, *A Matter of Principle* (Oxford: Clarendon Press, 1986); *Law's Empire* (London: Fontana, 1986).

about interpretation generally, that "an interpretation of a piece of literature attempts to show which way of reading . . . the text reveals it as the best work of art." There are constraints on this process. It must attend to the text that is, not one that might have been written. "All the words must be taken into account and none may be changed to make 'it' a putatively better work of art." It must also be guided by some consideration of the work's coherence or integrity. "An interpretation cannot make a work of art more distinguished if it makes a large part of the text irrelevant, or much of the incident accidental."

But this, as Dworkin notes, is only part of the judicial process. For judges are "authors as well as critics." They add to the tradition they interpret. Their decisions in new cases extend the body of precedent. The analogy he suggests, therefore, is a chain novel, in which a group of novelists write a book sequentially, each contributing a chapter. Each new writer has the task of making his chapter add to the development of the book, but in such a way as to make the completed work hang together as the work of a single author. He is therefore involved simultaneously in interpreting and creating: interpreting the chapters already written and creating a new chapter that will preserve the coherence of the book as a whole. That, he argues, is what a judge does in deciding a hard case:

> Any judge forced to decide a lawsuit will find, if he looks in the appropriate books, records of many arguably similar cases decided over decades or even centuries past by many other judges of different styles and judicial and political philosophies, in periods of different orthodoxies of procedure and judicial convention. Each judge must regard himself, in deciding the new case before him, as a partner in a complex chain enterprise of which these innumerable decisions, structures, conventions and practices are the history; it is his job to continue that history into the future, through what he does on the day. He *must* interpret what has gone before because he has a responsibility to advance the enterprise in hand rather

than strike out in some new direction of his own. So he must determine, according to his own judgement, what the earlier decisions come to, what the point or theme of the practice so far, taken as a whole, really is.[38]

That seems to me an admirable way of describing the halakhic process.[39] *Hiddush* renews the halakhic enterprise by adding a chapter to its continuing history but in such a way as to preserve the integrity and coherence of the whole. At its best it will not seem to be innovative at all. The new case will fit without strain into the pattern now revealed to be that which was implicit all along.

AN EXAMPLE OF HALAKHIC *HIDDUSH*

Let me give an example from my own experience. When my wife gave birth to our eldest daughter, we were overjoyed. We already had a son, and we had particularly wanted a daughter for personal reasons, and because of the *mitzvah* of *peru u-revu* (procreate and multiply). One thing, though, distressed me: that I was unable to make the blessing of *ha-tov ve-ha-metiv*. That blessing, we recall, is mentioned by the *Gemara* in connection with the birth of a boy, not a girl.[40]

On the one hand, there stood the ruling of the *Arukh ha-*

---

[38]Dworkin, *A Matter of Principle*, 159; see Dworkin's *Law's Empire*, 225–75.

[39]It also, incidentally, helps us to understand the hermeneutics of *halakhah*. For halakhists read texts in some sense ahistorically and non-contextually, without reference to authorial intention or the specific circumstances in which they were written. For the halakhist confronts the antecedent literature as if it were the work of a single author at a single time, and attempts to continue the enterprise in the same way. This is part of what gives *midrash* its primacy over *peshat* in the halakhic process specifically, and the rabbinic tradition generally.

[40]*Berakhot* 59b.

Shulhan[41] that "at the birth of a girl one does not make a blessing, because there is not so much rejoicing at such an event." On the other, there was the ruling—innovative in its own way—of the *Mishnah Berurah*.[42] From the absence of any ruling to the contrary, the *Mishnah Berurah* infers that *ha-tov ve-ha-metiv* is not to be said at the birth of a girl, even if the parents have already had many sons and long for a girl for the sake of fulfilling the *mitzvah* of *peru u-revu*. R. Israel Meir haCohen does not end there however. He adds: "Nonetheless it seems to me clear that the first time the father sees her, he makes the blessing *she-hehiyanu*. For can [his pleasure] be less than one who sees a friend after an absence of thirty days?" One who is overjoyed in such a case makes the blessing of *she-hehiyanu*. So, then, should the father on first seeing his daughter.

Several things disturbed me about this ruling. It ran counter to our feelings, of which the *berakhah* itself was an expression. We took delight in the birth of a girl no less than in a boy, and one component of that delight was *simhah shel mitzvah* (the joy of the *mitzvah*). It made a distinction between boys and girls that seemed irrelevant to the subject at hand, namely, the emotions of the parents. Moreover, the *Mishnah Berurah*'s analogy was difficult to understand. Why relate the case to seeing a friend after thirty days? Why not after twelve months, in which case the blessing would have been *mehayyeh ha-metim*? And so on.

I mentioned these reservations to my then *rav* and *posek*, R. Nachum Rabinovitch. Without hesitation he declared that it was his own belief that in such a case one should make the blessing *ha-tov ve-ha-metiv*. He explained why. Any occasion on which the Rambam does not codify a *halakhah*, explicit in the Bavli and unchallenged elsewhere, calls for explanation. Yet that was the case with the *halakhah* at hand. There is no reference in the *Mishneh Torah* to the *baraita*, "One whose wife gives birth to a boy makes the blessing *ha-tov ve-ha-metiv*." Instead, Rambam merely codifies the

---

[41]*Arukh ha-Shulhan, Orah Hayyim* 223:1.
[42]*Orah Hayyim* 223 n. 2.

general rule: Over whatever is good for oneself and others one blesses *ha-tov ve-ha-metiv*. Over whatever is good for oneself alone one blesses *she-hehiyanu*.[43]

How then are we to understand the *baraita*? It could be taken in two ways. First it could be an *independent law* in its own right. It could, as it were, be a halakhic stipulation that *this* event—unlike the birth of a daughter—demands *this* blessing. Alternatively, though, it could merely be understood as an *example* of the kind of event that is "good for oneself and others." The *baraita* chooses this example because it is uncontroversial. Elsewhere the *Gemara* discusses whether daughters evoke as much delight as sons. Some said yes, others said no.[44] All, then, could be assumed to take delight in the birth of a son. Not all could be assumed to feel likewise at the birth of a daughter.

Rambam clearly takes the second interpretation. The *baraita* is an example of a general rule, not a new law. Therefore he does not codify it. It follows that if both father and mother are delighted at the birth of a daughter—if it is "good for oneself and others"—they make the blessing *ha-tov ve-ha-metiv*.[45]

This seems to me a good example of a *hiddush be-halakhah*, an "innovative" ruling in the sense that, despite the fact that the subject it addressed was almost as old as the human situation, it gave a ruling that had not been given before. But here let me argue certain features of the case.

First: its innovative character is the least important thing about it. What commands respect is its cogency in interpreting the sources. It offers a persuasive reading of the talmudic *sugyah* (discussion). It provides a convincing explanation of the lacuna in the *Mishneh Torah*. It places the blessing over children in a more general framework—good for oneself/good for others. It reestablishes the

---

[43]*Berakhot* 59b; *Mishneh Torah, Berakhot* 10:7.

[44]*Baba Batra* 16b, 141a.

[45]The reasoning is reproduced in R. Nachum Rabinovitch, *Yad Peshutah* to *Mishneh Torah, Berakhot* 10:7.

connection between the blessing and the impact of the event over which it is made on the lives of those who make it. It reveals a new interconnectedness in the sources that we had not noticed before. In short, it satisfies Dworkin's requirement that a ruling should enhance the coherence and integrity of the law as a whole, rather than striking out in a new direction.

By contrast, the ruling of the *Mishnah Berurah* is technically far more innovative. It too yields a new, unprecedented decision. But it does so on the basis of a comparison between seeing a daughter for the first time and seeing a friend after thirty days that, to my knowledge, is not supported by the sources. It transfers the blessing over a daughter—unlike that over a son—from the category of *birkat hodaah* (thanksgiving blessing) to *birkat re'iyah* (blessings over sights). It does not proceed by interpretation alone. The *Mishnah Berurah*'s ruling, if true, is innovative. R. Rabinovitch's ruling, if true, is not. This, to my mind, gives the latter a halakhic cogency greater than the former.

The second point takes us into deeper waters. Dworkin, we recall, argued that a judge, ruling in a hard case, must "determine, according to his own judgement, what the earlier decisions come to, what the *point* or *theme* of the practice so far, taken as a whole, really is." Here we come upon an elusive but crucial consideration, and one to which I would give the name *Daat Torah* (the Torah's view).

In this sense: To be *dan din emet le-amitato* (to judge a law truthfully), it is not sufficient mechanically to extrapolate from a narrow range of precedent to the case at hand. A *posek* must view the case and the issues it raises in the total context of Torah. There is a difference between the considerations he may formally cite in justification of his ruling, and those that may, consciously or intuitively, play a part in his judgment that this ruling is not merely justifiable but also correct. *Aharonim* (postmedieval halakhists) have certainly been known to ground their rulings on biblical verses, *aggadot*, and even medieval exegetes and philosophers. That these sources occasionally surface in explicit argumentation suggests that they figure no less prominently in the *fore-understanding* that a *posek* brings to his rulings.

Daat Torah, in this sense, would be the broad constellation of values, and priorities between them, that emerges from the *posek*'s lifelong involvement with Torah in its broadest sense. It would be impossible to cite all such considerations in defence of a particular ruling. Indeed most rulings and responsa do not touch at all on these broader reflections. Yet we sense their presence, even if we can do no more than speculate as to what they are.

To return to the case at hand, for R. Yehiel Mikhal Epstein, author of the *Arukh ha-Shulhan*, the blessing of *ha-tov ve-ha-metiv* is entirely determined by whether the child is a boy or a girl. We recall that he asserts that "there is not so much rejoicing" at the birth of a girl. Later he adds that the blessing is made at the birth of a boy whether or not the parents "rejoice in their hearts." They may have had many boys; they may be profoundly disappointed that this child is not a girl; nonetheless they must bless. But for Rambam, however, as interpreted by R. Rabinovitch, the critical factor is the emotions of the parents. How are we to understand their disagreement?

There are two obvious alternatives. The first would be to see it as turning on whether *ha-tov ve-ha-metiv* is determined by individual or normal reactions—normal here being defined as the reactions of most Jews throughout Jewish history. Of the couple who rejoice in a girl as much as in a boy we would say, *batlah daatam etzel kol adam* (their view is nullified relative to everyone else). The second would be to see it as turning on whether the blessing is constitutive or regulative. Does *halakhah*, as it were, *define* certain events as good (for one person, for many)? Or does it begin with the fact that there are certain events—different events for different people—which are experienced as good and for which they wish to give thanks to God, and proceed to regulate the form which those thanks should take? If *halakhah* is constitutive, the couple who wish to say *ha-tov ve-ha-metiv* over a girl have simply failed to understand that neither their feelings, nor anyone else's, are relevant to the halakhic conception of good.

This second way of seeing the dispute leads us into the broadest possible debate about *halakhah*. As we noted earlier, in a famous *aggadah*, R. Yohanan ben Zakkai argued that the laws of *tumah* and *taharah* are constitutive. Death does not of itself defile, nor do the waters of themselves purify. *Tumah* and *taharah* are states created by the laws which govern them: outside those laws, they have no reality. The view of *halakhah* advanced by R. Soloveitchik in *Ish ha-Halakhah* is largely of this kind. *Halakhah* is a universe of theoretical constructs.

At the opposite extreme we recall that R. Judah Halevi, in the *Kuzari*, argued that even the laws of *tumah* and *taharah* are regulative. Death empirically (psychologically?) defiles.[46] In general, since the Giver of the Torah is the Creator of the world, the Torah's norms are mirrored in the structure of empirically discoverable reality.

Midway between these two views is one which has been stated with the utmost pungency and paradox by Yeshayahu Leibowitz. The laws between man and God are constitutive. Prayer is meaningful not as an expression of man's desire to pray, but solely as a fulfillment of the command to pray. All anthropocentric reasons for the commands are idolatrous. On the other hand, the Torah's entire range of social legislation is regulative, or what Leibowitz calls *bedi'avad (ex post facto)*. Marriage, divorce, government, exchange, and contract all exist independently of the Torah, which merely provides, *ex post facto*, the detailed forms these are to take for Jews. Therefore, the most radical halakhic innovation is warranted—both in relation to the state of Israel and women—because the social realities on which *halakhah* is predicated have changed.

Those who see *halakhah* as constitutive will be primarily concerned about the dangers of straying outside its formal boundaries. In the case of blessings, they will be concerned about *berakhah*

---

[46]*Kuzari* 2:60.

she-einah tzerikhah and *berakhah le-vatalah* (forms of unnecessary blessings). Those who see *halakhah* as regulative will be concerned in a different direction. They will be disturbed by the danger of *secularization of consciousness* when *halakhah* is increasingly dissociated from the lived experience of Jews. In the case of blessings, they will recall Moses' repeated warnings of the dangers of secularization implicit in national independence and prosperity.[47] The Israelites, says Moses, will find houses filled with all good things. They will eat and be satisfied. They may then forget God. They will attribute their success either to their own efforts, or to nature and its gods. The religious task is to "rejoice in all the good that God your Lord has granted you and your family." Bringing one's joy to God, in the form of *birkhot hodaah,* will be an overarching imperative, part of the cognitive-educative process whereby human delight is turned into religious joy by viewing events in the context of creation and covenant. Thus, two *posekim* can bring quite different "fore-understandings" to even the simplest *she'elah* (question): what blessing does one make over a girl?

The relevant question is not which is the more conservative, but which is conservative *of what?* Two opposed rulings may emerge from two sets of interpretations of the texts, which in turn flow from two different broad conceptions of the nature of the halakhic territory under review, and of the halakhic system generally. What gives each of them their cogency is their grounding in the totality of Torah. I do not know how this requirement is to be defined, or whether it has been defined. It is, though, to my mind, the crucial consideration in considering the nature of legitimate halakhic development.

BEYOND THE BOUNDS OF ACCEPTABILITY

Armed with these reflections, I want finally to consider a case of halakhic argument which proceeds entirely by a narrow, formal

---

[47]Deuteronomy 6:10–12, 8:10–17, 28:47.

consideration of "directly relevant" sources only. Joel Roth's responsum on the ordination of women as congregational rabbis seems to me a key example of the danger of understanding halakhic "creativity" or "innovation" in formal terms alone.[48]

The responsum turns primarily on two questions: may women be *shlihei tzibbur*, leading the congregation in prayer? And may they be witnesses on a *ketubah* (the Jewish marriage contract)? Let us focus on the first.

Roth gives an affirmative answer based on two considerations. Though women are exempt from public prayer, they may nonetheless exempt men because (1) one who is exempt from a command may not only perform it and pronounce the blessing over it, but also place himself under an obligation to do so in future, and (2) a self-imposed obligation has the same status as an other-imposed obligation.

The second point, critical to Roth's argument, is the difficult one, for what emerges, oddly enough, is that there is no direct source which rules on the question either way. Roth argues for its plausibility in an extended footnote on the ground that one who voluntarily performs a *mitzvah* does so in exactly the same way as one who does so because he is commanded. Thus women who voluntarily perform sacrificial acts [*semikhah*, for example, for those who hold *nashim somekhot reshut* (women are allowed to perform the sacrificial act of *semikhah*)] may do so even though the act—if done secularly—would involve the infringement of a *shevut* (a rabbinic prohibition). A blind man, even if exempt from the commands, may perform them and the blessings over them, despite the prohibition of a *berakhah she-einah tzerikhah*. The voluntary performance of a *mitzvah* is, in short, not a secular act. It is a *mitzvah*-act and thus overrides certain conflicting prohibitions. This line of reasoning has its advocates, notably the *baalei Tosafot*. What it amounts to is that the permission voluntarily to perform a *mitzvah* is the permis-

---

[48]*The Ordination of Women as Rabbis*, ed. Simon Greenberg (New York: Jewish Theological Seminary, 1988), 127–85.

sion to act as one who is commanded acts. And since one who is commanded may exempt others, so may one who voluntarily assumes the commandment.

The final inference is Roth's own. Now this *may* be true. But *is* it true? The claim is larger than it seems. For there is a difference between the status of an act and the status of an agent. The sources cited by Roth refer to the status of a voluntary act, and they offer at least prima facie evidence that a voluntary act can take on the status of a *mitzvah* act. But—if we follow Rashi and Ritva—the concept of *exempting others* has a different logic. It flows from the idea that *kol Yisrael arevin zeh ba-zeh*. All Jews are jointly responsible for their collective fulfillment of the commands. We stand halakhically not only in relation to God and to ourselves but to the rest of Israel also. Exempting others flows, then, from certain halakhically defined relationships between persons. The question then is: can women voluntarily enter into the covenantal relationship involved in commands from which they are exempt? Can we, in short, decide to change our halakhic ontology, our status as persons?

Halakhah knows of one case in which this is possible, namely, conversion. But it knows, surely, of others where this is not possible. An individual who voluntarily undertook all the obligations of priesthood would not thereby become a Cohen, with the power of acting as a *sheliah tzibbur* (the congregation's agent) in offering sacrifices and conferring the priestly blessings. Roth's proposal is tantamount to the suggestion that women should be able voluntarily to convert to halakhic malehood. Now this is a proposition that commends itself with great persuasive force to a modern consciousness in which the only ethically or religiously significant roles are those we choose. It is also one that conflicts at the most fundamental level with traditional Jewish belief, that there are significant roles, with differential obligations, into which we are born and which lie outside the range of choice.

My first point, then, is this: even if the sources could be read as Roth reads them, we would have reason for dissenting from his conclusion, for it ends in a halakhic *reductio ad absurdum*.

HALAKHAH AND THE SENSE OF HISTORY

The second point is more fundamental, for it touches on the crucial question of the relationship between *halakhah* and history. Roth's responsum fails precisely because it *ignores* the larger question of history.

The issue was the ordination of women as rabbis. Immediately we are faced with the question: what *is* rabbinic ordination? *Semikhah* (in the sense of "ordination") in the mishnaic sense no longer exists; nor could it exist outside Israel. Examining the sources, we immediately encounter a sharp ambiguity. On the one hand, Maimonides describes *hatarat horaah* (permission to decide halakhic questions) as an informal and personal transaction between teacher and pupil, whereby the former gives the latter permission to give halakhic rulings.[49] At the same time, in his letter to his disciple R. Joseph, he describes the rabbinate as a formal religious office for which one was dependent on the permission of the *Rosh ha-Galut* (Exilarch).[50]

His attitude to these two roles was markedly different. *Horaah* (decision-rendering) was an obligation: "A sage who is qualified and refrains from rendering decisions is guilty of withholding Torah and placing stumbling blocks before the blind."[51] On the rabbinate as part of the religious establishment, however, he wrote to his disciple: "It is far better for you to earn a drachma as a weaver, tailors, or carpenter than to be dependent on the license of the Exilarch."[52] That distinction, of course, still exists. A majority of those who obtain *semikhah* from traditional *yeshivot* do so not in

---

[49]*Mishneh Torah, Talmud Torah* 5:3.

[50]*Iggerot le-Rabbi Moshe ben Maimon*, ed. R. Joseph Kafih (Jerusalem: Mossad ha-Rav Kook, 1987), 137.

[51]*Mishneh Torah, Talmud Torah* 5:4.

[52]*Iggerot*, ibid. This is part of Maimonides' consistent stance against an economically dependent rabbinate (see *Commentary to Mishnah*, Avot 4:7 and *Mishneh Torah, Talmud Torah* 3:10–11).

order to practice as rabbis in an official capacity but as a private, informal qualification, an endorsement by one's teacher of the right to give rulings.

The question of the halakhic status of the contemporary congregational rabbinate requires precisely what Roth and the other Conservative respondents do not offer: an analysis of the office in the constellation of Jewish institutions. For even if it were hypothetically demonstrable that women could perform each of the discrete functions of the rabbinate—from delivering sermons and visiting the sick to leading the congregation in prayer and acting as a witness on a *ketubah*—the question would still remain: what is the character of the *office* over and above the activities it embraces?

It is just such an analysis, accompanied by sharp historical insight, that we find in the Hatam Sofer.[53] The question was: does a son have the right to inherit his father's rabbinical position? The talmudic sources point in two contradictory directions. There was the profound insistence that, as R. Jose ha-Cohen put it, "Torah is not an inheritance."[54] R. Joseph argued that "the sons of scholars are not scholars" so that "it should not be said that Torah is an inheritance."[55] A son of an *am ha-aretz* (common person) should never be allowed to say, "Since I am not a scholar, what benefit shall I gain by studying the Torah?"[56] These propositions go to the heart of the sages' concern for egalitarianism in the life of Torah. On the other hand, there was the talmudic passage which spoke of R. Judah ha-Nasi's instruction that he be succeeded by his younger son Gamliel.[57] From here it was clear that the laws of succession,

---

[53]*Responsa Hatam Sofer, Orah Hayyim,* no. 12. The question had, of course, been addressed by other authorities. See *Responsa Rivash,* no. 271; *Mabit* 3:610; *Maharashdam, Yoreh De'ah,* no. 85; *Rema, Shulhan Arukh, Yoreh De'ah* 245:22; *Magen Avraham, Orah Hayyim* 53:33.

[54]*Mishnah, Avot* 2:12.

[55]*Nedarim* 81a.

[56]*Sifre Devarim* 48.

[57]*Ketubot* 103a.

deriving essentially from monarchy, applied to the office of *nasi* (patriarch). Maimonides constructs the rules of communal appointments and succession on the paradigm of a king.[58]

So here were the egalitarian and dynastic tendencies in Judaism in conflict. The resolution lay in the distinction made by R. Yohanan and codified by Maimonides: "With three crowns was Israel crowned: with the crown of Torah, of priesthood and of monarchy. The crown of priesthood was bestowed on Aaron. . . . The crown of monarchy was bestowed on David. . . . But the crown of Torah is for all Israel. . . . It rests, available, before every Jew . . . whoever wishes may come and take it."[59] The crown of Torah could not be a privilege of birth. How then was the office of *nasi* dynastic? The Hatam Sofer argues that with the increasing estrangement of the sages from the Hasmonean monarchy, especially from Herod onward, the role of *nasi* was elevated to a quasi-governmental one. It became a rival *keter malkhut* (crown of monarchy). This perceptive analysis has been echoed by modern scholars.[60]

The Hatam Sofer duly ruled that *nesi'ut* (patriarchate) had no bearing on the contemporary rabbinate, to which the law of family succession did not apply. In a later responsum he was to change his mind, again on the basis of sociohistorical insight.[61] This time he distinguishes between the classic role of the sage as teacher and interpreter of Torah, and the contemporary rabbi who is *meshubad le-kehal laasot tzorkhehem be-skhar* (responsible to the community to fulfill their needs with compensation). He is like a *sheliah tzibbur*, to whom the rules of dynastic succession apply. Without saying so explicitly, the Hatam Sofer has linked the congregational rabbinate to *keter kehunah* (crown of priesthood).

There is a strong underlying logic of egalitarianism to the *keter*

---

[58]*Mishneh Torah, Melakhim* 1:4–7.

[59]*Mishneh Torah, Talmud Torah* 3:1.

[60]Daniel Elazar and Stuart Cohen, *The Jewish Polity* (Bloomington, IN: Indiana University Press, 1985), 122–24.

[61]Ibid., 13.

Torah, and this applies to the place of women among its wearers. The history of rulings on women and *talmud Torah* (Torah learning), from the *Sefer Hasidim* onward, shows a recognizable tendency toward leniency, culminating in the Hafetz Hayyim's radical statement that the prohibition against teaching girls Torah applied "specifically in the past" but not in the present.[62] As to whether a woman may be a *morah horaah* (rendering decisions), a number of authorities would reply in the affirmative.[63]

There is an equally strong underlying logic *against* the inclusion of women in the *keter kehunah.* Why this should be so is a matter for historical conjecture, but it is certainly not because priestesses and other women religious functionaries were unknown to the pagan background against which the Torah is a sustained protest.

It is stunning that the Conservative responsa pay no attention to this issue, surely the critical one in assessing the ordination of women as a symbolic issue, a battleground in the fight for sexual equality. The rabbinate of these responsa belongs to the value framework of contemporary America, not of classical Judaism. Compare this, for example, with R. Ben Zion Uziel's careful exploration of the difference between *keter malkhut* and a democratically elected representative in his classic responsum permitting women to be elected to governmental office.[64]

Roth's responsum is, in short, ahistorical, in the sharpest possible contrast to those of the Hatam Sofer and R. Uziel. It fails to set the congregational rabbinate in the historical context of the three crowns, and thus fails to distinguish between the different value considerations that apply to each. This should be sufficient to overturn the conventional wisdom that a Conservative approach to *halakhah* is "historical" and an Orthodox one is a- or metahistorical.

---

[62]*Likkutei Halakhot, Sotah* 21.

[63]*Sefer ha-Hinukh,* no. 158; *Birkhei Yosef, Hoshen Mishpat* 7:12; R. Eliyahu Bakshi-Doron, *Responsa Binyan Av,* no. 65.

[64]*Piskei Uziel* (Jerusalem: Mossad ha-Rav Kook, 1977), 44.

Hard cases necessarily involve historical assessment. Are the circumstances now equivalent in relevant respects to what they were then? To which paradigms of the past are contemporary cases functionally equivalent? The historical sense is firmly in evidence in the great *posekim*, as it must be if the interpretive role in *pesak* is to ensure the persistence of halakhic values through historical, social, and economic change. Indeed conservation requires a finer historical sense than revolution. A failure to relate halakhic questions to the inner history of Jewish law—its resistances no less than its accommodations—is a failure of what Dworkin calls integrity, and what I have termed *Daat Torah*.

HALAKHAH AND SOCIOLOGY

The final point is more fundamental still. For we can surely have no doubt that any Orthodox halakhist would rule that a woman may not be a leader of prayer in a congregation that included men, for quite different reasons from those adduced by Roth. The first: *kol be-ishah ervah* (a woman's voice is "nakedness"). The second: *mipnei kevod ha-tzibbur* (out of respect for the congregation).[65] The third: *Be-emet amru . . . ve-ishah mevarekhet le-baalah aval amru hakhamim tavo me'erah la-adam she-ishto u-vanav mevarkhim lo* (In truth they said: . . . a woman may make a blessing on behalf of her husband, but the sages said: Let a curse come upon a man whose wife and children make blessings on his behalf).[66] The fourth: Tosafot's argument that women may not exempt the congregation by reading the *Megillah mishum de-rabbim [hem] zilla behu milta* (because in a wide assembly, this would be disgraceful).[67]

The marginality of these considerations, not only to Roth's but to most of the other JTS responsa, vividly indicate the "sociological"

---

[65]*Megillah* 23a.

[66]*Berakhot* 20b, *Sukkah* 38a.

[67]*Sukkah* 38a, s.v. *be-emet*; see *Magen Avraham* 271:2.

nature of Conservative *"halakhah."* Others are candid. These dicta reflect "the inferior status of women" in an earlier age. They are "unconscionable," "sexist," and incompatible with the values of "Western democracies." Roth does not confront the issue directly but we can guess his response: *nishtannu ha-zemanim*: times have changed.

No Orthodox thinker would be quite so radical. But some have come close. Yeshayahu Leibowitz has argued that the sociopolitical status of women in Jewish law is determined by changing social convention. The proof that this is so, he argues, is that many of the laws are justified by phrases like *ein darkhah shel ishah le* . . . (it is not the way of women to . . .) or *ein kevodah shel ishah le* . . . (it is not honorable for a woman to . . .), phrases which refer to extant social norms.[68] Eliezer Berkovits has suggested that "there can be little doubt in the mind of any thinking Jew that those time-conditioned elements that, in talmudic times and later still, influenced the formulation of the laws regarding the status of the woman, have been overcome to a very large extent by the Jewish people of today."[69] Emanuel Rackman has suggested that the halakhic presumption of *tav le-meitav tan du*, that a woman prefers being married, even to a bad risk, to remaining a spinster, no longer holds.[70]

It is here that we come to a particular crux. For it is views of this kind that warrant the adjective "modern" Orthodoxy – where modern bears a normative sense – and that at the same time make many doubt whether there can be a "modern" Orthodoxy which is not an inherent contradiction. Certainly, in an address to the Rabbinical Council of America, R. Soloveitchik reacted strongly to R. Rackman's suggestion, arguing that such an approach would

---

[68]"Maamadah shel ha-ishah: Halakhah u-meta-Halakhah," in Y. Leibowitz, *Emunah, Historiah ve-Arakhim* (Jerusalem: Akadamon, 1982), 71–74.

[69]Berkovits, "The Status of Woman within Judaism," 369.

[70]Rackman, *One Man's Judaism*, 243.

constitute the destruction of Judaism. *Hazakot*, halakhic presumptions, rested—he suggested—"not upon transient psychological behavioral patterns, but on permanent ontological principles rooted in the very depths of the metaphysical human personality, which is as changeless as the heavens above."[71]

The relationship of *halakhah* to social change is complex and I am not sure that it can be reduced to a simple formula. There are some laws which explicitly allow for differential behavior depending on social circumstance. An example is the law that allows an *ishah hashuvah* (an important woman) to recline at the seder table in the presence of her husband. This enabled the Rema to rule, in the name of the Mordechai and Rabbenu Yeruham that "all our women are of high rank."[72] There are others which depend on convention. To some extent this is true of what counts as male and female clothing, and of what misinterpretations of human behavior are likely as far as the law of *marit ha-ayin* is concerned.

Changed social conditions may warrant the development of halakhic strategies to make Jewish life economically viable: *hetter iska, mekhirat hametz*, and the *hetter mekhirat karka*, for example. These are mandated under the general rubric of *hassah Torah al mammonam shel Yisrael*. There were *posekim* who reconciled the difference between talmudic and contemporary medical or scientific assumptions by using the phrase "nature has changed." But there does not seem to be, certainly in the posttalmudic literature, an instance where a ruling was given contrary to precedent on the grounds that *human* nature has changed, or that behavioral assumptions that were once halakhically normative are no longer so.

How are we to understand this fact? One way is that advocated by R. Soloveitchik, namely, that the *halakhah* is based on "permanent ontological principles." Another is that its assumptions are based on what is true most of the time in most societies. These approaches would give a kind of *natural law* status to halakhic

---

[71]R. Joseph Soloveitchik, "Surrendering to the Almighty," *Light* 17 (*Kislev* 5736): 13.

[72]Rema, *Orah Hayyim* 472:4.

behavioral presuppositions. Maimonides' strict view that any decree enacted by the sages as a protective measure cannot be annulled may be based on the juridical idea that courts may bind their successors; but it may also be grounded in the idea that the sages only enacted decrees against what they saw as permanent features of the human situation. Certainly Maimonides states that "one will not find a community at any time" that does not experience breaches of sexual morality.[73]

Not all halakhic presuppositions, though, are necessarily of this *hazakah* kind, rooted in universalities of human nature. It might have been argued in the case at hand that *ervah* ("nakedness") and *kavod* ("honor") – two reasons that would underlie a halakhic refusal to permit a woman to lead a mixed congregation in prayer – are culturally determined categories. Peter Berger, for example, has convincingly demonstrated that "honor" – the nearest equivalent to the rabbinic concept of *kavod* – is predicated on a particular kind of social structure and has become displaced, in modern societies, by the notion of "dignity."[74]

But Berger's analysis takes us to the heart of the matter. For he argues that "the concept of honor implies that identity is essentially, or at least importantly, linked to institutional roles." It is precisely this that makes it objectionable or unintelligible to a modern consciousness in which identity and worth are predicated on the self prior to its roles. "This democratised self which has no necessary social content and no necessary social identity can then be anything, can assume any role or take any point of view, because it *is* in and for itself nothing."[75] Modern consciousness, deeply affronted that there might be significant role differences given by birth, runs pervasively through the JTS responsa.

But surely we are sociologically and philosophically sophisticated

---

[73]*Mishneh Torah, Issurei Bi'ah* 22:19.

[74]Peter Berger "On the Obsolescence of the Concept of Honour," in *Liberalism and its Critics*, ed. Michael Sandel (Oxford: Blackwell, 1984), 149–58.

[75]MacIntyre, *After Virtue*, 30.

enough to realize—given the wealth of studies on this very point—
that *it is this modern consciousness that is radically subversive of tradition
of all kinds*. At the very heart of Judaism, biblical and rabbinic, is an
insistence on standing apart from, sometimes maintaining an op-
positional stance to, the secular ethos of the age. The very concept—itself biblical—of a "fence around the law" recognizes that
there may be behaviors which, while not directly in conflict with
Jewish law or values, are nonetheless subversive of them. It was
remarkable, therefore, to find a series of "responsa" rejecting a set of
halakhic assumptions in favor of an uncritical acceptance of a
late-twentieth-century American view of what is "sexist" or undem-
ocratic. This fails to pass a minimal threshold of sociological
insight, let alone halakhic integrity.

I would hazard this view: that concepts like *ervah* and *kavod are*
culturally determined, and that a general disposition to find them
meaningless testifies to a failure of cultural transmission. I have
argued that Roth's responsum fails the test of integrity, or what I
have called *Daat Torah*, by concentrating on narrow and formal
argumentation and ignoring the wider ambit of halakhic values. It
fails, in fact, exactly on those grounds in which Conservative
thinkers claim prowess: historical and sociological sophistication.
But this is part of a wider failure.

Halakhah is often taken to be a set of rules, and as such is
governed by the general jurisprudential considerations that apply
to rules. This view governs, for example, the entire presentation of
Roth's book, *The Halakhic Process: A Systemic Analysis*. But this is
not so, as Maimonides makes clear in the *Guide*.[76] The laws of
Torah, he argues, are intended to do more than govern behavior.
They are meant to shape character and cognition. That is why one
cannot be halakhically indifferent to secular culture insofar as it
shapes character and cognition in ways antithetical to or subversive
of Torah. We can go further. The extraordinary emphasis in both
biblical and rabbinic Judaism on Torah not only or even primarily

---

[76]Maimonides, *Guide* 2:40.

as law, but as *an object of perpetual study*, testifies to the degree to which Judaism finds its meanings *not* self-evident on the surface of either society or nature, but acquired through extended, indeed continual, education. A failure of *talmud Torah* will eventually lead to a failure of *halakhah*, for there will then be exactly the cognitive dissonance between law and sensibility that we find in the Conservative responsa. The answer to this is *not* halakhic change.

THE *SITZ-IM-LEBEN* OF THE *POSEK*

I have argued that a narrowly jurisprudential approach to halakhic "innovation" is seriously misleading. The formal powers of a *bet din* and the interpretive license of the *posek* may be wide. But the history of *halakhah*, especially after the closure of the Talmud, testifies to both constraint and restraint in the use of those powers.

That history is neither accidental nor "conservative" in the Burkean sense, that most change is for the worse and all change should be effected as slowly as possible. Instead, underlying it is a fundamental commitment: to conserve and preserve Torah as the immutable constitution of the covenant between God and the Jewish people. *Halakhah* only changes so that the Torah shall not change and that the Jewish people maintain its strict identity with Jews past and Jews yet to be.

Halakhah therefore requires a strong sense of history, not to admit change but to defeat it. A halakhic ruling gains its cogency by being set in the context, and enhancing the coherence, of Torah as a whole. The most innovative rulings may well be those that, if true, are the least innovative in that they reveal a pattern in the sources that we had not noticed before, and do so without strain. I instanced the example of a ruling on the blessing for girls. A halakhic ruling may fail by the questions it does *not* ask. Roth's responsum on the ordination of women is of this kind, and as a result violates basic considerations of halakhic integrity.

Above all, in modernity, the *posek* must have a critical historical and sociological awareness if he is to speak cogently to the contemporary situation without unconsciously admitting alien values into the halakhic system. The great *posekim* command admiration precisely for this quality of insight into what "the hour requires" while yet echoing eternity.

To my mind the most serious issue confronting contemporary *halakhah* is not lack of creativity, but the sociological divorce between the centers of *pesak*—nowadays, largely the *yeshivot*—and the centers of congregational life. *Pesak* involves applying Torah in its unchanging totality to Jewish life in its present specificity. A law-interpreter, no less than a law-maker, must have a clear, objective understanding of the lives he is called on to instruct.[77] R. Joshua once suggested that Rabban Gamliel's capacity to lead the Jewish community was compromised by his ignorance of the economic conditions in which they lived.[78] The same surely would be true of a *posek* who was ignorant of their intellectual and cultural circumstances.

I am not a *posek*; but I am a *sho'el* (questioner). And anyone who has asked a *she'elah* instinctively knows when his *meshiv* (responder) has understood the context of the question. Our lack is not of "modern Orthodox" *posekim* but of *posekim* who fully understand contemporary *am Yisrael*; not of those who find a way of saying Yes, but of those whose Yes and No address us equally with the *authority* of one who understands our situation and the *authenticity* of one through whom the whole of Torah speaks.

---

[77]See ibid. 1:54; 2:40.
[78]*Berakhot* 28a.

5

Personal Autonomy and Religious Authority

Moshe Sokol

THE SCOPE OF THE PROBLEM

For most halakhic Jews the idea of personal autonomy is likely to seem extremely remote. The halakhic life, after all, is characterized by strict obedience to a remarkably extensive system of laws governing every detail of life, from the most public to the most intimate, down to the order in which one cuts one's fingernails. When the halakhic Jew is in doubt about what to do, he typically asks his or her rabbi or *posek*, halakhic decisor, for guidance. Thus,

I would like to express my gratitude to Professor David Shatz for the very insightful comments he made on an earlier draft of this chapter delivered at the Orthodox Forum Conference, and to the participants of that Conference as well for their helpful comments during the discussion. I would also like to thank Professors Norman Lamm, Aaron Kirschenbaum, Norbert Samuelson, Eugene Borowitz, and Ya'akov Fuchs for their reactions to earlier drafts of this chapter.

there hardly seems to be room for even the most minimal exercise of personal autonomy. It will be the thesis of this chapter, however, that this view of the halakhic life is wrong, for at least one influential way of understanding Judaism. I will also argue, however, that an uncritical affirmation of the value of personal autonomy, as found in the writings of many non-halakhic, and even some halakhic writers, is also wrong, and that it fails to do justice to the force of the Jewish revelatory idea and its halakhic embodiment.

Most discussions of this subject, I believe, tend to be somewhat primitive in their conception of autonomy. By clarifying the very concept of autonomy, via a series of distinctions to be drawn in what follows, we shall be in a far better position to show which sort of autonomy may be compatible with Judaism, and which not. Having established that a certain form of autonomy is indeed compatible with, and probably embraced by, the tradition within which I shall be working, my argument will conclude by sketching out a theological model for explaining the importance of autonomy in Judaism, and for the role of *halakhah* in Jewish life. Given the constraints of brevity of this forum, however, full justice cannot be done to all the complex issues involved, and the reader should view the following analysis as a first step in what must clearly be a far more ambitious project.

A prefatory note: One of the most common flaws in philosophizing about Judaism is what might be called the *fallacy of homogenizing*. Those guilty of this fallacy make sweeping claims about Judaism based upon a limited number of texts, and, most significant of all, upon certain preconceived notions of what Judaism is all about. Thus, all of Judaism gets polemically homogenized into a single, complacent whole.

Of course, Judaism is in fact much too complicated for that, and important differences between schools of thought, periods of history, individual Jewish thinkers and leaders, and religious movements get obscured. Therefore, I should like to situate my approach explicitly, at the very outset: it is that of the halakhic rationalistic philosophical tradition which has its origins in the middle ages and which has continued in one form or another until the present day. I have in mind the sort of rationalism characterized by such Jewish philosophers as Saadya, Maimonides, and Bahya ibn Pakuda, all of whose views were articulated within a halakhic framework. Certainly there can be little doubt that an analysis of personal autonomy out of the mystical tradition will yield a very different picture, and this is especially so in light of Moshe Idel's recent claims, *contra* Scholem, that for many mystics *unio mystica* is in fact a central ideal.[1]

Similarly, an analysis of the question of personal autonomy out of an entirely nonhalakhic framework, such as that of Reform Judaism, and perhaps some versions of Conservative Judaism, would appear quite different.[2] And again, there is a voluntaristic strand within Judaism, not limited to the mystics, according to which personal autonomy is of no value whatsoever. All that counts in this view is strict obedience to God's inscrutable command. This tradition extends back to the rabbinic period, and perhaps further, and is expressed very clearly, among other places, in one amoraic interpretation of the famous *mishnah* in *Berakhot* concerning *kan tzippor*, according to which, whoever says that God's mercies extend to the bird's nest "makes God's qualities merciful, and they are only decrees" (*Berakhot* 33b). This Ockhamistic vision of Judaism has always had its protagonists, from

---

[1]Moshe Idel, *Kabbalah: New Perspectives* (New Haven: Yale University Press, 1988).

[2]See, for example, two articles by Eugene Borowitz, "The Autonomous Jewish Self," *Modern Judaism* 1 (1984) and "The Autonomous Self and the Commanding Community," *Theological Studies* 45 (1984), and the articles by Emil Fackenheim and others cited below, n. 18. These thinkers, Borowitz in particular, draw heavily on the work of Martin Buber and Franz Rosenzweig, both of whom, although especially Buber, write outside the framework of binding *halakhah*. See Walter Wurzburger's article, "Covenantal Imperatives," n. 42 below.

the medieval antirationalists to those of the modern era, most notably in the person of Yeshayahu Leibovitz.[3] I shall, however, not be able to take up Leibovitz's arguments here, except indirectly.[4]

What, then, are my assumptions? Put positively, it seems to me *prima facie* reasonable that personal autonomy in some form is—or at least ought to be—consistent with, if not essentially constitutive of, at least some standard versions of normative Judaism. This is so for two basic reasons, one external to Judaism and the other internal to it. The reason external to it is the very power of the concept itself. The idea that each human being by virtue of his rationality should think through and carry out a life-plan that expresses his authentic self; that each human being ought to be free to choose how to lead his own life; that what we truly believe ought to be the only real basis for choice; that human beings ought to take full responsibility for their choices and lives by virtue of their rational capacities; that ceding the power over choices to another person or institution evacuates the most peculiarly human of capacities, the ability to think and reason; these are all interrelated concepts (which I shall seek to separate out somewhat later on in this chapter) that carry with them a great deal of weight. That is, there seems *prima facie* to be *something* right about it all, and therefore, again *prima facie,* it ought at least partially and in some form to be consistent with, if not an essential part of, some standard Jewish teaching.

So much for reason one. Reason two is internal to Judaism, and

---

[3]See especially Yeshayahu Leibovitz, *Yahadut, Am Yehudi u-Medinat Yisrael* (Tel Aviv: Schocken, 1975).

[4]While I shall be considering the issue from the nonvoluntaristic stance, it is imperative that the sorts of arguments the voluntarists use be considered. While it is wrong to homogenize, and best to make clear one's assumptions at the onset, the voluntarist position, it seems to me, represents something authentic about Judaism to which even the nonvoluntarist must be responsive. I shall return to this point later.

rests on evidence from its classical sources. These have been marshalled extensively in a variety of places; I shall cite only several examples as illustrative of a larger body of material. The interested reader might consult these texts for a fuller rendering of the evidence.[5]

Starting with the Torah, perhaps the most striking evidence for the role of some form of autonomy in human life is the example of Abraham. In the process of bargaining over Sodom, Abraham tells God: "That be far from You to do after this manner, to slay the righteous with the wicked, so that the righteous should be like the wicked; that be far from You; shall not the judge of all the earth do justly?" (Genesis 18:25).

Here Abraham has the independence to challenge God Himself on the basis of what he autonomously believes to be correct. Even if Abraham learned the general imperative to act justly from God directly, the application of that general principle to this particular instance certainly appears to be autonomous. Moses too says much

---

[5]See, for example, David Hartman, *A Living Covenant* (New York: Free Press, 1985), and Louis Jacobs, "The Relationship Between Religion and Ethics in Jewish Thought," reprinted in *Contemporary Jewish Ethics*, ed. M. Kellner (New York: Hebrew Publishing Company, 1978), 41–57. Some of these sources come up in discussions concerning the autonomy of ethics in Judaism, and the question of whether the natural law doctrine finds a home in Jewish teachings, about which there has arisen a huge body of literature. It is important to distinguish the issue of personal autonomy, which is the subject of this chapter, from the issue of the autonomy of ethics in Judaism. Put somewhat baldly, the latter question is concerned primarily with whether ethical laws are right apart from whether God commanded them. The former question is concerned not only with ethical laws, but with all of life's decisions, with knowledge and with laws of all sorts, ethical or otherwise, and its concern in this regard is largely with how individuals *appropriate* and *determine* what is right or true, whether it is God who is the ultimate source of their rightness or truth, or whether they are right of their own accord apart from God.

the same thing: "O God, source of the breath of all flesh! When one man sins, will You be wrathful with the entire community?" (Numbers 16:22).

Whereas autonomy in the biblical period involved man's stance directly toward God, in the rabbinic period man's relation to God had become mediated by the Torah. Therefore, many (although not all) expressions of autonomy in the rabbinic period reflect a relationship to God via the sacred text, via God's laws as revealed in that text, and via the oral law which accompanied it. Perhaps the most famous of these, and certainly one of the most striking, is the story relating to the dispute between Rabbi Eliezer and the Sages concerning the oven of Akhnai:

> On that day Rabbi Eliezer brought forward every imaginable argument, but they did not accept them. Said he to them: "If the law is as I say, let this carob tree prove it!" Thereupon the carob tree was torn a hundred cubits out of its place—others say, four hundred cubits. "No proof can be brought from a carob tree," they retorted. . . . Again he said to them: "If the law is as I say let it be proved from heaven!" Whereupon a heavenly voice cried out: "Why do you dispute with Rabbi Eliezer, seeing that in all matters the law is as he says!" But Rabbi Joshua arose and exclaimed: "It is not in heaven" [Deuteronomy 30:12]. What did he mean by this? Said Rabbi Jeremiah: "That the Torah had already been given at Mount Sinai; we pay no attention to a heavenly voice, because You have long since written . . . 'After the majority must one incline' " [Exodus 23:2]. Rabbi Nathan met Elijah and asked him: "What did the Holy One, blessed be He, do at that moment?" He replied: "He laughed, saying 'My sons have defeated Me, my sons have defeated Me.' " [*Baba Metzia* 59b]

While the text and dating of this famous *aggadah* are problematic, it nevertheless constitutes a ringing affirmation of autonomy from God's will and knowledge in ascertaining halakhic truth, one which had a profound impact on medieval and modern conceptions of *halakhah*. Numerous other *aggadot* reflect much the same attitude in regard to *halakhah*; here, however, I shall cite a rabbinic text in which some form of human autonomy appears to be endorsed in a *non-legal* context. The following *midrash* describes Hannah's prayer for children at the Tabernacle:

> Rabbi Eleazar said: "Hannah said before the Holy One, blessed be He: 'Sovereign of the Universe, if You will look [answer my prayers], it is well, and if You will not look, I will go and shut myself up with [another man], with the knowledge of my husband Elkanah. And since I shall be alone with [this man who is not my husband] they will make me drink the water of the *sotah*, and You cannot falsify your Torah, which says "[If she is innocent of adultery] she shall be cleared, and shall conceive seed" ' " [Numbers 5:28]. [*Berakhot* 31b]

Here Hannah vigorously demands, rather than submissively beseeches, what she autonomously determines to be her just due, and threatens to force God's hand by a procedurally correct manipulation of the law in order to insure conception.

One final rabbinic text should be cited here in this abbreviated marshaling of *prima facie* evidence for some form of autonomy in the Jewish tradition; it relates to motive in carrying out the *mitzvot*. The *Midrash Tanhuma* quotes the following assertion:

> Whoever performs one *mitzvah* for its own sake [literally, "its truth"], it is as if he gave it himself at Sinai, as it says "you shall keep them and you shall do them" [Deuteronomy 26:16]; and what is the intent of "do them"? It is only to teach you that whoever fulfills the Torah and does it for its own sake, is as if he decreed it and gave it at Sinai. [*Ki Tavo, aleph*; Buber ed., 3:46]

While this text admits of many interpretations, certainly one plausible interpretation is that performing a *mitzvah* with the right

motive is akin to virtuous self-imposition of the *mitzvah*, which
sounds very much like an endorsement of autonomy.

During the medieval period many of the themes cited above
from rabbinic sources recur. New to the period, however, is a stress
on autonomous reason in nonhalakhic contexts. Under the influence of Greek and Islamic philosophy, the medieval Jewish rationalists stressed the competence of the human intellect and the
central role human reasoning should play in life. Certainly one of
the more striking examples of this phenomenon appears in Maimonides' *Letter on Astrology*. Criticizing those who rely on astrology,
Maimonides writes:

> What we have said about this [astrology] from the beginning is
> that the entire position of the stargazers is regarded as a
> falsehood by men of science. I know that you may search and
> find sayings of some individual sages in the Talmud and
> Midrashim whose words appear to maintain that at the
> moment of man's birth the stars will cause such and such to
> happen to him. Do not regard this as a difficulty; . . . it is not
> proper to abandon matters of reason that have already been
> verified by proofs, shake loose of them and depend on the
> words of a single one of the sages from whom possibly the
> matter was hidden. . . . A man should never cast his reason
> behind him, for the eyes are set in front, not in back.[6]

In this passage Maimonides expresses his willingness to set aside a
rabbinical teaching if it is contradicted by the laws of scientific
reasoning. These laws are of course discoverable by unaided human
reasoning, which says a great deal about the value Maimonides
places on autonomous thinking. In fact, Maimonides asserts that
the central *mitzvah* of love of God cannot be fulfilled *without* the use

---

[6]Moses Maimonides, *Letter on Astrology*, trans. R. Lerner, in *Medieval
Political Philosophy*, ed. R. Lerner and M. Mahdi (New York: Free Press,
1963), 234–35.

of human reason, by which Maimonides means philosophical speculation. As he says in his *Mishneh Torah:*

> One only loves God with the knowledge with which one knows Him. According to the knowledge will be the love. . . . A person ought therefore to devote himself to the understanding and comprehension of those sciences and studies which will inform him concerning his master, as far as it lies in human faculties to understand and comprehend—as indeed we have explained in the Laws of the Basic Principles of the Torah.[7]

This theme is a recurrent one in Maimonidean literature, and appears in one guise or another in almost everything he wrote, philosophical, halakhic, and otherwise. It is also a recurrent theme in rationalist medieval Jewish philosophical literature generally. Bahya ibn Pakuda, for example, devoted the introduction and first two chapters of his classic *Hovot ha-Levavot* to this issue. Bahya even goes so far as to compare those who believe in God's existence and unity on the basis of tradition alone, rather than on reason, to "blind men" walking single file "each with his hand on the shoulder of the man preceding." If the leader, or one of the middle members of the chain should go astray, everyone following will be lost, and may even fall into the pit.[8] Bahya, Maimonides, and many others maintained that the only way to fully satisfy the obligation to know God—no small matter—was by engaging in independent human reasoning.[9]

Even these limited illustrations drawn from premodern

---

[7]*Mishneh Torah*, *Yesodei ha-Torah*, *Teshuvah* 10:6. See also *Sefer ha-Mitzvot*, positive 3.

[8]*Hovot ha-Levavot* 1:2.

[9]See, for example, Saadya Gaon, *Emunot ve-De'ot* 1:6; Bachya, *Hovot ha-Levavot*, op. cit. and 1:3; Maimonides, *Guide for the Perplexed* 1:50 and 3:51, and *Mishneh Torah*, *Yesodei ha-Torah* 1:1–6; Joseph Albo, *Ikkarim* 1:19, 24.

sources should suggest that there is *prima facie* evidence that at least some important classical thinkers and texts affirmed some form of personal autonomy. It would be altogether wrong, however, to make any sweeping generalizations about the Jewish tradition as a whole on the basis either of the argument external to Judaism or of the evidence internal to Judaism. This is so because there are also arguments, both internal to Judaism and external to it, which suggest quite the opposite, that personal autonomy cannot be a central Jewish value. First of all, there is the hard evidence that certain important traditions within Judaism largely or entirely deny the value of autonomy, as noted earlier in this essay. Even in the context of the tradition being considered here, however, there are three *prima facie* arguments internal to Judaism that run counter to the claim that personal autonomy is a central Jewish value.

First, there is the brute fact that Judaism is a religion at whose theological core stands God's revelation. The Torah conveys God's heteronomous commands addressed to the Jewish people. The heteronomous character of *mitzvot* suggests that personal autonomy cannot be a central Jewish value. Second, there is the extraordinary *scope* of the halakhic life, and third the widespread role of the rabbinic decisor, both noted in the opening paragraph of this chapter. These three internal arguments, to which I shall return later, are of course only *prima facie* arguments themselves, and certainly much can be said in evaluating them. Nevertheless, they should lead us at least to suspect any sweeping claims made for autonomy: indeed, they stand at the heart of the voluntaristic approach to Judaism (particularly the first two arguments).

Supplementing these internal arguments are a set of external arguments, all of which grow out of a historical consideration. While the concept of autonomy may be rooted in the scholastic tradition of Aquinas, as some have suggested,[10] in its fully fleshed-out form, with all its philosophical, theological, and political ram-

---

[10]W. Ullmann, *The Individual and Society* (Baltimore: Johns Hopkins Press, 1966), especially 127.

ifications, it is clearly a creation of the Enlightenment. Jeffrey Stout has argued[11] that the development of the idea of autonomy is grounded in what he calls "the flight from authority." The breakdown in religious authority and consensus which characterized the Reformation, with all its attendant political upheaval and violence together with the need of certain minorities such as the Huguenots in the sixteenth century to maintain their religious rights, gave rise to the need to ground moral and political behavior in a nonreligious (and therefore noncontroversial) framework. The concept of autonomous "rights" that the individual bears independent of any religious or political authority emerged precisely to supplant the failures of religious authority. The modern concept of autonomy was thus born on the pyre of traditional religious authority.

If this historical account of the rise of autonomy is correct, then attributing autonomy to halakhic Judaism should surely give us pause. Halakhic Judaism, whatever else it is, is surely rooted in authority, both the authority of the *halakhah* itself, as well as the authority of the interpreters of *halakhah*. The putative marriage of halakhic Judaism and autonomy may in historical perspective thus be a particularly problematic one.[12] Moreover, this historical account might suggest that were religious authority to have functioned effectively, as it surely sometimes did and certainly was meant to, then the concept of autonomy might never have been born. Indeed, perhaps authority, justly exercised, isn't such a bad thing after all—and here we come to the heart of the matter. Perhaps justly exercised authority serves to correct self-indulgent error with the wisdom of accumulated experience, and with the insight of people not captured by the particular intellectual fashions of the day (even if they remained captives of the fashions of an earlier day), and with the perspective of individuals not pressed by

---

[11]Jeffrey Stout, *The Flight From Authority* (Notre Dame: University of Notre Dame Press, 1981), chap. 11.

[12]Stout defends this sort of "historicist" philosophical reasoning in *Flight From Authority*; see his introduction to the book and pt. 3.

the urgency of a particular situation. Perhaps it serves to prevent the anarchic potential of rampant individualism. Perhaps, as Alasdair MacIntyre argues, if society shared a common conception of the good and of the sort of virtue needed to achieve that good, as it once did, then shared moral discourse and behavior would be possible, and the fractured moral discourse embodied in individualism and autonomy would be seen as utterly counterproductive.[13] The historical perspective might thus suggest that even if the concept of autonomy is a powerful one, perhaps it ought not to be embraced with altogether uncritical enthusiasm.

Where does all this leave us? After summarizing what is, all told, fairly considerable evidence that strongly suggests that autonomy is indeed affirmed by at least some authoritative Jewish teachings, I have presented a range of considerations which suggest just the reverse. It seems to me that this leaves us in need of clarifying the very concept of autonomy itself. Thus far, the term *autonomy* has been used somewhat indiscriminately, largely to set up the problems that the remainder of this essay will attempt to solve. In fact, as noted earlier, many treatments of the subject, particularly those in the Jewish context, use the term quite imprecisely, resulting in a good deal of confusion not only about what autonomy is, but also about what place it has in the context of Judaism.

SOME PROPOSED DISTINCTIONS

In order to clarify the concept of autonomy, it may be useful to begin to distinguish among various kinds of autonomy. The three broad categories that can be sorted out at first pass I call *Nomic Autonomy, Epistemic Autonomy,* and *Haeretic Autonomy.*[14]

Nomic Autonomy, from the Greek word for law, *nomos* (whence

---

[13] Alasdair MacIntyre, *After Virtue* (Notre Dame: University of Notre Dame Press, 1981).

[14] I shall first describe these three kinds of autonomy somewhat broadly. Following the distinction I draw between "Hard Autonomy" and "Soft Autonomy," I shall attempt to define them with more precision.

the "nomy" in autonomy), relates to an individual's autonomy with respect to law. Thus, one might claim as does Kant that no law in itself places moral obligations upon a human being (apart from furthering some mere interest) unless it is self-legislated.[15] *Epistemic Autonomy*, from the Greek word for knowledge, *episteme*, relates to an individual's autonomy with respect to knowledge. Thus, one might claim that I can only be said to truly know something if I proved it to myself, whereas if I blindly accept it on someone else's authority, then I don't really know it. Finally, *Haeretic Autonomy*, from the Greek word *haeresis*, or choice, relates to an individual's autonomy with respect to personal decision-making and the choice of life-plans. Thus, one might claim that if a particular way of life or important decision was forced down my throat, or was unthinkingly adopted by me out of superficial social conformity, then that way of life or decision has no value at all.

What emerges from these distinctions is that autonomy is a complex concept — it can mean at least three different things. To prove that one form of autonomy is consistent with or affirmed by Judaism is not necessarily to prove that another form of autonomy is consistent with or affirmed by Judaism. We shall soon see how this pertains to the problems at hand.

The next distinction to be drawn is between what I shall call *Hard Autonomy* and *Soft Autonomy*. Broadly speaking, by *Hard Autonomy* I mean the strict view that holds that wherever autonomy is at all wanting, all is lost. A law is no law at all if not autonomously imposed *(Hard Nomic Autonomy)*; a belief cannot be counted knowledge unless one proves it for oneself *(Hard Epistemic Autonomy)*; a choice is no real choice at all unless chosen autonomously *(Hard Haeretic Autonomy)*. A further distinction, to which we shall return, should be drawn between hard autonomy as a *necessary condition* and hard autonomy as a *sufficient condition*.

---

[15]Immanuel Kant, *Groundwork of the Metaphysic of Morals*, trans. Lewis Beck White, Konigliche Preussische Akademie der Wissenchaft ed. (Berlin, 1902–1938), 431.

By *Soft Autonomy* I mean the more moderate view that considers departures from the ideal of autonomy to be significant, but not fatal. A law that is not self-imposed lacks the important value of autonomous self-imposition, but nevertheless may still be a binding law *(Soft Nomic Autonomy)*; a belief not rationally self-demonstrated lacks the important value, the epistemic force of self-demonstration, but it may nevertheless be knowledge *(Soft Epistemic Autonomy)*; a choice externally imposed lacks the important value of autonomous self-imposition, nevertheless it may still be a choice of value *(Soft Haeretic Autonomy)*. Again, the key point to bear in mind here is that proving that one or more forms of soft autonomy are consistent with (some strands of) Judaism does not imply that other forms of soft autonomy are consistent with Judaism. Far more important, it doesn't imply that any form of *hard autonomy* is consistent with Judaism, a very critical point.

THE DISTINCTIONS APPLIED:
HARD AUTONOMY

Armed with the distinctions we have delineated, we are now in a position to consider more precisely the relationship between personal autonomy and religious authority in the Jewish tradition. Ultimately, as will be seen, I shall argue that by using these distinctions a strong case can be made out for affirming the importance of some versions of personal autonomy, one of the central claims of this chapter.

Nomic Autonomy

Let us first look at the various forms of hard autonomy, beginning with hard nomic autonomy. The classic formulation of the principle of hard nomic autonomy is that of Kant: "The will is therefore not merely subject to the law, but subject in such a way that it must be considered also as self-legislated, and only for this reason subject to the law of which it can regard itself as author."[16]

Kant is saying here that no (categorical) obligation can arise which in itself places duties upon us independent of furthering some mere interest, unless that obligation is self-imposed. Of course, if I wish to satisfy some interest, such as self-preservation or meriting some reward, then it may be heteronomously obligatory for me to take a certain course of action. However, non-self-interested obligation, or law, requires self-imposition. What kinds of laws merit self-imposition? Kant would answer, according to one formulation of the Categorical Imperative, only those which are universal, which are stripped of all personal interest and are applicable to all human beings by virtue of their being rational agents. As Alasdair MacIntyre points out, Kant is responding in part to the breakdown of authority and the traditional worldview characteristic of the Enlightenment.[17] If no satisfactory form of authority exists outside the individual, it must reside somewhere within. Hence, (what I am here calling) hard nomic autonomy.

This Kantian thesis has generated perhaps the most extensive Jewish philosophical discussions regarding autonomy.[18] I have argued elsewhere that Kantian autonomy is indeed inconsistent with the revelatory character of the Jewish legal tradition: classical Judaism has always understood its adherents to be bound by God's laws irrespective of whether or not those laws are self-imposed. Even if the Jew doesn't autonomously accept *kashrut* he is still *legally* obligated to keep it, by virtue of God's omnipotence and, hence, ability to legislate irrespective of one's feelings about the matter. For Kant, however, heteronomous obligations are not true law, but

---

[16]Ibid.

[17]MacIntyre, *After Virtue*, chaps. 4–5.

[18]See, for example, Emil Fackenheim, "The Revealed Morality of Judaism and Modern Thought," in *Quest For Past and Future* (Boston: Beacon Press, 1970); Norbert Samuelson, "Revealed Morality and Modern Thought," *CCAR Journal* (June 1969); David Ellenson, "Emil Fackenheim and the Revealed Morality of Judaism," *Judaism* 25 (1976).

mere reflections of self-interest. For the Jewish tradition, these are true laws, and not mere obligations of self-interest. Nevertheless, I suggest that careful analysis of Kant's own reasons for affirming his Principle of Autonomy shows that if Kant were to accept basic theistic beliefs and premises, he himself might admit that God-derived norms satisfy his very own arguments for the Principle of Autonomy.[19] In any case, hard nomic autonomy is inconsistent with classical Judaism, and surely with halakhic Judaism. What this shows is that even if personal autonomy is a great value, it is not constitutive of true legal authority. According to traditional mono-theism, there is an authority outside the individual, a commanding God whose overarching plan for human life orients that life.

In the formulation of hard nomic autonomy I have used thus far, autonomy is conceived as a *necessary condition* for the obligato-riness of a law: a law is binding *only if* self-imposed. However, one might conceive hard nomic authority also (or only) as a *sufficient condition* for the obligatoriness of a law. One might argue, for instance, that a law is binding in case it is self-imposed, so that if I accept an obligation, I am in fact obligated to carry it out. Where this is an obligation of interest – say to get a raise I commit myself to work extra hours – then the obligation is not autonomous but heteronomous. But if I commit myself to something because I believe it to be the right thing to do, quite apart from whatever benefit I derive – or trouble I get myself into – then such a self-imposed obligation would be binding according to this formulation of hard nomic autonomy.[20]

In many instances, *this* formulation of the hard nomic au-tonomy principle is by and large consistent with classical Jewish tradition of all varieties. *Humra* is a time-honored Jewish religious

---

[19]Moshé Sokol, "The Autonomy of Reason, Revealed Morality and Jewish Law," *Religious Studies* 22 (1986): 423–27.

[20]I am bracketing for present purposes the question of whether any nonmoral law can be autonomous in the Kantian sense. See my article, ibid., for a full discussion of the issue.

category, and with certain important exceptions (such as where it is accepted for the wrong reasons or is lacking certain formal criteria), *humra* practices become binding.[21] Where the practice is accepted with certain formulae, then the obligation may even have the halakhic status of a binding oath (a *neder* or *shevuah*). Conscience thus binds.

The more serious question in the context of this chapter is what the scholastics called "erring conscience." What happens when I autonomously impose upon myself behavior I believe to be right knowing that halakhic sources say it is wrong? Or when I refrain from doing something because I believe it is wrong knowing that the halakhic sources say it is right? Is such autonomously imposed behavior obligatory?

The problem here needs to be considered in two contexts.[22] First, there is the more general, philosophical one: can any individual dissent from the *halakhah* on clearly nonhalakhic grounds, or on grounds that do not flow from "standard halakhic analysis," however we are to define that phrase? For example, if I am convinced that a certain law flows from a dated, ancient near-eastern practice, and is inconsistent with contemporary standards of morality, but I do not use any sort of halakhic analysis to prove the validity of those contemporary standards of morality, may I disregard that law? Second, there is the more technical context of halakhic decision-making: can a halakhic expert, the *posek*, using "standard halakhic analysis," dissent from halakhic precedent,

---

[21]For an extensive listing of classical sources relevant to *humra*, see Yehuda Leo Levi, *Shaarei Talmud Torah* (Jerusalem: Feldheim, 1982), 83–84, 103–22. An issue that merits further consideration is whether the formal limits placed upon *humra*, and the difference between *kabbalah be-lev* and engaging in *humra* practices three times, are consistent with the central idea of autonomy, which is simple self-imposition. My hunch is that they are, because these halakhic requirements are probably at least in part intended to legally establish self-imposition.

[22]I am grateful to Professor David Shatz for pointing to the significance of this distinction.

accepted practice, or accepted contemporary authority? I shall consider each context in turn, starting with the more general one.

On the face of it, it would be inconsistent for an individual to affirm the obligatory nature of the halakhic system and yet dissent from it when he chooses. All legal systems are taken to be binding, *halakhah* included, unless it can be shown otherwise. Thus sufficient hard nomic autonomy, in the general philosophical context, seems *prima facie* incompatible with halakhic Judaism. Nevertheless, one important contemporary Jewish thinker who professes an affirmation of the halakhic framework maintains that the *halakhah* in these cases would not be binding, and that is Michael Wyschogrod.[23] Wyschogrod presents an independent and interesting argument for hard nomic authority in its sufficient condition formulation; that is, he argues for the view that in Judaism erring conscience binds. It is worth considering his argument with some care, since if it is correct it will turn out that where my conscience tells me the *halakhah* comes out wrong, for example, in particular instances of an *agunah*, or a *mamzer*, then I will be obligated to follow my conscience and not the *halakhah*.[24]

Rabbinical halakhic judgment, says Wyschogrod, must be capable of being in error; if the rabbis can never be wrong, he argues, then they can never be right either. But what is halakhic error? Getting God's will wrong. Thus, it turns out that the rabbis must be capable of getting God's will wrong. But if my obligation as a halakhic Jew is precisely to obey God's will, and the rabbis are capable of getting God's will wrong, then in relying exclusively on

---

[23]Michael Wyschogrod, "Judaism and Conscience," in *Standing Before God*, A. Finkel and L. Frizzell (Hoboken: Ktav, 1981), 313–28. Wyschogrod develops the argument more fully in his later book, *The Body of Faith* (Minneapolis: Seabury Press, 1983), 189–90. Hartman, *A Living Covenant*, makes a similar claim, for different reasons, in his chapter on ethics. (See my brief discussion of Hartman's views below, n. 50.)

[24]Wyschogrod suggests an approach similar to the one I take here, but whereas he formulates an argument intended as a *response* to that approach, I argue that such an approach does not succeed.

the rabbis I may end up not obeying God's will. Therefore, if I am *convinced* that the rabbis are getting God's will wrong, it would be wrong for me to obey them: after all, the only criterion for my behavior can be obeying God's will.[25]

The problem I find with this argument is that it equivocates about the meaning of the phrase "God's will." God's will, in fact, can encompass many things. It can be His will that abortion for reasons of maternal mental health is wrong, and it can simultaneously be His will that if it is the consensus of rabbinic opinion that abortion for reasons of maternal mental health is right, then it is right for me to have an abortion. There can be no doubt that each individual, as Wyschogrod suggests, stands before God under the obligation to do His will, and stands responsible to Him for doing it. Nevertheless, the *halakhah* may very well be so constituted (as the *aggadah* concerning the oven of Akhnai suggests) that this responsibility is satisfied precisely by scrupulously following the halakhic procedures for adjudicating halakhic questions.

Does this mean, as Wyschogrod suggests, that halakhic Jews can find blanket security in blindly following these halakhic procedures? If the scrupulous search for satisfactory halakhic adjudication is easy, then perhaps yes, although I am not so sure how easy it really is. More important, however, if some form of *soft nomic autonomy* is in fact consistent with Judaism, which we shall soon consider, then his life will not be so easy after all. He will be charged with the task of figuring it all out for himself, of seeking to encounter God's will in the halakhic process on his own, of personally struggling with questions of right and wrong, of facing the terrifying quandary of Rabbi Eliezer who couldn't bring himself to follow the majority even though he knew just as well as Rabbi Joshua that the majority will prevails.

---

[25]For parallels to this issue in the sources see *Sifre*, Deuteronomy 17:11; the comments of Nachmanides and Abarbanel ad loc., and *Horayot* 1:1. These sources relate to the question of legal procedure. Wyschogrod, of course, is making a far broader claim.

If Wyschogrod's argument is unconvincing, as I think it is, then
we are left with the *prima facie* assumption that legal systems are
binding, and hence the conclusion that the laws of the Torah and
halakhah are binding on the individual Jew whether or not they are
autonomously imposed, and whether or not the individual's conscience urges otherwise. As will be seen, the classical sources cited
earlier, and others like them, support no more than a *soft autonomy
principle*. If that is correct, then we must at least tentatively reject the
principle of hard nomic autonomy in its more general, philosophical
context. Considering this question in the technical, halakhic context, however, yields a somewhat different conclusion.

The autonomy of the *posek* who follows "standard halakhic
procedure" is great indeed. One of the most influential Jewish legal
authorities in the history of *halakhah*, R. Moshe Isserles of sixteenth-
century Poland, asserts in his glosses to the *Shulhan Arukh*: "If it
appears to a judge and to members of his generation on the basis of
decisive evidence that the law is not as was decided by [earlier]
authorities, he may disagree with them, since it was not mentioned
in the Talmud."[26] Menahem Elon and others have argued that in
Jewish law, precedent is not binding: each individual judge has
"only what his eyes see."[27] Various writers have stressed the remarkable autonomy accorded to the decisor of Jewish law.[28] While the
issue is complicated, there is strong evidence that in practice the
posek indeed has substantial autonomy—whether or not he chooses

---

[26]*Hoshen Mishpat* 25:1, following R. Asher ben Yehiel *(Rosh) Sanhedrin*
4:6.

[27]Menahem Elon, *Ha-Mishpat ha-Ivri* (Jerusalem: Magnes Press, 1978),
223–38. See also his *Principles of Jewish Law* (Jerusalem: Keter, 1975),
115–16.

[28]Elon, *Ha-Mishpat*, n. 26; N. Lamm and A. Kirschenbaum, "Freedom
and Constraint in the Jewish Judicial Process," *Cardozo Law Review* 1
(1979): 99, and J. Roth, "Responding to Dissent in Jewish Law: Repression
versus Self-Restraint," *Rutgers Law Review* 40 (1987): 31. See also the
chapters by Lawrence Kaplan, Michael Ronsensweig, and Jonathan Sacks
in this volume.

to exercise it – a critical point in considering the question of hard nomic autonomy.

Nevertheless, affirming this hard nomic autonomy of the *posek* does not entail affirming hard nomic autonomy as a general principle. This is because it is precisely the halakhic sources and system which grants him what autonomy he has. It seems safe to say that were the halakhic system to deny him that autonomy, then the *posek* would not have it. And where it does deny him autonomy, i.e., where the *posek* fails to follow "standard halakhic procedure," such as where he dissents from decision recorded in the Talmud itself, then his decision is regarded by the halakhic system as illegitimate – in every sense of the word. An analogy to playing a game by the rules may be apt. The rules of the game may be very broad, granting the players a great deal of autonomy in creating novel, unprecedented moves. Despite this autonomy, they must still play by those rules, as broad as they are. If they fail to abide by them, they are no longer regarded as legitimate contestants. Similarly, the halakhic system may grant its experts substantial autonomy, a point of great significance. Nevertheless, they must abide by the procedural rules of the system, rules that cannot be autonomously disregarded.

Epistemic Autonomy

The principle of *hard epistemic autonomy*, however, is a different matter altogether, and a very complicated one in its own right. The principle of hard epistemic autonomy, formulated as a *necessary* condition for knowledge, holds that no individual can be said to know something unless he finds it out for himself.[29] I may hold the

---

[29]Of course, what counts as an adequate "finding out for yourself," or "self-demonstration," is itself an interesting and important question: Is deductive reasoning necessary, or is inductive reasoning using empirical evidence sufficient? and what degree of certainty, or probability, is required?

true belief that London is the capital of England because my teacher told me, but unless I go to London myself, make inquiries, inspect the Parliament, and so on, I can't truly be said to *know* it. More relevantly, I may believe that God exists because that is what I was taught, or I may know that it is wrong to cheat on my income taxes because that is what I was told, but unless I reason out for myself that God must exist, or examine the halakhic sources myself which yield the conclusion that it is wrong to cheat on my income taxes (or reason it out for myself on the basis of my ethical convictions), then I cannot be truly said to *know* any of these things.

Formulated as a *sufficient* condition for knowledge, the principle of hard epistemic autonomy holds that if after demonstrating something to my own satisfaction I am certain that it is true, then I can be said to know it is true, even if it contradicts other propositions I was taught or had reason to believe. For example, if I am convinced after a great deal of thought and what I regard as conclusive research that the earth revolves around the sun and not vice-versa, then I can be said to know that it is true even though certain passages in the Bible suggest otherwise.

Is hard epistemic autonomy as here formulated consistent with any strands of the tradition? Is it embraced by any? The central locus for these discussions in the tradition is of course that of medieval Jewish philosophy. In the case of theological knowledge, I am aware of no rabbinic sources that clearly maintain that self-demonstration is a necessary or sufficient condition for theological knowledge. Hints of the value of theological self-demonstration, which appear in isolated *midrashim* such as the *midrash* concerning Abraham who, it is said, reasoned out on his own that God exists,[30] are no more than that: hints, touching on the possibility of such an achievement, and perhaps its value, but certainly not asserting its necessity. Even if they do show sufficiency, it is far from evident that they would show sufficiency where self-demonstrated belief would contradict revealed belief, which is the really interesting

---

[30]Genesis *Rabbah* 14:2.

question. The great medieval rationalists, such as Maimonides, who had encyclopedic knowledge of rabbinic materials, would have produced such evidence if they had had it; apparently they didn't. Indeed, Saul Lieberman has demonstrated the extremely limited influence of Greek philosophical thinking on the rabbis of the Talmud.[31] *Hard* epistemic autonomy is a product of philosophical thinking (as against soft epistemic autonomy, which is not dependent upon abstract reasoning about the nature of knowledge, a typically philosophical enterprise). Its absence from the rabbinic (and of course biblical) tradition is therefore to be expected. Furthermore, biblical and rabbinic Judaism conceive of knowledge of God as deriving initially from direct revelatory experience, and then, for almost every Jew, from reports about revelatory experiences mediated by reliable transmission—the chain of tradition—or by sacred texts. The centrality of tradition would leave little room for self-discovery.

If hard epistemic autonomy in its necessary condition formulation is to be found anywhere in premodern Judaism, it is in the writings of the medieval rationalists, whom I cited earlier.[32] The extent to which it is present, however, is far from clear. Among the most influential of the medievals, Bahya ibn Pakuda seems to go the furthest in approaching, if not actually adopting, the hard epistemic position, as the text cited earlier about the blind man leading everyone into the pit would suggest. Yehuda Halevi of course would deny hard epistemic autonomy. Saadya and Maimonides fall somewhere in between.[33]

---

[31]Saul Lieberman, *Greek in Jewish Palestine* (New York: Jewish Theological Seminary of America, 1942); *Hellenism in Jewish Palestine* (New York: Jewish Theological Seminary of America, 1950).

[32]In the context of Torah knowledge, I am aware of no tradition holding that knowing a halakhic conclusion requires understanding the reasoning leading up to that conclusion. Therefore, I have limited the discussion to the philosophical literature.

[33]The issue is a complicated one in regard to both Maimonides and Saadya. Saadya, in his introduction to *Emunot ve-De'ot*, proposes four

The issue of hard epistemic autonomy as a sufficient condition for knowledge is joined in both the philosophical and the halakhic contexts. In the philosophical (and scientific) context it amounts to what is perhaps the central issue of Jewish philosophy: what happens if I am convinced that some (or all) Jewish teachings are false?[34] In Maimonides' *Letter on Astrology* we saw that Maimonides

---

roots of knowledge, one of them being the root of reliable tradition (ed. Kapah, 14), a position he argues for in chap. 3 (130–31). Nevertheless, in numerous instances he suggests that speculative demonstration produces a "superior" form. For example, he calls knowledge derived from demonstration "actual," as against what is taught via the prophets (24). Even more striking, in connection with the sufficiency condition formulation, he seems to maintain that if no fallacy can be found in an argument put forward by "someone who is not a member of our people," then "it is clear truth," which even Jews must accept (22–23).

With regard to Maimonides, the issue is similarly complicated. At the beginning of his *Letter on Astrology*, he maintains that it is reasonable to accept as trustworthy that which is received "from the prophets or from the righteous." Nevertheless, in the *Guide* (1:50) he seems to suggest that the only true knowledge of God derives from speculative reasoning. This is suggested as well by the famous palace metaphor in the *Guide* (3:51), according to which only men of speculation can enter God's palace. In connection with the sufficiency condition formulation, in 2:25 Maimonides asserts, "That the deity is not a body has been demonstrated; from this it follows necessarily that everything that in its external meaning disagrees with this demonstration must be interpreted figuratively." In this famous chapter regarding the creation of the world, the Straussian debate is fully joined. For (early, but classic) discussions of Saadya's theory of knowledge see I. Efros, "Saadia's Theory of Knowledge," and A. Heschel, "The Quest For Certainty in Saadya's Philosophy," both published in *Jewish Quarterly Review* (1943). For a comparison of Saadya with other medieval philosophers, see Wolfson's early article, "The Double Faith Theory," reprinted in *Studies in the History and Philosophy of Religion*, ed, I. Twersky and G. Williams, vol. 1 (Cambridge: Harvard University Press, 1973).

[34]For a summary of medieval attitudes toward rabbinic *aggadah* and science see M. Saperstein, *Decoding the Rabbis* (Cambridge: Harvard University Press, 1973), chap. 1.

was ready to reject at least certain traditional teachings on the basis of rational, scientific demonstration.[35] In many respects, the entire history of medieval philosophy, Jewish or otherwise, revolves around the question of the sufficiency of human reasoning against the background of tradition. It seems fair to say, however, that a limited number of medieval Jewish rationalists may have been willing to go quite far in according sufficiency to human reasoning;[36] it is altogether unclear, however, how many, if any at all, would have been willing to accord it total sufficiency, as hard epistemic autonomy requires. To use Wolfson's phrase, they were all engaged in "scriptural philosophy," and scriptural philosophy of its very essence pays attention to Scripture.[37]

---

[35]Whether Maimonides would reject more central Jewish teachings, such as the creation of the world, indeed whether he actually did reject certain central teachings on the basis of philosophical reasoning, hinges on the extent to which one adopts a Straussian reading of the Maimonidean oeuvre, an issue extensively debated in the scholarly literature on the subject, and one we cannot possibly even begin to summarize here.

[36]Especially relevant here is the debate in late medieval Jewish philosophy concerning what has been called "inadvertant heresy": Is someone a heretic if he denies what I believe to be true of Judaism, or affirms what I believe to be false of Judaism, in both cases inadvertently (i.e., he does not intend to rebel, but after careful reflection sincerely believes himself to be correct)? Shimon b. Zemah Duran maintains that he is not a heretic, a view that borders on, but does not quite embrace, according full sufficiency to human reasoning (the person in question is still a heretic). Menahem Kelner, in his *Dogma in Medieval Jewish Thought* (Oxford: Oxford University Press, 1986), traces this view back to R. Abraham ben David of Posquieres (twelfth century), notes Joseph Albo's ambivalent stance toward it, and argues that Hasdai Crescas may have affirmed the same view (both fifteenth century). Professor Norbert Samuelson has suggested to me that Crescas's view that belief cannot be commanded may also suggest the sufficiency of human reasoning. I am unsure if this is so, however.

[37]Cf. I. Twersky, *Introduction to the Mishneh Torah* (New Haven: Yale University Press, 1980), 500 n. 373. It should be noted that an influential trend within contemporary philosophy, especially as articulated by such

In the halakhic context (or any case of Torah knowledge, aggadic or purely theoretical) the issue is whether I may be said to know as true a conclusion arrived at on the basis of pure reasoning even if that conclusion is contradicted by traditional authority. The epistemic question is of course different from the nomic, where the conclusion has no normative consequences but is purely theoretical, such as the kind of analyses characteristic of many contemporary *yeshivot,* or where the halakhic conclusion has no practical ramifications. Can I be said to know something about the Torah which God Himself, or which traditional Torah authority, denies?

While the answer to this question surely depends upon what counts as "traditional Torah authority," it would be difficult to accept unconditionally sufficient hard epistemic authority. The oven-of-Akhnai debate shows that, remarkably enough, it does indeed seem possible to know something about the Torah which God Himself, so to speak, denies. This is surely a powerful endorsement of sufficient human epistemic autonomy vis-à-vis God. Nevertheless, this does not entail unconditional affirmation of the thesis in question, since autonomy from God is not the same as autonomy from the standards of halakhic procedures and reasoning, as I noted earlier in regard to hard nomic autonomy. Rabbi Joshua's point is precisely that those procedures must be followed, in his case that majority rules. It therefore seems altogether likely that, notwithstanding the oven-of-Akhnai dispute and the wide-

---

philosophers as W. V. O. Quine, W. Sellars, R. Kuhn, N. Goodman, and others, casts some doubt on the total sufficiency of human reasoning and scientific discovery to get at the truth. See, for example, Richard Rorty, *Philosophy and the Mirror of Nature* (Princeton: Princeton University Press, 1979). In considering the question of epistemic authority, R. T. DeGeorge argues that it is reasonable under certain circumstances to rely on authorities, much as Saadya argued in *Emunot ve-De'ot* (Kapan ed., 130–31). See his article, "Epistemic Authority," in *Authority: A Philosophical Analysis,* ed. R. B. Harris (Birmingham, AL: Alabama University Press, 1976), 76–93.

ranging literature generated over the centuries reflecting "autono-mous" halakhic *pesak*, there are some constraints upon what would count as legitimate legal procedures and reasoning, and those constraints are themselves rooted in traditional authority.[38]

But what if I follow those standards rigorously? Can I then be said to know a halakhic conclusion even where it contradicts the conclusion of traditional authority? Although this question surely needs further exploration, on the basis of the literature cited above it is my hunch that the answer is probably "Yes."[39]

In summary, I argued above that while there is evidence for considerable practical hard nomic autonomy in the technical, halakhic context, there is no evidence for a broad theoretical affirmation of the concept itself. With respect to hard epistemic autonomy, there is some evidence that, at least in its necessary condition formulation, it is embraced by one and perhaps more influential medieval Jewish rationalists. Hard epistemic autonomy in its sufficient condition formulation is probably also accepted in some quarters, although only in the purely theoretical halakhic context, and in the writings of one late medieval philosopher.[40]

Haeretic Autonomy

Finally, we must consider the issue of hard autonomy in its haeretic formulation. Hard haeretic autonomy as a necessary condition holds that no choice has moral or religious value unless it is autonomously made.[41] If I choose to enroll in medical school because that is what my parents always expected me to do, and I

---

[38]See nn. 27 and 28 above.

[39]See Joseph B. Soloveitchik, *Halakhic Man*, trans. Lawrence Kaplan (Philadelphia: Jewish Publication Society, 1983), 78–82.

[40]See n. 36.

[41]As I see it, the claim that a choice not autonomously made isn't even a real choice relates more to traditional philosophical (and halakhic) questions regarding freedom of the will (in the halakhic context, inten-tionality) than it does to the question of autonomy.

never really thought through the question of whether it was
something that I really wanted to do, or should do, then my
decision to enroll in medical school, while perhaps "technically" a
decision that I made (no one forced me), has no value as a decision.
Conversely, any decision I do make autonomously has full value as
a decision—even if it turns out to have been a wrong or counterproductive one—since it was made autonomously. This of course is
the sufficiency formulation of the hard haeretic autonomy principle. Both of these positions are closely associated with the existen-
tial schools of thought.

To the best of my knowledge, the traditional sources address
the question of choice only in a religious context: choices which
have no direct bearing on the religious life are simply not addressed.
Insofar as a choice is made in a religious context, I know of no
influential tradition which denies the rabbinic dictum *mi-tokh she-lo
lishma ba lishma*[42] (by performing [a *mitzvah*] not for its own sake,
one will be led to performing it for its own sake). While this saying
is not addressed explicitly to the realm of choice, it seems to me that
its inner logic would require that it be applied to precisely this
realm. Performance of a *mitzvah* is regarded by the rabbis as a good,
even if performed for other than the right reasons: the Torah
explicitly commanded performance; it did not stipulate that a
necessary condition for minimal performance is the right rationale.
As we shall see, there can be little doubt that the right rationale
enhances, perhaps immeasurably, the performance; nevertheless,
provided that the person intends to perform a given act (e.g., he is
not asleep when he shakes the *lulav*), a good is achieved. A decision
to perform a *mitzvah* has value as a means to the end of performance, even if that decision was not arrived at autonomously.
According to this argument, with respect to doing what is right,
hard haeretic autonomy as a necessary condition for a decision to
have value would not be consistent with the Jewish tradition. In the

---

[42]*Nazir* 23b and elsewhere.

case of a choice that does not involve doing what is right, I am unaware of any relevant evidence internal to Judaism.

The principle of hard haeretic autonomy formulated as a sufficient condition would appear to follow a similar argument, with which many existentialists might even agree. If the decision leads one to do wrong, then it seems altogether likely that the rabbis would regard it, despite its having been arrived at autonomously, as bearing a preponderance of negative value—for doing wrong is inherently bad, even if the motive is good.[43]

In sum, we must tentatively conclude that in a religious context the principle of hard hearetic autonomy is inconsistent with classical Jewish teachings; in a religious-neutral context it could well be consistent, since there is no internal evidence one way or the other.

---

[43]Cf. the rabbinic saying, *hirhurei aveirah kashim me-aveirah* (thinking about doing wrong is worse than doing it) (*Yoma* 29a). Note Maimonides' interesting explanation of this assertion (*Guide* 3:8). The concept of *aveirah le-shma*—performing a sin for a good reason—is relevant here (see *Nazir* 23b), but (1) it seems not to have had a profound impact on normative rabbinic Judaism, and (2) it is far from clear that any autonomous action would by virtue of its autonomy alone satisfy the *le-shma* condition. In any case, this concept merits a detailed study in its own right. Note also the comment of *Sifre* (Deuteronomy 26:5, 301) on the verse *Arami oved ami*, which asserts that since Laban intended to do evil, it is as if he did it. However, Rashi in his *Commentary*, ad loc., appears to distinguish between a Jew and non-Jew in this regard.

Where a choice to do the right thing is autonomously made, but only because the chooser believes it to be right, exclusive of God (whose existence he denies) and His commands, the question is somewhat more complicated. This issue is joined in the context of Maimonides' *Mishneh Torah* (*Melakhim* 8:11), where he discusses the noachites. For the first in a long series of discussions of this subject, see Stephen Schwartzchild's now classic essay, "Do the Noachites Have to Believe in Revelation?" *Jewish Quarterly Review* 52 and 53 (1962).

In sum, our review of the evidence for *hard* autonomy in Judaism appears to have yielded decidedly mixed results. This of course is not surprising given the central role that authority must play in a religion grounded in revelation. The range of arguments external to Judaism, which I summarized earlier and which call into question the value of autonomy, have, it seems to me, made their mark in Judaism. Perhaps the tradition did not wholeheartedly embrace autonomy because it *should not* have wholeheartedly embraced it. Hard autonomy in most of its manifestations runs up against perfectly sound external reasons for questioning its validity.

SOFT AUTONOMY

In the case of *soft* autonomy, however, the situation is altogether different. Some form of authority is affirmed, and hence these external arguments against autonomy lose their sting. Moreover, and especially important, the internal illustrative texts cited earlier in this paper speak far more clearly. The principle of soft autonomy holds that personal autonomy is an important value, but that it is neither necessary nor sufficient in itself. A law is binding whether or not it is autonomously imposed; a belief may be knowledge even if the holder didn't find it out for himself; a choice may have value, even if it wasn't made authentically. Nevertheless, if I obey a law *also* because I deeply believe it is right, then my obedience has far greater value; if I believe something because I figured it out myself, then my belief is even more certainly held, is *mine* in a way that it wasn't before; if I choose to do something because, after much reflection, that is what my most essential self wants to do, then that choice has far greater value. Soft autonomy, properly speaking, is always a property of the state of mind or behavior of the agent (and not, for example, of the law itself), and it makes the value of his behavior or state of mind partially (but not entirely) dependent upon the extent to which autonomy is exercised in any of the three spheres we have discussed here. The distinction between the necessary and sufficient condition formulations, so important for understanding hard autonomy, loses much of its relevance in the case of soft autonomy.

Let us return briefly to the illustrative sources cited at the beginning of this chapter. That Abraham challenged God with a moral claim exemplifies all three forms of soft autonomy. Abraham reasoned independently that God ought not to kill every Sodomite, and he chose to challenge God and His decree on that basis, presumably out of the deepest of his convictions. Nevertheless, in the end, he abided by God's will. There is thus evidence for at least some forms of soft autonomy, and perhaps even all, but not for hard autonomy. The oven-of-Akhnai dispute, as noted above, shows the great value attached to independent halakhic reasoning, and to the sufficiency of human halakhic reasoning vis-à-vis God. It does not show, however, that human reasoning is sufficient if the rules of halakhic reasoning are not followed, nor does it show that independent halakhic reasoning may actually be followed contrary to traditional authority. The medieval rationalistic texts discussed above do show, for at least one Jewish philosopher, and perhaps more, that hard epistemic autonomy in a philosophic context is necessary for knowledge of God.

What of the necessity for the self-imposition of law (hard nomic autonomy)? While we argued earlier that requiring self-imposition is inconsistent with halakhic Judaism, the *value* of imposing the law on oneself can indeed be demonstrated within some strands of traditional Judaism. The entire medieval (and subsequent) rationalistic enterprise of *taamei ha-mitzvot*, articulating reasons for the *mitzvot*, is an attempt to ground *mitzvot* in canons of rationality, and surely strongly suggests the importance of nomic self-imposition. The Jew who understands the reasons for the *mitzvot* does them because he understands them to be inherently right; in so doing he makes God's wisdom his own. Indeed, Maimonides urged that the highest stage of wisdom is that "which teaches us to demonstrate the opinion of the Torah."[44] Contemplating God's commandments leads ultimately to knowledge of God Himself.[45] On this view it can even be argued that God's intention in issuing norms is precisely that the Jew come to internalize those norms as if they are his own. Only by appropriating God's commands, by absorbing their inherent wisdom and value and by following them because of these qualities (in addition to doing them because God so commanded), has the Jew fully satisfied God's will.[46] This, of course, is the spiritualizing quality of the rationalistic enterprise, one which has certain latent antinomian tendencies built into it, but which was adopted by the rationalists nonetheless.[47] What Isadore Twersky calls the spiritualist critique of "halakho-centrism"[48] — rationalist, mystical, or otherwise — has during its long history built within it to one degree or another a quest for the inner meaning of the *mitzvot* rather than their rote, legalistic performance. The quest for inner meaning in all these traditions may be seen in part as an attempt to assimilate and appropriate what lies behind the *mitzvah* into the will and mind of the Jew, what in our terms amounts to a search for realizing the values expressed in haeretic autonomy.[49]

---

[44]*Guide* 3:54.

[45]*Sefer ha-Mitzvot*, positive 3.

[46]See my article, "The Principle of Autonomy," 432–33, where I develop this idea more fully.

[47]See, among other sources, Isadore Twersky, *Introduction to the Mishneh Torah* (New Haven: Yale University Press, 1980), 393–96; and Yosef Dan, *Sifrut ha-Musar ve-ha-Derush* (Jerusalem: Keter, 1975), especially chap. 3.

[48]Isadore Twersky, "Religion and Law," in *Religion in a Religious Age*, ed. S. Goitein (Cambridge: Association for Jewish Studies, 1974).

[49]*Shabbat* 88a, where the Talmud notes approvingly that during Purim the Jews accepted the Torah willingly, unlike at Sinai, where according to one tradition the Torah was accepted under duress, may suggest that according to this *aggadah* there is value in the autonomous imposition of the law. I am grateful to Dr. Norman Lamm for this point.

But is this really possible? Can one really freely impose upon oneself laws that were in fact already imposed from without? This, of course, is a critical question; if answered in the negative, soft nomic autonomy becomes impossible to sustain. My intuition—and I have no more to go on here than intuition—leads me to believe that it is indeed possible, that one can freely assimilate laws already imposed from without, that one can become so convinced of their power and rightness that one comes to believe them quite independently of their original source. If so, then at least within the tradition we are exploring in this paper, a strong case can be made for soft autonomy in all its manifestations. Contrary to our initial negative intuitions about the possibility of autonomy within Judaism, soft personal autonomy is indeed affirmed by one important Jewish tradition.

THEOLOGICAL REFLECTIONS ABOUT THE VALUE OF AUTONOMY

Two tasks remain. First, I shall consider briefly the kind of theological model which can best support the sort of affirmation of personal autonomy proposed here. Second, I shall consider once again a central objection to the role of personal autonomy in Judaism.[50]

---

[50]See also the interesting article by Walter Wurzburger, "Covenantal Imperatives," in *Samuel K. Mirsky Memorial Volume*, ed. G. Appel, in which he suggests a positive role for conscience and personal autonomy based upon what he calls "covenantal imperatives," the message of God's presence before it becomes concretized into law.

See also David Hartman, A *Living Covenant*. Hartman devotes much of this recent book to arguing the case for personal autonomy in Judaism. He bases his thesis upon the husband–wife model of the covenant between God and the Jewish people, according to which God, the covenantal lover of the Jewish people, wants His beloved to achieve the fullest possible dignity and autonomy. Hartman's theological program is a rich one;

The theological issue is at least partly addressed by R. Joseph B. Soloveitchik, one of this century's most important Orthodox Jewish thinkers. R. Soloveitchik forcefully projects the role of personal autonomy in the halakhic life, although clearly distinguishing the autonomy possible within halakhic Judaism from Kantian autonomy (what we would call hard nomic autonomy in its necessary condition formulation).[51] The autonomy R. Soloveitchik projects is that of the halakhist who creatively and freely fashions his own image of the world via halakhic interpretation, and who then assimilates the norms of this world into his own self and soul. "The essence of the Torah," says R. Soloveitchik, "is intellectual creativity."[52] Halakhic man in this respect is like a great theoretical physicist who creates a world of abstract theories to account for the universe. The intellectual creativity of halakhic man lies in his capacity to create abstract halakhic models. Unlike the models of the theoretical physicist, however, these halakhic models have normative implications, implications for ordering and transforming the world. Since halakhic man has himself created a model for those very norms, his identification with them is complete.

---

nevertheless, he does not distinguish between the various forms of autonomy, and therefore takes evidence for soft autonomy to be evidence for hard autonomy, and evidence for hard epistemic autonomy to be evidence for hard nomic autonomy. Moreover, his exclusive reliance upon the husband–wife model of the covenant excludes certain important dimensions of the relationship between the Jew and God that have been long regarded as at least partially constitutive of that relationship. See my article,"David Hartman" *Contemporary Jewish Thinkers* (Washington, DC: B'nai B'rith, 1992).

[51]Soloveitchik, *Halakhic Man*, 153 n. 80: "The freedom of halakhic man refers not to the creation of the law itself . . . but to the realization of the norm in the concrete world."

[52]Soloveitchik, *Halakhic Man*, 82. See, generally, 78–82, and also pt. 2 for a fuller description of the role of creativity in Judaism, particularly self-creativity.

> We have a blending of the obligation with self-consciousness
> . . . a union of an outside command with the inner will and
> conscience of man. . . . We do not have here a directive that
> imposes upon man obligations against which he rebels, but
> delightful commandments which his soul passionately desires.
> When halakhic man comes to the real world he has already
> created his ideal a priori image which shines with the radiance
> of the norm. . . . And this ideal world is his very own, his own
> possession; he is free to create in it, to arrive at new insights, to
> improve and perfect. . . . Therefore he is free and independent
> in his normative understanding.[53]

This model of (soft nomic, haeretic, and possibly hard epistemic)
personal autonomy is embedded in R. Soloveitchik's rich portrait of
halakhic man. While powerful in its own right, its applicability to
nonhalakhic scholars is somewhat limited. Very few halakhic Jews,
even scholars, can approach the sort of wide-ranging abstract
talmudic analysis necessary to embody the vast freedom and creativity R. Soloveitchik portrays. Hence, very few Jews will have the
capacity to identify with the halakhic norms in the way R. Soloveitchik describes. Although R. Soloveitchik's model is an important one, it cannot (and almost certainly wasn't intended to)
provide an inclusive theological basis for personal autonomy in
Judaism.[54]

---

[53]Soloveitchik, *Halakhic Man*, 65–66.

[54]In R. Soloveitchik, "Lonely Man of Faith," *Tradition* 7 (1964–1965),
scientific and technological achievement are theologically affirmed. A
careful reading of the text will show, however, that the Adam I/Adam II
distinction provides no grounds for a religious affirmation of nomic and
haeretic autonomy; at most, epistemic autonomy is affirmed. Moreover,
Adam II submits his "self" in sacrifice to the covenantal community, a
religious impulse quite distant from autonomy. I have, therefore, concen-
trated here on *Halakhic Man*. A fuller treatment of the subject would
explore in some detail the "Lonely Man of Faith" essay, as well as several
others. See my "Joseph B. Soloveitchik: Lonely Man of Faith" (with David

At this point I should like to sketch out a different theological model, one which would provide this sort of inclusive theological basis for the role of personal autonomy in Jewish life, and which is designed to be helpful to us later as well, when we consider the role of *halakhah* in light of the kind of affirmation of soft personal autonomy I have argued for.[55] This approach, which is a kind of theistic humanism, is grounded in the doctrine of *imago dei*. According to this doctrine, human beings were created in the image of God, from which it follows that since God is all good, all human characteristics must be essentially good as well. This is, of course, not to say that people cannot do evil, since they obviously do. Rather, each human characteristic, while *essentially* good, has the capacity to degenerate into evil if not given proper attention.[56] Samuel, in this famous *midrash*, appears to have taken a similar view:

> And God saw everything that He had made, and behold it was very good [Genesis 1:31]. R. Nahman said in the name of Samuel: Behold it is very good'—that is the *yetzer ha-ra* (will to

---

Singer), *Modern Judaism* (1982), for a lengthy discussion of the overall philosophical views of R. Soloveitchik.

[55]See my "Attitudes Towards Pleasure in the Jewish Tradition: A Typological Proposal," in *Reverence, Righteousness, and Rahamanut: Essays in Honor of Rabbi Dr. Leo Jung* (Northvale, NJ: Jason Aronson, 1992), in which I spell out this approach in slightly greater detail. Given space constraints, I am unable here to locate this theological sketch within the classic sources, or within any theological traditions. It should be apparent, however, that my approach owes a great deal to the thought of Samson Raphael Hirsch, the nineteenth-century neo-Orthodox German thinker and communal leader. For a discussion of this issue, and for a number of important references to Hirsch's writings, see I. Grunfeld's introduction to *Horeb*, vol. 1 (London: Soncino, 1961), lxxxi–lxxxiv and lxxxix–xcvii.

[56]This distinction, of course, requires far more elaboration than is possible here.

evil). But is the *yetzer ha-ra* good? That is astonishing! Yet were it not for the *yetzer ha-ra* man would not build homes, or take wives, or propagate, or engage in business.[57]

Samuel thus regards even the *yetzer ha-ra* as good. Presumably, this is not to say that all human characteristics are *equally* good, but only that they are all inherently good. One way of ranking the goodness of human characteristics may be the extent to which they match the basic description of God's attributes as expressed in the thirteen *middot*. We shall soon consider another, perhaps more important way.

In any case, if all human characteristics are essentially good, it further stands to reason that to express and develop those characteristics is inherently good as well, since in doing so one is expressing and developing that which is essentially Godlike. Thus, for example, it is inherently good to refine and express human capacities for art, music, or just plain thinking, and they should therefore be pursued for their own sake, and not only as a means to a higher spiritual end.[58]

It is at precisely this juncture that theistic humanism parts company with secular humanism. To claim that expressing human qualities is a good is not to claim that it is an unqualified good; put differently, to say that expressing human qualities is an end in itself is not to say that it is *only* an end in itself and not also a means to some higher end. For the theist, only God can be an end in Himself. Anything else is idolatry. If a source of value existed apart from God, then God's value would be partially dependent upon that source. This, of course, is inconsistent with traditional theism: at the very heart of the classical monotheistic belief in God is the belief that only He can be a source of value. Therefore, to claim that

---

[57]Genesis *Rabbah* 9:9.

[58]In my paper, "Attitudes Towards Pleasure," I suggest that this thesis can be extended to account for what I call there the liberal attitude towards bodily pleasure, which one finds in certain rabbinic and medieval sources.

developing the human capacity to think is an end in itself cannot be to claim that it is only an end, that its value is self-sufficient. Rather, the theistic humanist would maintain that it must *also* be pursued as a means to the highest of goods, to that which is an end in itself, namely, to God.

For the theistic humanist, therefore, while it is inherently good to express and develop human capacities, this is only one good among many subordinate to the highest good whereby all other goods in life are measured and ordered. To the extent that the pursuit of lower order goods impinges upon the pursuit of God, then the value of pursuing that lower order good is diminished, even nullified. Thus, although the capacity to be aggressive is a human trait and therefore good—God Himself is described in Exodus 15:3 as a "man of war"—nevertheless, like all other human characteristics its expression is not an unqualified good, that is, it is not good in all contexts. Indeed, in most instances the expression of aggressiveness would on balance be wrong, precisely because in most instances, motivated by selfishness, egoism, and the like, it subverts the higher order pursuit of God.

We can now see how the doctrine of *imago dei* provides a theological model that affirms the value of personal autonomy, while situating it within the overall constellation of Jewish values. We have been considering the question of personal autonomy largely within a rationalist framework. Within that framework, human reason is that human characteristic which most mirrors God. All forms of autonomy express human reasoning, the thinking through on one's own how one should behave and what kind of life one should lead. Moreover, God is, after all, the very paradigm of the autonomous being. For both these reasons, then, autonomy in its various forms would surely be a high-ranking good. Nevertheless, it is not only an end in itself; it must also be pursued as a means to some higher end, an end intimately related to God and defined by Him in His Torah. In our terms this point accounts for the different approaches we found in the sources between hard and soft autonomy. In order to explore this more fully, however, we need to return to what is perhaps the strongest internal argument against the value of personal autonomy in halakhic Judaism.

HALAKHAH, PERSONAL AUTONOMY, AND PLURALISM

At the very outset of this chapter I pointed out that the halakhic system seems to govern every detail of Jewish behavior, down to the order in which one cuts one's fingernails. Isn't this abstract philosophical discussion of the value of autonomy, then, utterly belied by the reality of the halakhic life? Why is the *halakhah* so all-embracing, and reliance on halakhic authorities so extensive, if autonomy is really valuable?

A number of points need to be made in response. First, it is simply mistaken to construe *halakhah* to be as all-embracing as this argument would have it appear. After all, what percentage of the typical Jew's time is actually spent praying, studying Torah, and eating *matzah* on Passover? The fact is that most of one's waking hours are spent at work, or with one's family. Certainly these situations call for obedience to appropriate standards of behavior: it is wrong to cheat at work, for example, or hurt a spouse's feelings. Nevertheless, for great stretches of the day each individual must decide for himself how he will work, with what commitment, how warm he will be toward his children, how much time he will spend working for good causes, and so on. There is thus far more freedom than one might at first suspect.

Related to this point is another: there is in fact a whole range of Jewish categories that are normative but nonhalakhic, and which serve to orient the way in which each Jew will decide on his own to fill in these stretches of time. These categories include such values as *lifnim mi-shurat ha-din* (acting within the line of the law), *kedoshim teheyu* (be sacred), *hasidut* (piety), and so on.[59] I have suggested

---

[59]For an extensive listing and detailed discussion of these categories, and this issue generally, from within a classical perspective, see *Shaarei*

elsewhere that *lifnim mi-shurat ha-din*, which taken loosely has extremely broad ramifications, is best construed as an extrahalakhic category, and represents what might be called a Jewish ethic of virtue as against a Jewish ethic of action. That is, *halakhah* governs behavior or action. But God directs His norms not only to the things Jews do, but to the kind of person He wants each Jew to be, the kinds of virtues he expects each Jew to embody. There are, to paraphrase Bahya ibn Pakuda, obligations of the limbs and obligations of the heart. Both kinds of obligations are *mitzvot*, but only quantifiable obligations of the body – of behavior – are, properly speaking, *halakhah*. The rest reflect God's expectations about the kind of human beings He wants us to be. Are we generous or stingy, temperamental or easygoing, diligent or lazy? While the *halakhah* addresses certain behaviors that may reflect these qualities (e.g., giving a specified percentage of one's income to charity), God also addresses each Jew as a human being and, via the categories of *lifnim mi-shurat ha-din* and others like them, commands the Jew to embody certain virtues, virtues which will naturally flow over into certain forms of behavior. Nevertheless, it is the virtues rather than the behaviors which are the subject of God's norm. How each individual embodies those norms, to what extent, in what context and in what ways, is necessarily left up to each individual to decide. The normative life is not coextensive with the halakhic life, and that huge extrahalakhic side of life is ample domain for the serious expression of personal autonomy.[60]

It should also be noted that the Jewish people, and hence the

---

Talmud Torah, 55–91. An analysis of this subject is extremely important, and quite relevant to this undertaking, but unfortunately impossible in this chapter. For a discussion of an aspect of this problem, see my article, "Jewish Ethics," in the *Encyclopedia of Ethics.*

[60]See my article, "Jewish Ethics." This is, of course, no more than a summary of a complicated subject. The approach I take here is different from the one taken by Aaron Lichtenstein in his "Is There an Ethic Independent of Halakha?" reprinted in *Contemporary Jewish Ethics*, ed. Kellner.

halakhah they live by, has a history. The halakhic life of the Israelite in the desert was different from the halakhic life of the Jew of Samuel's time, which in turn was quite different from the halakhic life of the Jew living in fifth-century Babylonia, and so on. Changing circumstances gave rise to new halakhic needs, which became embodied in the form of *takkanot*, *gezerot*, halakhically sanctioned *humrot*, and other mechanisms. Thus was *halakhah* extended and further quantified. A good example of this quantification phenomenon is the first *mishnah* in *Pe'ah*, which teaches that the obligation to study Torah but does not prescribe the amount of time one should devote to it. By the Middle Ages, however, Maimonides could write that each Jew should study Torah nine hours a day.[61] The pressure to quantify is a persistent one in *halakhah* for a variety of context-specific as well as general reasons. One of the most important of these general reasons is the ever-growing concern on the part of halakhists that each new generation is not quite up to the achievements of the earlier one. It is worth pointing out, therefore, that *halakhah* in its earlier and less, so-to-speak, worried form might have allowed for even more autonomy than the *halakhah* does as it presents itself today. Insurance policies necessarily constrain.

A further point: since, as we have argued, soft personal autonomy is indeed affirmed by at least one important Jewish tradition, it would surely be of great value to be able to make halakhic decisions on one's own, without depending upon others, and with the creativity and autonomy so eloquently described by R. Soloveitchik. Of course, where the necessary skills are not achieved, it is certainly justifiable to have recourse to a halakhic expert, and to abide by his halakhic opinion, in much the same way that it is justifiable to have recourse to expert medical opinion when in need of medical care. Still, to the extent that halakhic Jews are unable to arrive at their own halakhic decisions, they fail to fully realize the value of personal autonomy (not to mention Torah study).

---

[61]*Mishneh Torah, Talmud Torah* 1:14.

Finally, and here we come to the very heart of the matter, historical Judaism presents not a single, unitary conception of the good, but multiple conceptions of the good. The good for some sacred Jewish figures has been intellectual knowledge of God; for others it has been ecstatic union with Him. For some the good has been making life better for fellow human beings; for others it has been furthering Jewish national aspirations. All of these conceptions of the good—and there are more to add to the list—have been embodied in Jewish hagiography by varying saintly figures, and all have been fervently endorsed by classical Jewish sources. Abraham, Isaac, and Jacob are taken by the rabbinic tradition to embody the lives of loving-kindness, service to God, and intellectual knowledge of His Torah, respectively. The mystical ecstasy sought by such figures as Abulafia is quite different from the sober Torah knowledge sought by Rashi, the philosophic knowledge sought by Maimonides, or the national salvation sought by Jepthah.

Each of these figures as enshrined in the tradition clearly maintained a different conception of the good, and from these widely varying conceptions of the good there flowed widely varying patterns of life. Rabbi Simon Bar Yohai was so intensely involved in Torah study that he was under no obligation to pray.[62] On the other hand, the "early pietists" described in the *baraita* prayed nine hours a day; their Torah knowledge was miraculously preserved.[63] Surely the lives of the heroes of the *Book of Judges* (whatever faults they had, they were portrayed in the Bible as largely heroic figures) were quite different from the lives of Rashi, the Tosafists, and the Gaon of Vilna. Different conceptions of the good thus yield widely divergent life-plans, and halakhic Judaism does not mandate any one of them.

It should be stressed that this is not simply a function of historical change, in which for historical reasons new models gain ascendancy and eclipse older ones. While this surely occurred, it is

---

[62]*Shabbat* 11a.
[63]*Berakhot* 32b.

likely that within each major historical period itself multiple models existed, if not always in practice, then at least in theory. The following *derash* suggests as much, at least for the rabbinic period:

> "Like goats on the grass": Just like these goats go down on the grass and bring it up, some [grass] is green, other grass is red, some is black and some is white. So it is with the words of the Torah. There are those who have great analytic capacities; those who possess wide knowledge; those who are righteous; those who are pious; [and] those who are proper. . . .[64]

The author of this statement did not evaluate the relative merits of these ways of leading a Jewish life (however they are to be interpreted). Each was equally affirmed as deriving from the Torah.[65]

It might be objected here that the pluralistic model I have proposed, which affirms the possibility of multiple legitimate Jewish conceptions of the good, would probably be denied by many advocates of these individual conceptions themselves. For example, Maimonides explicitly argues against what we today might call a Litvak conception of the good, according to which knowledge of (nonphilosophical) Torah is the highest of Jewish goods; similarly, advocates of the Litvak conception of the good have argued vigorously against the Maimonidean conception. According to the thesis advocated here, is there no truth of the matter? Are they all equally good? If they aren't all equally good, how then does one argue in favor of one position while conceding the "legitimacy" of the others, particularly for the rationalist, who would be committed to some form of rational adjudication?[66]

These problems inhere in all pluralistic models, and it would be impossible in the context of this particular essay to analyze the matter fully. Nevertheless, several preliminary points are in order.

---

[64]*Sifre* to Deuteronomy 306.

[65]See *Shaarei Talmud Torah*, 63–64 n. 22, where other sources are cited reflecting the same idea.

[66]I am grateful to Professor David Shatz for raising these issues with me.

First, my argument here is primarily a historical one. The raw data of Jewish history unequivocally show that multiple conceptions of the good were embraced by Jewish figures whose centrality to Judaism has been endorsed by serious constituents of the Jewish normative tradition. My claim is that the *historically conscious* advocate of any of these positions would be forced by the weight of Jewish history to advocate his position nonexclusivistically. Certainly, many partisans of a particular conception of the good have been exclusivistic, but many of these partisans were not historically conscious in the modern sense, often because they lived in premodern times. Historical consciousness has forever altered the contours of Jewish thought.

Second, to concede that the Jewish tradition embraces multiple conceptions of the good is not to concede that these conceptions are all *equally* good. The contemporary Maimonidean would still argue that knowledge of God is superior to all other goods, but unless he wanted to write off such figures as Rashi, who was a model for millions of serious Jews, he would be forced to concede that knowledge of nonphilosophic Torah is sufficiently good to justify devoting one's life to its attainment, even if in so doing one forfeits the superior good, philosophical knowledge of God. The question, however, remains what theological or philosophical reasons could justify this apparently paradoxical position?

Oddly enough, it may well be that a theological framework provides sounder grounds for justifying a pluralistic but hierarchical stance than would a secular, nontheological framework. God, as recorded in sacred Jewish literature, revealed Himself in many guises throughout human history: lawgiver, warrior, lover of the Jewish people, source of wisdom, helper of the needy, and so on. In Aristotelian/Maimonidean terms, God exhibits multiple attributes of action. The obligation to imitate God, a linchpin of Jewish theology, is thus a complex matter. First, which aspect of God is most essentially Him such that we should devote most of our energies to emulating that aspect over the others? After all, we can't do everything equally well. This is an essentially theological question. Second, which aspect of God is it most appropriate for human beings in general, or for specific individuals in particular, to emulate? This turns on the answers to questions about human nature and society, and the personal characteristics of individual people, and is partially a theological question, and partially a social scientific one.

To argue for a particular conception of the good in the language of *imitatio dei* is at least in part to argue over what God essentially is, or to argue over what aspect of Him it is most appropriate for Jews generally, or for the chooser particularly, to emulate. Now there are surely grounds to advocate one particular view of what God most essentially is, or what it is most appropriate for the Jew to emulate, as the works of Jewish philosophers, kabbalists, or masters of Jewish ethics amply demonstrate. These may be theological and philosophical, or social scientific and psychological grounds; the argument may even be based upon personal religious experience. But whatever the grounds, in a theistic system criteria for evaluating conceptions of the good are clearly available.

However, to argue that God is essentially a saviour of the needy, for example, as opposed to a knower of truth, is not to deny that God is, in some sense, both. The same holds when we ask what it is most appropriate to emulate in God. In neither case do we deny that these alternatives are indeed God's attributes of action as recorded in the sacred texts of Judaism. Even though they may fail to capture what God essentially is, therefore, it would not be unreasonable to think that they are worthy of emulation, perhaps worthy of devoting one's life to their achievement. Whatever one's conception of the paramount divine attribute, God *also* is the others: God *is* a saviour of the needy, *and* a knower of wisdom, *and* a warrior. It turns out, then, that in a theological framework one can simultaneously affirm multiple conceptions of the good and provide grounds for arguing that one of these conceptions is superior to the rest, whether for the Jewish people generally or for the individual Jew.

I argued earlier that the doctrine of *imago dei* may serve to
ground a Jewish humanism. It seems to me that its sister doctrine,
imitatio dei, may serve to ground a sister thesis, that of a Jewish
hierarchical pluralism.

This is of course no more than the barest sketch of a response
to the paradoxes of pluralism, but one which for the purposes of this
chapter will have to suffice. To return to our central concern,
personal autonomy and Judaism, it is my contention that the role
and value of (soft) personal autonomy makes itself most powerfully
felt in the choice each individual makes of a personal conception of
the good. If historical Judaism affirms the possibility of different
conceptions of the good, then it is up to each individual Jew to
choose his own. He may choose intellectual achievement of varying
sorts, the *via contemplativa*; or he may choose the *via activa*, a life of
social action, devotion to family and friends or Jewish national
advancement; or he may choose a life of intense spirituality of
varying forms. This freely—indeed autonomously—chosen personal conception of the good will fashion his life until the end of his
days, because the life-plan he constructs will flow from the personal
conception of the good he has chosen.

Despite this vast freedom to shape one's life, however, autonomy is not unlimited, nor should it be, for all the reasons put
forward earlier in this chapter against an uncritical affirmation of
autonomy. Although Judaism affirms multiple conceptions of the
good, it also affirms the thesis that there is only one *highest* good.
While intellectual perfection or social service may be ends in
themselves, goods in their own right, they must also be pursued as
means to the highest end, and that highest end, that good of goods,
is of course God. Thus, for example, the pursuit of intellectual
perfection, while good in itself, is not wholly good unless it also has
the effect of yielding better knowledge of God or His Torah. If it has
the effect of *distancing* one from knowledge of God or His Torah,
then whatever inherent good it has is outweighed by the greater evil
of distance from God. Similarly, where the pursuit of autonomy,
while good in itself, results in beliefs, feelings, and actions that are

independent of God Himself, a kind of rebellion against Him, then autonomy's inherent good is outweighed by the greater evil of such results.

The theistic dimension thus provides an overarching conception of the highest good, which in turn orients and shapes each individual's personal conception of what can never be more than a penultimate good. It places all lower order goods, including autonomy, in proper perspective. It also grounds the great divide between the religious conception of personal choice, and that of contemporary secular liberalism and humanism, which tolerate multiple conceptions of the good, but which provide no means for ordering or shaping them. What is left for secular liberalism, then, is the realm of fractured moral discourse, with different conceptions of the good competing for social sanction, and with no means to adjudicate these differences.[67]

But what prevents each individual Jew from veering off on his own, severing the bond between his personal conception of the good and God? It is here, I would argue, that *halakhah* plays a decisive role. *Halakhah*, on the model I have been exploring here, serves three discrete and critical functions. First, it serves to prevent precisely this dissociation. We can sometimes get so passionately caught up in our pursuit of knowledge or our pursuit of social justice that we lose sight of the religious dimension to that pursuit. *Halakhah* reinforces the individual's link with God. As consuming as my work for the needy is, I must still pray in the morning. *Halakhah* thus sustains the theistic perspective on life.

Second, *halakhah* helps to rule out of bounds certain possible conceptions of the good. Not every conception of the good can be affirmed in a theistic context. Hedonism, for example, ethical egoism, or radical individualism, are ruled out of the Jewish constellation of goods by virtue of halakhic requirements for charity, Torah study, fasting, and so on.

Finally, and perhaps most important, *halakhah* serves to pre-

---

[67]See MacIntyre, *After Virtue*, especially his introduction and chap. 1.

vent the exclusion of certain goods by excessive preoccupation with others. One ought never to be so preoccupied with Torah study, for example, that one fails to attend to the needs of the starving. The image of the ivory-towered scholar insensitive to the needs of real people is unfortunately all too often justified. *Halakhah* thus legislates a set of minimum requirements for the complete Jewish life, preventing an obsession with one virtue from leading to the neglect of another.

The need for the halakhic system, in the end, reflects the theistic origin of Judaism, its conception of the highest of goods that orders all other goods. The thesis of hard autonomy in all its dimensions thus could never be reconciled with a theistic system, in which religious authority, via revelation and *halakhah*, provides the critical link between varying conceptions of the good and God Himself. Within the theological model I have proposed, it is thus entirely to be expected that hard autonomy runs into the kinds of difficulties we discussed earlier in some detail. Within this theological model, however, the good of soft personal autonomy is indeed affirmed. Each individual Jew may choose his own personal conception of the good, and he may choose among the myriad ways in which to carry out that conception throughout his life. Indeed, the thesis of soft personal autonomy affirms the value of making that choice, and of taking responsibility for its consequences.

6

Toward a Sociology of *Pesak*

Chaim I. Waxman

This chapter is entitled "Toward a Sociology of *Pesak*" for several reasons. One is to emphasize its tentative nature. Rather than definitive, it is intended to be suggestive, both in terms of the realm of the subject matter and any and all specific issues which the chapter raises.

Second, it is by no means exhaustive. Rather, although it points to a variety of areas and issues which might well belong in a

This chapter is a revision of a paper delivered at the Orthodox Forum, sponsored by Yeshiva University, which was held at The Jewish Center, New York City, September 10–11, 1989. The critical comments of the participants in that forum and those of Rabbi Emanuel Feldman, who chaired the session in which it was presented, as well as those of Rabbi Chaim Bronstein and Rabbi Ari Waxman on an earlier draft of the chapter, are greatly appreciated. A slightly different version of this chapter appeared in *Tradition* 25:3 (Spring 1991): 12–25.

sociology of *pesak*, it admits that there are many others that have not even been touched upon. Hopefully, this article will stimulate further deliberation which will lead to broader and deeper analyses of the entire area. Ideally, a sociology of *pesak* should include, in the first place, an analysis of the role of the social in *pesak*. This would comprehend the role of social conditions in the determination of *halakhah*; the social factors that influence who is viewed as the *posek*, in general and in particular; and an analysis of which segments in the community are likely to seek out *pesak* and from whom.

To some, the whole notion of a sociology of *pesak* is heretical. As Haym Soloveitchik suggests, "If law is conceived of, as religious law must be, as a revelation of the divine will, then any attempt to align that will with human wants, any attempt to have reality control rather than to be itself controlled by the divine norm, is an act of blasphemy and inconceivable to a God-fearing man."[1]

If not necessarily heretical, the notion of a sociology of *pesak* might at least be viewed as inherently untenable as a result of the very phrase being viewed as a contradiction in terms. As some see it, to speak of *pesak* is to speak of pure *halakhah*, which is rendered solely on the characteristics of the specific case involved. It is rendered by a *posek*, an expert in *halakhah*, on the basis of principles that are centuries old, in an almost scientific manner, and is impervious to either social forces or social patterns. The greater the knowledge of the *posek*, the more widely known and accepted will his *pesakim* be. It is as simple and as complex as that.

Such an understanding of *pesak* is probably widespread in what Helmreich calls "the world of the Yeshiva,"[2] but might also be

---

[1]Haym Soloveitchik, "Religious Law and Change: The Medieval Ashkenazic Example," *AJS Review* 12:2 (Fall 1987): 205.

[2]William B. Helmreich, *The World of the Yeshiva* (New York: Free Press, 1983). This is the "world" known as the *haredi*, "black-hat," "right-wing," or "ultra-Orthodox" community. Actually, Helmreich also includes Yeshiva University's Rabbi Isaac Elchanan Theological Seminary (RIETS) in his

inferred from the writings of certain "centrist" authorities as well. For example, it can readily be read into the writings of David Bleich, although he may well not subscribe to such a view. At least at first glance, Bleich appears to concur when he writes:

> The ability to formulate definitive psak is the product of highly specialized skills. It is in choosing between conflicting precedents and opinions that the consummate expertise of the decisor is apparent. The decisor . . . must carefully weigh not merely on the basis of sheer number but also on the relative stature of the scholars whose opinions are under consideration, and must at the same time assess the complexities and relative importance of any number of component factors.[3]

Despite the tendency, particularly within the right-wing Orthodox communities, for an almost reflex-action rejection of the role of social forces in *pesak*, the more carefully one considers the issue the more it is apparent that *posekim* are not simply computers and that, indeed, there are many social forces which enter into *pesak*, both in terms of specific rulings made for individual cases and in terms of who is recognized at any given time as a reputable *posek*. Nor is this an issue over which there is any implicit dispute between "right-wingers" and "modernists." A few examples from history should suffice to indicate the role of social forces and conditions in *pesak*.

Probably the most often cited example is that of the *prozbul*, instituted by Hillel lest Jews cease lending money to their fellow

---

analysis. However, RIETS is clearly peripheral to the world of the *yeshivah* and not considered to be part of that world by the overwhelming majority of its members. As he suggests, it "is viewed by many in the other major yeshivas as not being part of the community because it not only permits secular education but maintains a college on its campus that is a required part of study for all undergraduates" (p. 36).

[3]J. David Bleich, *Contemporary Halakhic Problems* (New York: Ktav and Yeshiva University Press, 1977), xvii.

Jews. However, within the context of this chapter, this is probably
also the least effective example because that case has been so
frequently abused and made to serve as part of the legitimation for
unacceptable reform.[4] Indeed, it might be suggested that one of the
strongest barriers to the development of a sociology of *pesak* is the
well-founded fear that the mere suggestion that social factors can
influence pesak may lend support to those who seek to have social
factors be the *determinants* of *pesak*.[5] It should, therefore, be stated
at the outset that no such argument is intended herein. Such an
argument is to be rejected not solely on ideological grounds; I would
argue that an empirical examination of the *pesakim* of the most
widely accepted *posekim* in this and every other generation would
indicate that it is simply not true that social factors alone determine
halakhah.[6] On the other hand, that same examination would
uncover numerous instances where social conditions affected *halakhah*. For example, the concept of *hefsed merubah* (great financial
loss) is the basis for lenient halakhic decisions, not only those
involving rabbinic prohibitions *(issurei de-rabbanan)* but, apparently, in several involving Torah prohibitions *(issurei de-oraita)*, as
well.[7] Although *hefsed merubah* alone is clearly not a valid basis for

---

[4]A case in point: Michael A. Meyer, in his comprehensive work,
Response to Modernity: A History of the Reform Movement in Judaism (New
York: Oxford University Press, 1988), begins with a discussion of the
precedents for reform and specifically cites the case of *prozbul* (p. 5). For a
broader discussion of Hillel's innovation, see the symposium, "Prozbul:
Was Hillel True to Tradition?" *S'vara* 2:2 (Winter 1991): 61–73.

[5]Such a stance is the basis of the argument of David E. Ostrich,
"Creativity in the Halachah," *Sh'ma* 17/339 (October 16, 1987): 147–48.

[6]Cf. Emanuel Feldman's response to Ostrich's assertions, "The Torah,
More God's Law than Ours," *Sh'ma*, ibid., 148–50.

[7]Cf. Eliezer Berkovits, *Ha-Halakhah: Kohah ve-tafkidah* (Jerusalem:
Mossad ha-Rav Kook, 1981), 64–74. Also see Jacob Katz, *The Sabbath
Gentile: The Socio-Economic and Halakhic Background of the Employment of
Gentiles on Jewish Sabbaths and Festivals* (Jerusalem: Zalman Shazar Center,
1983) (Hebrew).

determining *pesak,* it can influence halakhic decisions in that it can provide the necessary basis for adopting a minority halakhic position, one which otherwise would not be adopted.

But it was not only in the case of great economic loss that the *halakhah* took the social situation into account. Ephraim Urbach cites a number of the Tosafists who adopted rather lenient stances on matters dealing not only with the permissibility of engaging in commercial enterprises with Christians but also in dealing in those objects which would overtly contribute to religious worship in Christianity.[8]

Likewise, without going into all of the details about their application, there are also such principles as *eit laasot la-Shem, heferu Toratekha,* which allows the actual breaking of a Torah law in order to preserve the corpus, and *Ein gozrin gezeirah im ein rov ha-tzibbur yekholin laamod bo,* which dictates that an edict with which the majority of the community is not capable of complying cannot be pronounced. Although the latter pertains only to the enactment of an edict, not to its specific applicability once it has been enacted, both of the principles cited, as well as numerous others, clearly indicate that the social factor is, indeed, very important in *halakhah.*

---

[8]Ephraim E. Urbach, *Baalei ha-Tosafot: Toldoteihem, Hibbureihem, Shitatam,* 4th exp. ed. (Jerusalem: Bialik Institute, 5740), 1:350–52. Earlier, in his discussion of Ramban's having permitted the selling of clothing and other objects to non-Jews and even priests despite the possibility that they might be used in the service of Christian worship, Urbach starkly asserts that even though Ramban does derive the permission from talmudic discourses, "the conditions of the situation were those which forced upon him the derivations and distinctions" (p. 177). For a critique of Urbach's assertion, see Jacob Katz, *Halakhah and Kabbalah: Studies in the History of Jewish Religion, its Various Faces and Social Relevance* (Jerusalem: Magnes Press, 1986), 340–49 (Hebrew). Also see Soloveitchik, "Religious Law and Change," 207–21; Avraham Grossman, *The Early Sages of Ashkenaz: Their Lives, Leadership and Works (900–1096)* (Jerusalem: Magnes Press, 1981), 126–27 (Hebrew).

Nor is it only with reference to economic factors that the social plays a role in *pesak*. Haym Soloveitchik deals at length with the issues of suicide and the killing of one's children in the face of forced apostasy in the Ashkenazic community during the period of the Crusades. Although heretofore "one knows of no allowance for committing suicide to avoid forced conversion," the scholars of the Ashkenazic communities

> evolved, in the course of times, a doctrine of the permissibility of voluntary martyrdom, and even allowing suicide. They did this by scrounging all the canonized and semi-canonized literature for supportive tales and hortatory aggadah, all of dubious legal worth. But by massing them together, Ashkenazic scholars produced, with a few deft twists, a tenable, if not quite persuasive case for the permissability of suicide in times of religious persecution. For murder of one's children few could find a defense, and almost all passed that over in audible silence.[9]

Neither this case nor those cited previously should be mistaken as providing the basis for virtually unlimited freedom to revise *halakhah* in accordance with perceived needs at any given time. The innovations of the Ashkenazic scholars were not undertaken to conform with the demands of an increasingly secularized community. On the contrary, "the Franco-German community was permeated by a profound sense of its own religiosity, and of the rightness of its traditions, and could not imagine any sharp difference between its practices and the law which its members studied and observed with such devotion."[10] The condition of Ashkenazic Jewry since the Enlightenment is radically different and, accordingly, the stances of its scholars have frequently also been very different.

---

[9]Soloveitchik, "Religious Law and Change," 208–10.
[10]Ibid., 211–12.

Nevertheless, even within the twentieth century there have been occasions when the most outstanding *posekim* supported major change based on contemporary social conditions. Consider, for example, that no less a figure than the Hafetz Hayyim, who was neither a "modernist" nor a "centrist," declared that the prohibition, cited by the Rambam, against the teaching of Torah to women is no longer relevant today *because of the social conditions of the present*: "All the doubts about the prohibition of teaching one's daughter Torah are without basis and cause for apprehension in our days (*"ein shum beit mihush la-zeh be-yameinu eileh"*) because our generation is different from previous generations where every Jewish home had a tradition to follow the path of the Torah."[11]

It should be emphasized that this is not meant to suggest that either the Rambam or the Hafetz Hayyim maintained that *halakhah* is actually determined or even influenced by environmental or sociological factors. Rather, they would undoubtedly have insisted that when a particular *halakhah* varies from time to time and place to place, it does so only because its application changes under changing conditions. In other words, the *halakhah* as originally conceived applies in one way under conditions X and in another way under conditions Y. They would have insisted, however, that

---

[11]Israel Meir HaCohen, "Letter to the Supporters of Torah in the City of Pristik," 23 *Shevat* 5693 (February 19, 1933). Reprinted in *Dos Yiddishe Vort* 31:252 (March [*Adar-Nissan* 5745] 1985): 51. In his *Likkutei Halakhot*, vol. 2, *Sotah* (Jerusalem: Sacks Family, circa 1980), 21–22, where the text mentions that, *a priori (lekhathila)*, one should not even teach one's daughter the written Torah (*Torah she-bi-khtav*), the Hafetz Hayyim asserts that that no longer applies. On the contrary, he says, "In our time . . . parental traditions have become very, very weak, and it is common that one does not at all live in the same place as one's parents, and especially since females take courses to learn to read and write in the languages of the nations, it is definitely a great *mitzvah* to teach them Humash, Neviim and Ketuvim, as well as ethical works of Haza'l, such as the Tractate *Avot*, *Menorat Hamaor*, and the like. . . ."

every *pesak* derives from the traditional *objective* process of halakhic decision-making.[12]

Nevertheless, as suggested initially, Orthodoxy in general, and especially its more traditionalist *haredi*, or "right-wing," components, would have a negative gut reaction to the notion of a sociology of *pesak*. In part, this is probably related to the nature of contemporary Orthodox religiosity, which, somewhat similar to the Ashkenazic community of the twelfth and thirteenth centuries, is characterized by the "simplicity of religious belief."[13] The further right one goes along the Orthodox spectrum, the less concern one finds for religious philosophy. Religion is *halakhah*, and *halakhah* has a self-evident status; it is taken for granted. "It is so because it is so." *Halakhah* is *mesorah*, tradition, which Moshe Rabbeinu gave to Yehoshua who in turn gave it to the Judges, and on down the line, until it reaches us.

But there is another way in which the social affects *pesak*, one with which the more right-wing element would probably have no

---

[12]See the quote from David Bleich below. For evidence of the sensitivity of this issue within contemporary Orthodox rabbinic circles, see the exchange between Rabbis Dovid Cohen and Israel Poleyeff, *Journal of Halacha and Contemporary Society* 15 (Spring 1988): 125–28. But the matter actually seems more complex than that. There do appear to be situations in which conditions do affect *pesak*. Specifically, certain social conditions may affect the degree to which one seeks a more lenient position, a *heter*. For example, virtually every halakhic authority asserts that conversion for the sake of marriage, especially where it is evident that the individual involved will not be an observant Jew, is invalid. Nevertheless, it is a common practice in Israel and even with many sectarian Orthodox rabbis of considerable stature to attempt to convince the non-Jewish spouse in an intermarriage to convert. For a survey and analysis of responsa on this issue, see David Ellenson, "Representative Orthodox Responsa on Conversion and Intermarriage in the Contemporary Era," *Jewish Social Studies* 47:3–4 (Summer-Fall 1985): 209–20.

[13]That is how Soloveitchik characterized the Ashkenazic community. See his "Religious Law and Change," 213.

disagreement. When the socially accepted norms are even more "rigorous," "stringent," *mahmir*, than strict *halakhah* requires, they become part of the *pesak* process. There is nothing new in this development; as Soloveitchik points out, it was prevalent in Ashkenaz during the era of the Tosafists.[14] There is, however, one basic difference between stringent behavior of the masses in Ashkenaz and the pattern that is prevalent in contemporary Orthodoxy, and that is that today there is a conscious, almost ideological, drive to be more stringent in the observance of certain areas of *halakhah*. To some extent, this is what Rabbi Simcha Elberg, editor of *Hapardes*, the oldest extant Torah journal in the United States, and a prolific writer who espouses right-wing Orthodoxy, had in mind when he described *Bnei Brakism*.

> The character and stature of Bnei Brak express themselves not only in religiosity and traditional piety . . . it consists of its own unique and independent approach. . . . A yeshiva student under the spiritual influence of the *Hazon Ish* of Bnei Brak actually lives and breathes the *Shulhan Arukh* with all of its *humrot* [stringencies]. When he takes the *Shulhan Arukh* to look up any question, his perspective is toward the *mahmir*, and he will neither seek out nor favor the more lenient opinion. His intention is not to be lenient but to be more stringent. He constantly makes an effort to search and dig; perhaps one of the commentaries tends toward greater stringency. And when he finds a more stringent opinion, it is as if his very being was refreshed and rejuvenated, and this *humra* becomes the norm which he established in his home and which he realized in his daily life.[15]

---

[14]Ibid., 220.

[15]Editorial, *Hapardes* 38:3 (*Kislev* 5724/November-December 1963): 5 (Hebrew). For a somewhat different rendition of Elberg's concept, based perhaps on the translation of another version of the Elberg editorial, which also appeared in the Israeli Agudat Israel periodical, *Digleinu*

Elberg attributes the growth of Bnei Brakism to the continuing influence of the powerful, almost charismatic, quality of the
late Rabbi Avraham Yeshayahu Karelitz, the *Hazon Ish*
(1878–1953). The *Hazon Ish* was one of the most widely revered
halakhic authorities of his time and, although many of his rulings
were lenient, his disciples normally tended to emphasize and follow
his more stringent rulings. The most obvious examples are those
which relate to the quantities specified for the fulfillment of certain
mitzvot, as with the wine and *matzah* at the *seder* on Pesah.[16]

Menachem Friedman astutely argues that the source of Bnei
Brakism goes far beyond any one individual, even one so influential
as the *Hazon Ish*. Rather, he suggests, its source is to be found in the
very structure and culture of the higher *yeshivah*, the *yeshivah
gedolah* of the Eastern European type, of which the model is the
yeshivah in Volozhin. Among its many features, the *yeshivah gedolah*

> is a total-like institution whose students are, for the most part,
> alienated from their surroundings and cut off from their
> families for most of the year, as a result of which they are
> united amongst themselves, especially around the figure of the
> *rosh yeshivah* (head of the *yeshivah*) and his family.[17]

(*Kislev-Tevet* 5725) see Menachem Friedman, "Life Tradition and Book
Tradition in the Development of Ultraorthodox Judaism," in *Judaism
Viewed From Within and From Without: Anthropological Studies*, ed. Harvey
E. Goldberg (Albany: State University of New York Press, 1987), 235.

[16]Friedman, "Life Tradition and Book Tradition," 236–38. Also see
David Singer, "Thumbs and Eggs," *Moment* 3:9 (September 1978): 36–37.

[17]Friedman, "Life Tradition and Book Tradition," 242. For further
developments in his analysis of the implications of the *yeshivah gedolah* of
the Volozhin type, see Menachem Friedman, "Haredim Confront the
Modern City," in *Studies in Contemporary Jewry*, ed. Peter Y. Medding, vol.
2 (Bloomington, IN: Indiana University Press, 1986), 74–96; Menachem
Friedman, "Mifgash Yahadut Torah Im Derekh Eretz Im ha-Harediut
ha-Mizrach Eiropit," in *Torah Im Derekh Eretz Movement*, ed. Mordechai
Breuer (Ramat Gan, Israel: Bar-Ilan University Press, 1987), 173–78
(Hebrew).

Although not quite along the same lines as Friedman, I too would argue that the rapidly expanding "world of the *yeshivah*" accounts for much of what Elberg has termed *Bnei Brakism* and that the widely observed "shift to the right" within Orthodoxy has determined the trend of contemporary accepted *pesak*. Specifically, the fact that *yeshivah* students are separated from their families and the outside world means that the regular ties with those traditional sources of influence, socialization, and social control are broken. Within the *yeshivah*, it is the *rosh yeshivah* who is the central authority figure and who determines the proper norms of behavior.

What this means is that, whereas historically the traditions of both the family and the local community played a central role in setting the standards of proper behavior within the religious realm—*minhag*, custom, often took on the authority of *halakhah*[18]— with the growth of the *yeshivah gedolah* a new pattern emerged. The *rosh yeshivah* now determines proper behavioral norms, and the folkways and mores of the family and local community are often no longer taken very seriously. Likewise, whereas traditionally the local *rav*, or rabbi, served as the halakhic authority for his community, the emergence of the *yeshivah gedolah* has resulted in a growing struggle between the *rav* and *rosh yeshivah* for halakhic authority.

To clarify and amplify this last point, mention must be made of another basic feature of the *yeshivah gedolah*. As Friedman points out, the *yeshivah gedolah* of the Volozhin type "is not an institution *of the community*, but rather an economically independent organization supported by the contributions of individuals from many regions. . . . The vast majority of the yeshiva students are not from the community but come from near and far for the purpose of studying there."[19]

---

[18]On the status of *minhag*, see Yedidya Alter Dinari, *The Rabbis of Germany and Austria at the Close of the Middle Ages: Their Conceptions and Halakhah-Writings* (Jerusalem: Bialik Institute, 1984), 190–228 (Hebrew).

[19]Friedman, "Life Tradition and Book Tradition," 242. Emphasis added.

Until the beginning of the nineteenth century, there was no struggle between *rav* and *rosh yeshivah* because the *yeshivah* was a local institution, and the *rav* and *rosh yeshivah* were usually one and the same. Not only did these two roles not conflict, they frequently complemented each other and compensated for conflicts in other areas. Jacob Katz has analyzed the pre-nineteenth-century *yeshivah:*

> The identity of purpose of the rabbi and yeshiva head, which was customary in this period, was another typical feature. . . . Since the nucleus of the yeshiva consisted of students whose only loyalty was to their rabbinic head, an atmosphere was created conducive to the creation of a close personal link between them. These circumstances facilitated the formation of an educational framework of an unusually intensive nature. The combining of the tasks of president of the local rabbinic court and yeshiva head decreased rather than increased the prospects that this would happen. The advancement of the yeshiva was, after all, only one of the rabbi's many tasks. . . . The relationship of the *kehillah* to the rabbi, which was not lacking in conflict and tension, was likely, for its part, to have its equilibrium restored through the halo which surrounded the rabbi in the line of his yeshiva duties. The honor accorded the rabbi as head of the yeshiva and as disseminator of learning among the people, values that were universally esteemed, also strengthened his hand as he carried out his function as arbiter of the values of the entire community.[20]

By the nineteenth century, when R. Chaim of Volozhin (1749–1821) established the *yeshivah* there (1802), the basic roles had changed because the relationships were radically altered. Although R. Chaim was the rabbi of Volozhin, when he wanted to establish a *yeshivah* there he went outside of his community for the

---

[20]Jacob Katz, *Tradition and Crisis: Jewish Society at the End of the Middle Ages* (New York: Schocken Books, 1971), 197–98.

requisite financial resources.[21] Although that is the common pattern today and many strong arguments can be made in its defense—it eases the financial burden of the local community, for example—the fact remains that this then new approach radically restructured some of the basic patterns within the traditional Jewish community. Specifically, it restructured the nature of the relationship between the *yeshivah* and the local community, between the *rosh yeshivah* and the local community, and between the *rosh yeshivah* and the rabbi. Broadening the base of financial support for the *yeshivah* meant that the *yeshivah* was no longer under the direct control of the community within which it was located, and that the *rosh yeshivah* as well was now much more independent of the local community; moreover, not only were the *rosh yeshivah* and the rabbi no longer one and the same, they were now potentially in competition for the loyalties of the members of the community as well as for those of the *yeshivah* students from within the community. Not infrequently, each attempted to enhance his own stature at the expense of the other. Within this development, the tendency toward stringency, *humra*, played a special role insofar as the more stringent ruling is frequently posited as and viewed as the more "authentic" one.[22]

---

[21]On the founding of the *yeshivah* in Volozhin, see S. Shtampfer, *Shalosh Yeshivot Litaiot ba-Me'ah ha-Tesha Esrei* (Ph.D. diss., Hebrew University of Jerusalem, 1981), 12ff.; Samuel K. Mirsky, *Mosdot Torah be-Eiropah be-Vinyanam u-ve-Hurbanam* (New York: Histadrut ha-Ivrit be-America, 1956).

[22]Cf. R. Yeshayahu Horowitz (1565–1630) (a.k.a. Shelah Hakadosh), *Shnei Luhot ha-Brit* (Jerusalem: 5735/1975), 1:19a, wherein the author gives a somewhat mystical reason for what he describes as the continuously increasing prevalence of sin. The increasing prevalence of sin, he says, is actually the constantly spreading venom of the snake, for which he prescribes *humrot*, stringencies, as the "antitoxin," and defines them not as rabbinic stringencies but as *humrot* ordained by the Torah: "Therefore, in each *generation* when it is proper to add stringencies, then all of that is from the Torah *(mi-de-oraita)*." Although both Menachem Friedman and I

Several related points should be made at this juncture with respect to the approach to and the use of *humra*. Although the vast majority of authorities define it, at most, as within the realm of rabbinic law, the authority to institute stringencies is defined as rooted in the Torah itself, deriving from the dictum, *Asu mishmeret le-mishmarti* (make a guard for my guard). Thus, rabbinic leaders in each generation have not hesitated to impose restrictions whenever they deemed them necessary to the prevention of further deterioration of religious life. Since many of the traditional rabbinic leaders viewed modernity itself as threatening, they not infrequently instituted stringencies against any innovations simply because innovation itself was deemed to be inherently destructive. The classic statement in this regard is probably that of Rabbi Moses Sofer, the Hatam Sofer, who, by way of a pun, declared that all innovations are prohibited by the Torah—*hadash assur min ha-Torah*.[23] He opposed all innovations and frequently adopted stringencies, particularly in opposition to the nascent movement to reform Judaism.[24] Following the lead of the Hatam Sofer, traditionalists who are ideologically opposed to modernity and innovation often legitimate their opposition and the stringencies they impose under that same banner. This may be one of the major reasons why

---

emphasize the role of the *yeshivah* movement in the tendency toward *humra*, I am grateful to Rabbi Emanuel Feldman for pointing out that mention should also be made of the influences of both Hasidism and the *Musar* movement on this development.

[23]See, for example, *Teshuvot Hatam Sofer: Orah Hayyim* (New York: M. P. Press, 1958), 68b, responsum 181, and *Teshuvot Hatam Sofer: Yoreh De'ah* (New York: M. P. Press, 1958), 8a, responsum 19. For biographies of the Hatam Sofer, see Eliezer Katz, *Ha-Hatam Sofer* (Jerusalem: Mossad ha-Rav Kook, 1960), and Yehuda Nahshoni, *Rabbeinu Moshe Sofer: ha-Hatam Sofer* (Jerusalem: Hotzaat Mashabim, 1981). Also see Jacob Katz, *Halakhah and Kabbalah*, 353–86; Moshe Samet, "Kavim Nosafim le-Biographiah shel ha-Hatam Sofer," in *Torah Im Derekh Eretz Movement*, ed. Mordechai Breuer, 65–73.

[24]Michael A. Meyer, *Response to Modernity*.

Orthodox militancy was greater in Hungary than in Russia during the nineteenth century. Modernity and secularization were already being felt in Hungary at the end of the eighteenth century, whereas they did not manifest themselves in Russia almost until the twentieth century.

Although the number of *yeshivot gedolot* grew significantly throughout Eastern Europe in the nineteenth and early twentieth centuries,[25] the most dramatic growth in both the number of such institutions and the number of students learning in them has occurred within the past three decades. In 1945, there were nine *yeshivah* high schools in United States; thirty years later, in 1975, the number had grown to 138.[26] On the post-high school level, the growth has been even more dramatic, and it is at its greatest with respect to *kollelim*. By 1976, David Singer observed that "the number of students . . . studying Talmud on an advanced level . . . [compared] quite favorably with the number who were enrolled in the great yeshivot of Eastern Europe during their heyday – and this despite the fact that the yeshivot have made no concessions to modernity, and few to the American environment."[27]

---

[25]In addition to the works by Shtampfer and Mirsky cited in my n. 21 above, see R. Baruch Halevi Epstein, *Mekor Baruch*, 4 vols. (Vilna: Rom, 1928), in which he describes the surge of Torah learning in Eastern Europe during the nineteenth century. I specifically use the term *learning*, rather than *studying*, because of the unique character of that process in *yeshivot gedolot*. It is perhaps best captured in Samuel Heilman, *The People of the Book* (Chicago: University of Chicago Press, 1983), wherein he uses the term *lernen*.

[26]Egon Mayer and Chaim I. Waxman, "Modern Jewish Orthodoxy in America: Toward the Year 2000," *Tradition* 16:3 (Spring 1977): 99.

[27]David Singer, "The Yeshivah World," *Commentary* 62:4 (October 1976): 70. Also see Herbert W. Bomzer, *The Kollel in America* (New York: Shengold, 1985). This, of course, is not to say that the extent of learning is the same in the United States today as it was in Eastern Europe. Obviously, a much greater percentage of Jews in Eastern Europe spent some hours each day in learning than do American Jews today. Equally

All of this has translated into the growth of right-wing or
"sectarian" Orthodoxy—the "*yeshivah* world" is, overwhelmingly,
the world of right-wing Orthodoxy—and the rise of perspectives
which are more punctilious and stringent, both in terms of *pesak*
and in terms of observance. To clarify and demonstrate this point,
it is necessary to distinguish between two types of modern Orthodoxy. One may be called philosophical, while the other is more
appropriately characterized as behavioral. Within the category of
philosophical modern Orthodox, or centrist Orthodox, would be
those who are meticulously observant of *halakhah* but are, nevertheless, philosophically modern. Within this context, being
modern means, at minimum, having a positive perspective on
general education and knowledge and being well disposed to Israel
and religious Zionism.

The behaviorally modern Orthodox, on the other hand, are
not deeply concerned with philosophical ideas about either modernity or religious Zionism. By and large, they define themselves as
modern Orthodox in the sense that they are not as meticulously
observant as the right wing states one should be. In many ways,
they define themselves as modern Orthodox on the same basis as
did those who Marshall Sklare found to define themselves as
Conservative. When asked, "What do you mean when you say you
are Conservative?" they typically responded, "Now—I'd guess you'd
call it middle of the road, as far as (not) being as strict as the
Orthodox, yet not quite as Reformed as the Reformed" or "I don't
like the old-fashioned type, or the Reform. I'm between the two of
them."[28] Similarly, most of those who define themselves as modern

---

obvious is the fact that observant Jews comprise a much smaller proportion of today's American Jewish population than they did of Eastern
Europe's Jewish population. Singer is only dealing with the number of
students in higher *yeshivot*. Likewise, although I am not as convinced as
Singer that the American *yeshivot* have made no concessions to modernity, that is an issue that is not directly germane to my argument.

[28]Marshall Sklare, *Conservative Judaism: An American Religious Movement*, aug. ed. (New York: Schocken Books, 1972), 208.

Orthodox do so in reference to right-wing or "sectarian" Orthodoxy, and they define themselves as modern in the sense that they
are not as observant. As Heilman and Cohen put it,

> Others, the so-called "Modern Orthodox," have tried to find a
> way of remaining linked to the contemporary non-Jewish
> world in which they find themselves and to the traditions and
> practices of Judaism to which they remain loyal. For some,
> this has meant little more than a nominal attachment to
> Orthodoxy while for others it has meant little more than a
> partial attachment to the demands of the tradition.[29]

Lest it be suspected that Heilman and Cohen's description is
in itself ideological, and would not hold up under scrutiny, they do,
in fact, present empirical evidence to substantiate their assertion.
Using a range of ritual practices, they demonstrate that the traditionalists, those on the right, are consistently much more observant
than are those who identify themselves as centrist or modern.[30]
Much as the ideological modern Orthodox may protest and argue
that they disapprove of the prevalent laxity of ritual practice as
much as do those on the right, the fact remains that the majority of
those who define themselves as modern Orthodox are of the
behavioral category, and are considerably less conscientious about
ritual observance than are those on the right.

The implications of all of this for *pesak* should by now be
evident. Specifically, the *yeshivah* is likely to "produce" an individual who is more punctilious in observance and who is likely to
adopt a more stringent pattern of religious behavior. He is much

---

[29]Samuel C. Heilman and Steven M. Cohen, *Cosmopolitans and Paro-
chials: Modern Orthodox Jews in America* (Chicago: University of Chicago
Press, 1989), 39.

[30]Ibid., 40–81. Also see Samuel C. Heilman and Steven M. Cohen,
"Ritual Variation Among Modern Orthodox Jews in the United States,"
in *Studies in Contemporary Jewry*, ed. Peter Y. Medding (Bloomington, IN:
Indiana University Press, 1986), 2:164–87.

more likely to turn to his *rosh yeshivah* on halakhic matters, and the *rosh yeshivah* is more likely to adopt a more stringent position on practical issues than is the rabbi of the community. (This may be due to any of a variety of factors: he may be less vulnerable to community pressures; he may be possessed of deeper learning than the communal rabbi; he may have less contact with daily communal issues.) Furthermore, the sectarian, or right-wing, segment of Orthodoxy has much more of a say in whose *pesakim* are accepted since its followers are more observant and are, therefore, the ones who are most likely to abide by those halakhic decisions.

Communal organization is a further element adding to the virtual monopoly of the right in determining who is the *posek*. Structurally, sectarian Orthodoxy is at least potentially, much more organized than modern Orthodoxy in a number of respects. The right-wing is more likely to live in close-knit sectarian Orthodox communities. Although unofficial, there is a strong tie between the "*yeshivah* world" and Agudat Israel of America, which is not only a political organization but a vast social welfare agency as well. And there is nothing in the Modern Orthodox community which comes even close to that kind of organization. Thus, not only in terms of its educational institutions, the *yeshivot*, but also in terms of its broader political and social welfare institutions, the right-wing has a much firmer structural base than modern Orthodoxy. And, since sectarian Orthodoxy commands the loyalty of its adherents on religious grounds, they are, in fact, much more loyal to their leaders than are the modern Orthodox.

Finally, no analysis would be complete without touching on the role of technology in the diffusion of *pesak* through the larger Orthodox community and its effect on the status of *posekim*. One cannot but be awed by the speed with which halakhic decisions are spread through the population today compared with, say, a century ago. Many more religious books, *sefarim*, are published today than ever before, and many individual Orthodox Jews have the financial ability to purchase those *sefarim*, and they do. This is a very important aspect of the sociology of *pesak* because, as in all fields of knowledge, it is not necessarily the greatest expert who becomes the authority. Rather, it is the scholar whose works are known. Publishing is crucial to the process of being known. This, of course, does not mean that publishing is either a prerequisite or a guarantee of wide acceptance as a *posek*. On the one hand, there are and have been some "world-class" *posekim* who have not published widely. On the other hand, there are some widely published *posekim* who are, nevertheless, not uniformly recognized as authoritative. Obviously, there are many other factors, such as breadth and depth of learning, rigorousness of analysis, and perceived *yirat shamayim* (fear of God), which are prerequisites for being accepted as a *posek*. But publishing is an increasingly important means by which those qualities become widely recognized; publishing allows a much wider community of scholars access to the scholarship of the *posek*. Therefore, all other things being equal, the *posek* who publishes will likely become much more authoritative than one who does not.

In addition to the more traditional *sefarim* of the *yeshivah* world, there is a whole new type of Orthodox Jewish book being published today. However one may judge the intellectual quality of most of the books published by Art-Scroll,[31] there can be no question of the major impact of what may be termed the "Art-Scroll phenomenon." It most assuredly does enhance the sectarian perspective. In addition, it has probably also led some who might have otherwise been completely ignorant of Jewish learning to become

---

[31]For a critique of the Art-Scroll phenomenon, see B. Barry Levy, "Judge Not a Book by its Cover," *Tradition* 19:1 (Spring 1981): 89–95. For a retort, see the response by Emanuel Feldman, *Tradition* 19:2 (Summer 1981): 192. For a more extensive version of Levy's critique, see his article, "Our Torah, Your Torah and Their Torah: An Evaluation of the Artscroll Phenomenon," in *Truth and Compassion: Essays on Judaism and Religion in Memory of Rabbi Dr. Solomon Frank*, ed. Howard Joseph, Jack N. Lightstone, and Michael D. Oppenheim (Waterloo, Ontario: Canadian Corporation for Studies in Religion/Wilfrid Laurier University Press, 1983), 137–89.

aware of some aspects of it and, presumably, to seek out authorities for both Torah knowledge per se and for halakhic guidance as well.

There also exists today a series of English-language periodicals that appear on a quarterly, monthly, and weekly basis which often serve as vehicles for the dissemination of *pesak*. Among these are the *Journal of Halacha and Contemporary Society, Tradition*, the *Jewish Observer*, and even the *Jewish Press*. Periodicals such as these are significant not only in terms of the speed with which they are able to communicate *pesak*, but also for the size of the audience they reach. Obviously, it varies, and many more read the *Jewish Press* than read the *Jewish Observer*, just as the *Observer* probably has many more readers than either *Tradition* or the *Journal of Halacha and Contemporary Society*. Nevertheless, if one were to compare the number of people reading such periodicals today with the number reading similar periodicals several decades ago, one would almost certainly find that the numbers have grown significantly.

In addition to the printed media, the advent of the telephone has undoubtedly had great impact on the dissemination of *pesak*. One can now just pick up the telephone and immediately get an answer to virtually any halakhic question (assuming, of course, that it is the kind of question for which an immediate answer is actually appropriate). Thus, halakhic decisions can be publicized worldwide in a matter of moments. Obviously, this has many benefits.

However, the feasibility of instantaneous communication of *pesak* may also have negative consequences. Because a *pesak* can no longer be considered a private, individual, or even local community matter, some *posekim*—although probably not the "giants" among them—may have become more cautious. They may hesitate to open themselves up to such potentially broad criticism, or at least to criticism from such a broad public. This may, therefore, inhibit *pesak* and cause the *posek* to be much more consensus-oriented than he might otherwise be. In essence, he and his followers may become "victims" of the politics of *pesak*.

As for the community rabbi, all of these developments have had an impact on his position. Aside from the growing tendency among the Jews of the community to consult with a *rosh yeshivah* rather than the community rabbi, with the increase in the numbers of those who learned in *yeshivot gedolot* there are now more *yeshivah*-educated laymen who feel competent to render *pesak* on their own, without consulting anyone else, especially not the community rabbi. Not only have they learned in the *yeshivot*, they have the necessary tools—the *sefarim*—in their own libraries. And, should there arise a case in which they do not feel competent to render a *pesak*, they can easily pick up the telephone and get a decision from the *posek* whom they feel is the best authority.

Lest one conclude that these developments have had a solely negative impact on the status of the rabbi as *posek*, it should be emphasized that rabbis, too, are able to take advantage of these same tools. Community rabbis can now much more easily turn to their halakhic mentors for *pesak*, without having to wait the weeks and even months that might have been required in the past.

Finally, the fact that there is a larger community of *yeshivah* alumni may result in the emergence of a new type of rabbi in the United States, one much more akin to the rabbi of the past. More congregations may seek out rabbis who are primarily Torah scholars and authorities in the world of *pesak*, rather than community leaders in a broader sense. If this should indeed turn out to be the case we may see a realignment and much closer interaction between rabbi and *rosh yeshivah* in the not too distant future.

Contributors

Dr. Lawrence Kaplan is Associate Professor of Rabbinics and Jewish Philosophy in the Department of Jewish Studies at McGill University and co-editor of *The Thought of Moses Maimonides* and *Rabbi Abraham I. Kook: His Thought and Legacy*.

Dr. Aaron Kirschenbaum is Professor and Chairman of the Department of Jewish Law, the Faculty of Law, Tel Aviv University. He is author, most recently, of *Equity in Jewish Law*.

Rabbi Michael Rosensweig is *Rosh Yeshivah* at Rabbi Isaac El-chanan Theological Seminary of Yeshiva University.

Dr. Jonathan Sacks is Chief Rabbi of the United Hebrew Congregation of the British Commonwealth. He is editor of *L'Eylah: A Journal of Judaism Today* and is author, most recently, of *Arguments for the Sake of Heaven*.

239

Dr. Moshe Sokol, editor of this volume, is Associate Professor and Chairman of the Department of Philosophy at Touro College.

Dr. Chaim Waxman is Professor of Sociology at Rutgers University and Adjunct Professor at Yeshiva University's Azrieli Graduate Institute of Jewish Education and Administration. He is author, most recently, of *American Aliya.*

Index